DISCARD

EXPERIENCING JEWISH MUSIC IN AMERICA

The Listener's Companion
Kenneth LaFave, Series Editor

Titles in **The Listener's Companion** provide readers with a deeper understanding of key musical genres and the work of major artists and composers. Aimed at nonspecialists, each volume explains in clear and accessible language how to *listen* to works from particular artists, composers, and genres. Looking at both the context in which the music first appeared and has since been heard, authors explore with readers the environments in which key musical works were written and performed.

Experiencing Alice Cooper: A Listener's Companion, by Ian Chapman
Experiencing the Beatles: A Listener's Companion, by Brooke Halpin
Experiencing Beethoven: A Listener's Companion, by Geoffrey Block
Experiencing Bessie Smith: A Listener's Companion, by John Clark
Experiencing Big Band Jazz: A Listener's Companion, by Jeff Sultanof
Experiencing Billy Joel: A Listener's Companion, by Thomas MacFarlane
Experiencing Black Sabbath: A Listener's Companion, by Nolan Stolz
Experiencing Broadway Music: A Listener's Companion, by Kathryn Sherrell
Experiencing Carl Maria von Weber: A Listener's Companion, by Joseph E. Morgan
Experiencing Chick Corea: A Listener's Companion, by Monika Herzig
Experiencing Chopin: A Listener's Companion, by Christine Gengaro
Experiencing David Bowie: A Listener's Companion, by Ian Chapman
Experiencing Film Music: A Listener's Companion, by Kenneth LaFave
Experiencing Jazz: A Listener's Companion, by Michael Stephans
Experiencing Jewish Music in America: A Listener's Companion, by Tina Frühauf
Experiencing Led Zeppelin: A Listener's Companion, by Gregg Akkerman
Experiencing Leonard Bernstein: A Listener's Companion, by Kenneth LaFave
Experiencing Mozart: A Listener's Companion, by David Schroeder
Experiencing Ornette Coleman: A Listener's Companion, by Michael Stephans
Experiencing Peter Gabriel: A Listener's Companion, by Durrell Bowman
Experiencing the Rolling Stones: A Listener's Companion, by David Malvinni
Experiencing Rush: A Listener's Companion, by Durrell Bowman
Experiencing Schumann: A Listener's Companion, by Donald Sanders
Experiencing Stravinsky: A Listener's Companion, by Robin Maconie
Experiencing Tchaikovsky: A Listener's Companion, by David Schroeder
Experiencing Verdi: A Listener's Companion, by Donald Sanders
Experiencing the Violin Concerto: A Listener's Companion, by Franco Sciannameo

EXPERIENCING JEWISH MUSIC IN AMERICA

A Listener's Companion

Tina Frühauf

ROWMAN & LITTLEFIELD
Lanham • Boulder • New York • London

Published by Rowman & Littlefield
An imprint of The Rowman & Littlefield Publishing Group, Inc.
4501 Forbes Boulevard, Suite 200, Lanham, Maryland 20706
www.rowman.com

Unit A, Whitacre Mews, 26-34 Stannary Street, London SE11 4AB

British Library Cataloguing in Publication Information Available

Library of Congress Cataloging-in-Publication Data

Names: Frühauf, Tina, author.
Title: Experiencing Jewish music in America : a listener's companion / Tina Frühauf.
Description: Lanham : Rowman & Littlefield, [2018] | Series: Listener's companion | Includes bibliographical references and index.
Identifiers: LCCN 2017053148 (print) | LCCN 2017054480 (ebook) | ISBN 9781442258402 (electronic) | ISBN 9781442258396 (cloth : alk. paper)
Subjects: LCSH: Jews—United States—Music—History and criticism. | Music—United States—History and criticism.
Classification: LCC ML3776 (ebook) | LCC ML3776 .F88 2018 (print) | DDC 780.89/924073—dc23 LC record available at https://lccn.loc.gov/2017053148

Printed in the United States of America

To immigrants of all faiths, cultures, and walks of life

CONTENTS

SERIES EDITOR'S FOREWORD

The goal of the Listener's Companion series is to give readers a deeper understanding of pivotal musical genres and the creative work of its iconic composers and performers. This is accomplished in an inclusive manner that does not necessitate extensive music training or elitist shoulder rubbing. Authors of the series place the reader in specific listening experiences in which the music is examined in its historical and social contexts. By positioning the reader in the real or supposed environment of the music's creation, the author provides for a deeper enjoyment and appreciation of the art form. Series authors, often drawing on their own expertise as both performers, scholars, and audiences, deliver to readers a broad understanding of musical genres and the achievements of artists within those genres as lived listening experiences.

Following in this vein, Tina Frühauf's book provides a deep, informative, thoughtful study of Jewish music in America—its history, its influences, and its many expressions. Jewish music extends to every conceivable genre, both sacred and secular. Jews, for example, have made up a large percentage of major classical and popular musicians. Violin mastery without international Jewish artists would be unthinkable. Yehudi Menuhin, Fritz Kreisler, Jascha Heifetz, Nathan Milstein, David Oistrakh, and Isaac Stern are but a sampling of the names that made up what critic Virgil Thomson, not without controversy, once called "the Jewish fiddle mafia." (He meant it as a compliment.) In the first half of the twentieth century, Jewish songwriters embraced

American popular music to such an extent that an old joke went as follows: "How do you remember which songwriters are Jewish? Answer: With two words, 'Cole Porter,' the name of the only one who isn't." The punch line ignores Harry Warren and a few other non-Jewish tune smiths. But not many.

Classical music, pop, and rock hardly exhaust the well of music produced by Jewish musicians, as you are about to find out. From the stage and the screen to arenas and nightclubs, Jewish musicians have vigorously contributed to the musical life of America. And yet, this very range of artistry—one is tempted to call it a veritable diaspora of talent—gives rise to a vexing question. As Frühauf puts it in her introduction, "Given this diversity, how then does one construe the concept of 'Jewish music'?" She takes the length of her book to approach that question, which comes down to two different ways of thinking about the concept of "Jewish music." One way might be called the positivist and the other the descriptive. The positivist is simply that Jewish music is any music made by Jewish people, while the descriptive requires an explanation of what, for example, makes Jewish liturgical or klezmer music distinctive. We know, for instance, that *Fiddler on the Roof* contains musical elements traceable to Hasidic music, qualifying it without question as "Jewish music." But is Rupert Holmes's late 1970s hit "Escape" (aka "The Pina Colada Song") an example of Jewish music because Holmes, whose birth name was David Goldstein, is Jewish? Frühauf weaves a dialectic of seeming opposites to paint a picture that grasps the complexity of her subject.

Is it perhaps possible to come up with a provisional notion of what makes music *Jewish* if we operate on the premise that the music is such if we can recognize a conspicuous element within it as "Jewish"? Take as an example one of the most ubiquitous songs of the past twenty years, Leonard Cohen's "Hallelujah." Its rolling 12/8 meter recalls rock-and-roll ballads from the 1950s, while the chorus of the title word repeated over simple chords plugs into the energy of gospel. The lyrics make biblical reference that qualifies them as Jewish in origin. The first, famous opening lines go as follows:

> Now, I've heard there was a secret chord
> That David played, and it pleased the Lord.

The words point to the music itself—"a secret chord"—as the key to some kind of sacred understanding. But what chord? And how can its "secret" please the Lord? In one of the more amazing feats of pop music, Cohen's words go on to describe the very harmonic progression that is happening beneath them! Shortening what could easily be a lengthy technical description, both the words and the progression lead to a condition that blends hope with despair; the king is "baffled," yet he composes "Hallelujah." How can hope come from despair? Our secret chord—in technical terms a secondary dominant—is the answer. Landing on the second syllable of the word "composing," the secret chord leads with finality to a minor chord, where previously only major chords have been heard. The minor implies a darkness or even hopelessness, yet it is precisely the arrival of the minor that makes the praiseful chorus of "Hallelujah" possible. This is the "crack" where "the light gets in" that Cohen sings of in another song, "Anthem." A divine connectedness is implied: the life connection of sorrow to joy is the connection of the relentless minor to all our strivings for the major. And that can be perceived as "Jewish music."

Or at least, it's one way of hearing it. Jewish music is a multifaceted crystal, and Frühauf turns the gem in every direction to give universal perspective in the context of the American soundscape. Her commentaries will prompt readers to listen in a refreshing new way to Jewish music, opening doors to understanding.

Kenneth LaFave

A NOTE ON TRANSLITERATION, SPELLING, AND TRANSLATION

Transliterating from Hebrew and Yiddish can be tricky, as different sources have different ways of doing it. For Hebrew, I follow the transliteration system of the Library of Congress; for Yiddish, I follow the transliteration system established by the YIVO Institute for Jewish Research in the 1930s. There are a few exceptions, however, such as when I quote from a source that uses a different spelling. The same goes for titles of musical works; terms for Jewish holidays and selected prayers; names of characters; and names of musicians, composers, and writers. In this book, names appear in their most common form, whether original or adopted, and variant forms are given only occasionally. Similarly, Hebrew and Yiddish words that have found their way into English appear in their modern spellings (e.g., hazanuth, not *chazzanut* or *ḥazanut*). In cases where common spelling warrants it, I follow the orthography of *Merriam-Webster's Collegiate Dictionary*, eleventh edition (2003). For quotations from and indirect biblical allusions to the Hebrew Bible, I rely on the English translations of the New JPS version (1985). The numbering of Psalms follows Masoretic (i.e., Hebrew) conventions. Finally, all translations in this volume are by the author.

INTRODUCTION

Imagine you are visiting a record store looking for "Jewish music." What would you find? In the same rack, there might be cantorial classics sung by Yossele Rosenblatt and klezmer music. You might find Israeli folk music and songs in Yiddish and Ladino. You might see one of the CDs by Hasidic pop star Lipa Schmelczer or stumble over John Zorn's experimental sounds. For sure, you will find an abundance of classical music by composers of Jewish heritage. The inventory of a record store is as much a microcosm of Jewish music as America is a microcosm for the Jewish cultures of the world, from the Bukharian Jews in Queens to the Syrian Jews in Miami and Persian Jews in Los Angeles. Indeed, there are several subgroups of Jews in America with different customs. The Sephardim (the Jews of Spain and Portugal and their descendants) were the first to set foot in the New World in 1584; the Ashkenazim (Jews of France, Germany, and eastern Europe and their descendants) followed thereafter. In later modernity, Jews from North Africa and the Middle East and other subgroups, such as Yemenites and Ethiopian Jews, settled in the United States as well. Within these groups, some are religious to various degrees (the main denominations are Reform, Conservative, and Orthodox, with several smaller movements alongside and in between), and some are secular. Diversity is inherent in Jewish culture, musically and otherwise.

Given this diversity, how, then, does one construe the concept of "Jewish music"? This question opens a door to the impossible, though we cannot afford to ignore it. In recent years, the growing market for world music and the placing of Jewish music in that context has sparked a fierce debate over what defines it. Like many terms, "Jewish music" is a construct, a young concept of later modernity. In the United States, it first appeared in print in Sam L. Jacobson's (1873–1937) essay "The Music of the Jews" of 1898, published in the monthly magazine *Music*. This essay, conceived in defense against the claim that Jewish music is a nonentity, relies on synagogue music and its modes as counterargument. Decades before Jacobson, composer Richard Wagner, in his anti-Semitic tract "Judaism in Music," had already attempted to single out "the Jewish elements" in the music of eminent composers of Jewish heritage. Since then, attempts to define Jewish music have faced many difficulties and have stirred up controversies.

In the early twentieth century, Abraham Zvi Idelsohn, an ethnologist, musicologist, and composer born in Latvia, perpetuated the idea of the underlying cultural unity of the Jewish people throughout and in spite of their dispersion over the centuries. He put forth the notion that the music of the various Jewish communities conveys the linearity of a history dating back to ancient Jerusalem. This view has been contested based on the evolving heterogeneity of the Jewish people in various Diasporas. More so, many Jews did not *continue* existing traditions; rather, they *created* new ones—a process difficult to accept by Orthodox Judaism, where preservation, not creation, is the defining norm. Music, used in sacred and leisure time, has played a key role in ideological debates about tradition and innovation.

Considerations on the meaning of Jewish music took a new turn when the modern State of Israel was founded in 1948. Curt Sachs's famous definition in 1957, "music by Jews, for Jews, as Jews," celebrated for its poignancy and widely applied, has also received much criticism. It begs an answer to the overarching question of who is a Jew, and this answer all depends on who you are asking. For some, Jewishness is in the genes, transmitted based on matrilineal succession since the time of Ezra; for others, Jewish identity is constructed by society, whether by members of the group or by outsiders. Indeed, what does it mean to be Jewish in the modern world? Capturing Jewishness broadly, it can be understood as a racial, cultural, ethnic, or religious category. The dilemma of Jewish music comes down to what is Jewish and what is a Jew.

Clearly, there are competing notions in defining Jews and music. Accordingly, Jewish music denotes different meanings for a diverse conglomerate of people at different places and at various times. The answer to what "Jewish music" is, then, all depends on who defines it and when and under what circumstances. Some insist on a Jewish ritual context and traditional languages (Hebrew, Yiddish, and Ladino) or melodies; others see the Jewish heritage of the musicians as sufficient even when non-Jewish musical influences are dominant, and still others embrace music by non-Jewish musicians based on Jewish themes. The term also carries expectations of "authenticity" or, rather, originality, sometimes leading to heated debates in the evaluation of musicians, composers, and their works, especially in recent years when musicians pushed the limits of "Jewish music" through eclectic borrowing from surrounding cultures. But music can also serve to deliberately preserve and promote Jewish culture in an ever-increasingly assimilated world. A contributing factor in the overall discourse is music's fundamentally variable nature. As organized collections of sounds that both accept and resist fixed notated forms, music easily acquires, communicates, and negotiates meaning long after the sounds themselves have faded.

In spite of breadth and difficulties, "Jewish music" remains the over-arching working term of record in scholarship, the synagogue, and the communal world, used as shorthand for an expansive and disparate series of conversations. In this way, "Jewish music" brings into play religious, national, cultural, social, and musical aspects. It encompasses a complex and multifaceted relationship between Judaism and sound from ancient times to the present day. This time span alone attests to music's role as a product and process through which cultural identity can be constructed and Jewish consciousness kept alive both inwardly and outwardly.

Whether one defines it as music made by Jews, for Jews, or in a Jewish style (whatever that may be) or music with Jewish subject matter, there will always be counterexamples for any such singular definition. Jewish music, just like its venues and contexts, is accepted as diverse, defying any *one* definition. It ranges from religious music to classical music; it includes folklore and popular music—all relating to the notion of Jewishness. A more narrow definition would depend on the perspective of those who attempt it.

Following this, what does Jewish music mean in the context of the *Listener's Companion*? Whichever argument the listener accepts, each chapter offers selective representative examples of 400 years of a diverse history of Jewish music. Aside from a focus on core names, works, and events, the general premise for these selections is that "Jewish" is understood by association, as an idea that in its combination with music can take on different roles: from accompanying religious ceremonies to leisure activities, from denoting Jews in contrast to other cultural groups to defining one group of Jews against another and characterizing local Jewish experiences, from bolstering the adherence to Jewish law or heritage to reinforcing specific ideas of Jewish communal history and identity. It can also be understood as music by affiliation. Composers and artists of Jewish heritage who somehow express their Jewishness in their work will be at the core of this volume; though, in a delicate balancing act, many others will receive mention in passing. In this way, reading about Jewish music will provide selective insight into the vast soundscape of music in America through the lens of its Jewish experience. Indeed, the image of the lens is apt and refers not only to Jewishness.

A second lens used in this volume is that of genre or type of music as we explore repertoires from classical to klezmer, from religious music to film music, from pop music to alternative styles. Here, Jewish music ever more becomes music by association; we hear it, and we associate Judaism or Jewishness with it. In this vein, the *Listener's Companion* presents a network of repertoires all tied to the Jewish as broad concept. The volume approaches these genres by specifically asking, What do we listen to when we listen to Jewish music? It relies on a wide variety of styles, some of them simple, others complex, some spiritual, and others secular.

A third lens that defines the overall structure of the book is the venue. Based on the premise that music does not lose its power if it travels outside the Jewish community, the *Listener's Companion* will explore sounds in many different contexts of musical activity. So pick a place, and I will find a piece that is related to the Jewish experience. Together, we will explore various locations of Jewish music—from the synagogue to the Broadway theater, in cafés and clubs, at the family table, and in the formal setting of the concert hall. Our journey will begin in 1654, when we visit the Spanish and Portuguese Synagogue in New York City, known as the first Jewish congregation established in North America. We proceed to other venues in subsequent chapters, tracing Jewish music's history and development, roughly chronologically to the twenty-first century, when hip-hop and other popular styles influenced Jewish musicians in pubs and clubs. Each chapter focuses on a selection of works that relate to a specific venue and adds one piece to the mosaic of Jewish music. As such, Jewish music is omnipresent in America. Let's approach it with an open mind and with respect to enjoy its full breadth.

1

SOUNDS OF THE SYNAGOGUE

Imagine, if each cantor contributes only one wrong note and one change into our *nusach ha-tefilah*, how disfigured it can become in only one generation. —Abraham Binder (1961)

In September 1654, twenty-three Jews arrived in what was then the Dutch settlement of Nieuw Amsterdam on the southern tip of today's Manhattan. These were refugees from Recife in Brazil, which Portugal had just reconquered. Reason enough for the Sephardi Jews to promptly flee. Governor Peter Stuyvesant was at first unwilling to accept them but succumbed to pressure from the Dutch West India Company, itself pressed by Jewish stockholders. As he imposed numerous restrictions and taxes on the new immigrants, many of them left, and those who remained were allowed to practice their faith only in their homes. No one knows the precise date of the first formal service. The mayor and the New York City Council (then called Common Council) banned all public worship except for Dutch Reformed until 1691. It thus took nearly four decades until a steady and organized congregation emerged: Shearith Israel (Remnant of Israel), also known as the Sephardic and Portuguese Synagogue. Its first known meeting place of 1695 was on Beaver Street, followed by a synagogue on Mill Street (now South William Street), a good distance away from the Dutch town and from the land the community had purchased decades earlier for their first cemetery on St. James Place, which today is surrounded by Chinese shops. Since 1897, the congregation has been located on the Upper

West Side in Manhattan, after moving slowly uptown by way of establishing new and larger houses of prayer in different neighborhoods.

Shearith Israel is known as the first Jewish congregation to be established in North America and until 1825 was the only Jewish congregation in New York City. In the course of the seventeenth and eighteenth centuries, Sephardic and Ashkenazic Jews from different parts of the world came in larger numbers to the New World, founding congregations in Newport, Rhode Island, in 1658; Savannah, Georgia, in 1735; Philadelphia in 1747; and Charleston, South Carolina, in 1749. Until the early nineteenth century, synagogues followed Western Sephardi practice.

Imagine yourself in a synagogue in America some 400 years ago. What would the service sound like? Little is known about specific musical practices. Religious melodies were transmitted largely orally from generation to generation. But we can safely assume that the sounds the congregants heard during weekly gatherings on the Sabbath were the ritual chanting of readings from the Hebrew Bible—the Psalms, the five books of Moses known as the Torah—as well as the recitation of statutory prayers by a single unaccompanied prayer leader. The chanting would vary depending on the time of the year and the point in the service. Overall, the melodies were simple, constructed of a patchwork of motives sung to flowing and free rhythms, some of which recurred (as such they constituted the *nusah*, melodic patterns that are often specific to a congregation and holidays). This presumed simplicity of early synagogue music relates to the prohibitions to make joyful music (especially on instruments) on the Sabbath, for since the destruction of the Second Temple in 70 CE, the Jewish people have been in perpetual mourning. An early exception to the use of instruments is the shofar, a biblical instrument usually made from a ram's horn whose sound resembles that of a trumpet. Its sounds on Rosh Hashanah, the Jewish New Year, and at the end of Yom Kippur, the Day of Atonement, are permissible because of their extramusical significance as a sacred signal of alarm and remembrance. Similarly, the chanting of liturgical texts was considered not music per se but rather a melodic inflection of sacred texts as they should not be spoken in the manner of everyday speech. Indeed, there is a difference between reciting and singing, and over time the names for those who recite and sing have changed as well. Depending on the status and ability of the prayer leader, he has been called *sheliaḥ tsibur* (delegate of the congregation), *baal tefilah* (master of ceremonies, preceptor), or hazan. During the colonial period, the office of the hazan was not chiefly a musical position. In the absence of ordained rabbis until the 1840s, hazanim were jacks-of-all-trades, some serving as kosher butcher or *mohel* (circumciser), teacher, and prayer leader presiding over burials and chanting the service but not necessarily having musical training. The function and musical ability of the hazan has been largely dependent on the needs and demands of individual congregations.

Shearith Israel is a case in point. Initially, the congregation relied on a *hakham* (literally, wise man), one of the elders who had profound liturgical knowledge. The first to be documented is Saul Pardo (Brown), who came to New York in 1685 and served the community until circa 1702. He and his successor's musical roles remained undefined. Only with Gershom Mendes Seixas (1745–1816), who served the congregation from 1768 to 1776 and, interrupted by the Revolutionary War, again from 1784 to 1816, is the musical function of the prayer leader documented. Who was Seixas? As the first American-born spiritual leader of Shearith Israel, a descendant of both Ashkenazim and Sephardim, and raised and educated on New York soil, he represents an early example of the American melting pot. Seixas's functions were clearly demarcated. He served as communal leader, mohel, and hazan. But he was also fully integrated in American society. In 1789, he participated in George Washington's inauguration ceremony and was active in a wide range of civic organizations, for example, as regent and trustee of Columbia University. His duties as hazan were outlined in 1795 but without any references to melodies or other music specifics.

Beyond the question of *what* music was sung, there was also the question of *who* should sing. Colonial Jews believed in general and unregulated participation, or what today would be called congregational singing. Men and women sang together in Sephardic synagogues: the women above in a separate section and the men below. But by the turn of the century, change was under way. Shearith Israel's bylaws of 1805 declared that "every member of this congregation shall, previous to the singing [of] any psalm, or prayer, remain silent until the [hazan] shall signify the tone or key, in which the same is to be sung. Those who are so inclined may then join therein, with an equal voice, but neither higher or louder than the *hazan*." Another change came on a special occasion, the consecration of the second synagogue in 1818, during which a mixed choir performed, consisting of five members of the Seixas family, who rehearsed especially for this event. However, the board did not support the establishment of a permanent choir for all services. It feared that a formal, institutionalized choir would dominate services and inhibit congregational singing as a hallmark of Western Sephardic customs, introduce elitism, and ultimately create dissension.

With the opening of the congregation's third synagogue, on Crosby Street in 1834, the musical qualities of the congregation's hazan, Isaac Benjamin Seixas (1828–1839), are documented for the first time. Seixas was vocally gifted and liked to soar in the upper registers. The *Times* called his voice "impressive." An all-male choir sang on this occasion as well—another exception, but not for long. In 1859, the trustees announced that they were prepared to advertise the position of a permanent choirmaster. The congregation remained torn, fearing that the introduction of a choir would transform worship and ultimately diminish the congregants to becoming passive auditors. Introducing choral music certainly had benefits. Sounding within the new grand synagogue architecture, it could enhance decorum and contribute to a refined atmosphere, one that reflected Jews' rising status in society and sought to bestir worshippers to elevated thoughts, introspection, and moral improvement. However, it was not until the 1870s that Shearith Israel had a standing choir whose primary function was to lead the congregational singing. The four-part choir, consisting of boys' and male voices, sang on the Sabbath, High Holy Day, and festivals and harmonized choral music of Sephardic melodies that the congregation sang in unison.

Although by 1825 the Ashkenazi members had seceded from Shearith, founding their own congregation, Shearith continued to be a synagogue for everyone and culturally inclusive. This extended to the personnel the congregation hired and the new repertoire they introduced from the late nineteenth century on. Between 1883 and 1941, Leon M. Kramer (1866–1943) served as choir director. He was a well-known director of Jewish choruses in the New York area who immigrated from Berlin. He is said to have been associated there in some capacity with Louis Lewandowski, the music director at the New Synagogue in Berlin, who was one of the central figures in the development of a new Ashkenazi synagogue music for liberal synagogues. Under his baton, the repertoire expanded to include traditional Sephardic music arranged for choir, new Sephardic compositions by English composers Joseph Barnby and Charles Kensington Salaman, the congregation's rabbis Henry Pereira Mendes and David de Sola Pool, and Ashkenazic choral music by Salomon Sulzer and Louis Lewandowski. In the following decade, Shearith continued to hire German émigrés as choral conductors, thus fostering an encounter of Ashkenazic and Sephardic musical culture. From 1881 on, Shearith also used instruments on weddings and special occasions. In 1936, George Gershwin donated his harmonium before moving to Hollywood. In spite of the adoption of the instrument, Shearith considers itself neither Reform nor Conservative nor Orthodox. Such denominational designations do not exist in Sephardic culture.

The custom of Shearith Israel is in many ways unique. There are thousands of synagogues in the United States today, and with that come innumerable customs. Accordingly, religious music differs from synagogue to synagogue, depending on the cultural makeup of the community—from Ashkenazi to Western and Eastern Sephardic with its different strands that reach from Bukharian to Syrian to Yemenite Jews—and on the denomination it represents. Liturgical music can be different in and within each branch of Judaism, although boundaries between the main streams are not always clear-cut, as we shall see. Also, if repertoires transcend these boundaries, their function remains the same. Additionally, religious music in America has evolved over the course of 350 years. Thus, providing comprehensive insights into synagogue music in America is a futile endeavor.

If Shearith Israel serves as an example for a Western Sephardic synagogue that musically evolved and over time adopted repertoires associated with the Ashkenazi Jews, we might ask whether a unique American style of synagogue music came to exist. By way of giving one possible answer, fast-forward to January 30, 2011. Temple Israel in Boston hosts a tribute to legendary performer, composer, recording artist, teacher, and passionate Jewish visionary Deborah Lynn Friedman. "Remembering Debbie" opened with the concluding episode of the 2003 documentary film *A Journey of Spirit*, which followed her from 1997 to 2002. In the clip, she softly begins strumming her guitar, joined on the piano by Chris Hardin, her longtime accompanist. After the short instrumental introduction, we hear the opening words of her famous song "Mourning into Dancing," her English setting of Psalm 30, later released on the album *One People* (2006). Words appear in clear diction and music in irregular flowing phrases, sung with intense spiritual conviction. The first line moves seamlessly into the second, effortlessly between on- and offbeats. Phrases and sections are repeated with an internal logic that engages the listener. The song ends with the phrase that opened it—"You turn my mourning into dancing"—sung just once and ending in a satisfying final chord. Although not intended as such, the song's message sums up the history and development of sounds in the synagogue—from the mourning for the Second Temple to contemporary and celebratory expressions of Judaism. Debbie herself called "Mourning into Dancing" her theme song. Indeed, its larger message—the power of transformation—relates Friedman's lifework as it largely became her credential. Through music, but even more so through the process of creating and presenting music as a liturgical experience and spiritual process, she also promoted healing. Tragically, the song also highlights the limitations of healing. After prolonged illness (Friedman suffered from a neurological condition), she unexpectedly passed away on January 9, 2011, at the age of only fifty-nine.

A public figure in the Jewish musical world, Friedman's passing triggered countless acts of remembrance through performances of her music. Dozens of events were staged at synagogues across the United States and the world. Thousands attended. Tens of thousands more watched these ceremonies online. The Hebrew Union College-Jewish Institute of Religion's School of Sacred Music in New York, where she taught rabbinical and cantorial students beginning in 2007, was renamed the Debbie Friedman School of Sacred Music. (Her appointment was striking for two reasons: first, because she was a largely self-taught musician who did not know how to read music, and, second, because her work—inclusive, progressive, and strongly feminist—was perceived as a threat to established liturgical music when she began her career in the early 1970s.) No other Jewish musical figure had received such an outpouring of remembrance in decades, which attests to her wide reception. Indeed, her songs had become liturgical staples. Shortly after her untimely death, the World Union for Progressive Judaism aptly summarized her achievement as changing the nature of synagogue music: "While Reform worship was once characterized by organs and choirs . . . Debbie taught us to sing as communities and congregations."

Obituaries hailed Friedman as a "revolutionary" whose music "transformed" Jewish liturgy in America. Although Friedman's impact was strongest within the Reform movement, her repertoire is sung across the Jewish spectrum and beyond.

Who was Debbie Friedman? Born in Utica, New York, in 1951 to parents who belonged variously to Conservative and Reform synagogues, Friedman grew up in Minnesota. As a teenager, she was captivated by Jewish and folk music; she taught herself to play the guitar from the records of the American folk group Peter, Paul and Mary, and her music would be likened to theirs. She began her work as a song leader beginning in 1967 at Reform movement summer camps in Wisconsin. The camp system originated in the 1950s and relied on music to get campers participating, having fun, and learning the basics of Jewish culture through song texts that leaned on prayers, rabbinic sayings, or lines of Scripture in Hebrew, English, or a mix of the two. The music had to be engaging and easy to learn and suitable for groups large and small. This musical environment shaped Friedman's approach.

In the fall of 1969, after high school, Friedman left for six months to Israel to work on a kibbutz where she cultivated her work as a song and youth leader. Not long thereafter, she began songwriting: "One night I went to synagogue, and realized, sitting there, I was bored," she told the *Los Angeles Times* in 1995. "I realized the rabbi was talking, the choir was singing and nobody was doing anything. There was no participation." In 1970, an original melody came to her, and as an experiment, she set to it the words of "V'ahavta" (You Shall Love), a prayer drawn from Deuteronomy that commands Jews to love God. She recalled of that song,

> That turned the liturgy upside down . . . that was the first thing I wrote and that was the first thing that kids sang and when they sang it they stood arm in arm, and they were just weeping and it was like all of a sudden they realized that they could take ownership of their tefillah [prayer], they could take ownership of what was theirs anyway but they could take it back. They didn't have to use other people's poetry anymore in order to have a meaningful worship experience.

With "V'ahavta," Friedman had found her calling. Her first album, *Sing unto God*, a collection of Sabbath songs, was released in 1972.

Hundreds of songs for Jewish worship, education, and meditation on twenty-one more albums followed during her lifetime. She toured beginning in the early 1970s, and her audience became broader as she moved from camps to synagogues to institutions, such as Jewish community centers. Her status as a popular Jewish artist was cemented in 1996 when she played her twenty-fifth-anniversary concert at Carnegie Hall in New York.

Friedman wrote songs for all ages and all musical abilities. Acutely aware of the lack of congregational participation in sacred service and herself musically illiterate, Friedman actively pursued music as a form of oral transmission. By making the songs accessible to those who could not read music, she encouraged a level of participation that until then was unequaled. Her approach was not uncontroversial. It conflicted with a contemporary movement promoting intellectual musical literacy and professionalization in liberal Jewish circles, with scholars, composers, and cantors trying to assert a long, evidence-based lineage of Jewish sound that could stand alongside similarly established rabbinic interpretation. While some rabbis and cantors welcomed her music as a democratizing force, others saw it as a subversive breach of time-honored customs in which the cantor was typically white-haired, always male, and usually vocally imposing and the congregants were passive listeners. From this side, Friedman's tunes faced criticism of being campy and schmaltzy and "happy clappy." Her most receptive audiences were among those groups familiar with the sounds of the folk revival and predisposed to questioning social norms: youth movements, college students, and liberal clergy.

Friedman's work is strongly connected to Jewish texts. She has contributed dozens of new tunes for well-known and lesser-known passages in the siddur (prayer book) and other Jewish texts, such as the Tanakh (Hebrew Bible). She also adapted such texts to English, sometimes with Hebrew mixed in. In this way, Friedman blurred the boundary between prayer and song. This is especially evident in "Mi Shebeirach," which became a means for reconnecting to the prayer and to healing resources in general.

The story of "Mi Shebeirach" (The One Who Blessed) begins in 1987 when one of Friedman's friends decided to hold a Simhat hokhmah, a ceremony celebrating wisdom and aging. For this, Friedman, together with Rabbi Drorah Setel, created the "Mi Shebeirach" prayer song. The original prayer designates the opening for special blessings spoken or chanted from the *bimah* after the weekly Torah portion is read and while the Torah scroll is still undressed. Each of the blessings opens with the words "mi shebeirakh" (The One who blessed our fathers). They may be offered for those who read Torah, a bar or bat mitzvah, a couple soon to be married, or new parents. Generally, however, they refer to the version recited for the ill and dedicated to named individuals. Current, nonorthodox prayer books alter the wording of the Mi Shebeirakh in various ways to reflect liberal sensibilities. Regardless of prayer book or denomination, the opening phrase remains central to the theology of healing and forms the basis of poetic adaptations.

Friedman and Setel adapted the widely known formula used in blessings, preserving the first two words and maintaining theological language to maintain the connection to the practice of praying to God for a sick person. Their setting consists of two verses. Both open with "mi shebeirach" and close with "And let us say: Amen." Internal lyrics reference "refuah sh'leimah" as well as body and spirit. Alongside these familiar allusions, Friedman and Setel offer their reinterpretation of the prayers. To ensure gender inclusivity, the authors invoke both the patriarchs and the matriarchs. Instead of replacing the opening line, "mi shebeirach avoteinu" (The One who blessed our fathers), the authors added the words "makor habrachah l'imoteinu" (Source of blessing for our mothers). These lines are reversed in the second stanza to prevent affixing gender to certain godly attributes and to create gender balance. The words "makor habrachah" (source of blessing) were borrowed from Lekhah Dodi, a core prayer of the Friday evening liturgy that welcomes the Sabbath bride. Such creative efforts influenced the awareness of gender issues and inclusivity in Jewish life, empowering women in worship and music. Repeated phrasing gives space for both a meditative and an interpretative response.

The combination of Hebrew and English lyrics, which largely translate the Hebrew in a single liturgical composition, is a striking element of "Mi Shebeirach" and follows songwriters' general trend of the 1960s and 1970s to create bilingual songs. Through this bilingual approach, those with limited or no knowledge of Hebrew are able to understand prayer in new ways. Previously, combining the languages was limited to children's songs. Friedman first began mixing the languages in the late

1970s to meld the heritage of the "holy language" with the vernacular of American life. More so, the Hebrew comes in short phrases that worshippers can easily learn. The English lyrics do not translate the Hebrew verbatim in order to maximize the poetic potential of each language and to offer alternative readings, thus enabling deeper engagement. The English segments in "Mi Shebeirach" emphasize and reenvision healing in subtle but significant ways. In the first stanza, the passive reception of blessing receives a sense of individual agency and the empowerment to take an active role in the process of healing through the phrase "help us find the courage to make our lives a blessing." In the second stanza, the rabbinic phrase "refuah sh'leima" is redefined as the renewal rather than the repair of body and spirit. Because the Hebrew and English lyrics offer complementary understandings of the original, many consider Friedman's works "musical midrash," referencing rabbinic literature that interprets and expands sacred texts.

Friedman's musical style is rooted in the American folk revival and action songs of the 1960s and 1970s. Some have mentioned a semblance to Joan Baez, and others have drawn parallels to Shlomo Carlebach. Many refer to Friedman's "gift for melody" to describe simultaneously her music's beauty and power, but also simplicity and accessibility. Congregants easily relate to her melodies and learn them quickly. The melody of "Mi Shebeirach" supports these qualities. Written in a major key, the melody is emotionally evocative and lyrical with stepwise motions and occasional small leaps upward, especially on key words such as "habrachah" (this blessing), as if musically expressing the appeal to the heavens. It spans the range of only one octave, which makes it more easy to sing, and is harmonized with a simple chord progression. The tempo is slow, inviting for liberties in rhythm. The second stanza shows only moderate variation.

One cannot separate Friedman's compositional output from her performance and transmission. Friedman insisted on singing the song twice: first, individually for listening ("I'll sing it first for you," she would say). After her clear, strong voice finished the tune, she would sing it with her audience in unison, accompanying them on the guitar. In this way, the song becomes both personal and communal. If in her songwriting Friedman embraced song and prayer as a social practice, in performances Friedman could easily oscillate between social hall and sanctuary. She compelled her audiences to sing and dance, connect with each

other, and create spiritually elevated moments no matter the context.
As such, her work defies simple division between liturgical and nonli-
turgical music and rather creates a general feeling of spiritual together-
ness perceived as profound and pressing. Although "Mi Shebeirach" is
particularly well suited to a more ritualistic context, Friedman included
it in nearly every concert. In this way, it became widespread and popular beyond the synagogue. But without her personal connection and
compassion, it is difficult to imagine that her piece would have reached
the level of broad usage that it has. First released on the album *And
You Shall Be a Blessing* (1989) and rereleased on *Renewal of Spirit*
(1995), "Mi Shebeirach" may be Friedman's most often requested song
in congregations across the spectrum and has even been sung in some
Christian churches.

Friedman was by no means the first or the only to represent a new
style of synagogue music and contribute initiatives that led to unique
and relevant forms of congregational worship, revitalizing it for a generation of postwar American Jews. Other talented musicians and religious
innovators around the country active in the Reform and Conservative
movements—among them Jonathan Klein, Raymond Smolover, Jeff
Klepper, Daniel Freelander, and Michael Isaacson—created so-called
Contemporary Jewish Music, which are works that frequently use English lyrics and borrow extensively from a restricted set of contemporary
popular music styles. In the Orthodox world, it was Shlomo Carlebach
who represented this new approach. To educate and engage listeners,
he turned to the folk revival for inspiration. He used musically uncom-
plicated (i.e., easy-to-sing-along-with tunes with repeated phrases) and
outside of worship accompanied himself on the guitar. But here the
comparison with Friedman ends. Carlebach, who once shared a stage
with Bob Dylan, sang only in Hebrew and provided few clues on how
his audience had to respond.

Independent of their denomination, the above-mentioned individuals challenged the boundaries and strict demarcations of liturgical music. In this way, they had a significant, even radical effect on Jewish
communal and religious practice. The increased popularity of their
works in synagogue services was part of a trend toward greater participation by the congregation during worship. This went hand in hand
with a decline of hazanuth, that is, the formal vocal style sung or
chanted by the hazan (sometimes combined with choir and organ),

which up to then had largely represented synagogue music. These changes triggered criticism and substantial resistance as they affected the more rigid barriers between the leader of the service and the congregation. They also initiated fundamental questions about the relationships between liturgy, music, and community.

Debbie Friedman, Shlomo Carlebach, and their contemporaries initiated one of the many transformations that synagogue music in America had undergone in its history. Drifting away from European models, synagogue music embraced popular music and engaged congregants with Hasidic tunes, folk and Israeli compositions, blues and jazz, and many other styles. As the Jewish community of America continuously changed and transformed, so did its sacred music.

Let us fill the historical gap between the Sephardic Colonial Jews and Contemporary Jewish Music by way of exploring some of the nineteenth- and early twentieth-century developments in the synagogues of America. One of the biggest transformations occurred when in the first half of the nineteenth century, a quarter of a million German Jews arrived in the United States and began to form separate Ashkenazi congregations (among the first were Rodeph Shalom in Philadelphia and B'nai Israel in Cincinnati). With the second big wave of immigration, between 1880 and 1920, this time of eastern European Jews, diversification of Jewish life, ritual, and music took its course, shifting to various Ashkenazi practices.

Earlier in the century, the *Haskalah* (Jewish Enlightenment) and Jewish emancipation had triggered efforts to modernize worship service in Europe. In the course of these reforms, synagogue music underwent radical changes to appeal to a public that was increasingly educated in classical music but with stark resistance by traditionalists. The hazan was now called "cantor." With the shift in nomenclature came changes in the profession as well. The cantor possessed a thorough knowledge of liturgy like the hazan but also had a more profound knowledge of music from outside the synagogue and was able to write music and in some cases conduct, but his role throughout the nineteenth and twentieth centuries would continuously change. If until the nineteenth century vocal music was mostly orally transmitted, from the early nineteenth century it began to be written down, thereby replacing the improvisation inherent to hazanuth with rhythmically strict and structurally fixed melodies.

Organized congregational singing in unison, and not necessarily in Hebrew, became a central part of Jewish worship. Larger communities employed a (semi-)professional chorus (depending on the congregation's denomination, either mixed voices or male voices only, to avoid *kol ishah*, the prohibition for a man to listen to a woman singing) and sometimes hired instrumentalists as well. Torah cantillation was practiced only in a very few Reform congregations because the reformers believed that cantillation and biblical chant no longer had validity, as both were a "postbiblical invention." Besides, the Reform movement found cantillation to be antiquated and unattractive and not in line with the current fashion of synagogue song. One of the most strident markers of newness, however, was the organ as accompaniment and solo instrument on the Sabbath and holidays (the first synagogue in America to introduce an organ was Kahal Kadosh Beth Elohim in Charleston, South Carolina, in 1841).

With new repertoires, Classical and Romantic styles began to influence the structure and expression of synagogue music. The orientation toward Western European composition of liturgical music, often associated with the names of Salomon Sulzer (Vienna) and Louis Lewandowski (Berlin), had profound consequences for synagogue music and was tied to new movements and branches of Judaism variously known as Progressive, Reform, Liberal, or Neolog. Many of the immigrants from the western parts of Europe brought these new repertoires with them to the United States, which began to infiltrate the Ashkenazi synagogues from the mid-1800s on.

In contrast, when the huge waves of eastern European Jews from Hungary, Poland, Romania, and Russia began to arrive on America's shores in the 1880s, they brought with them the familiar melodies of the shtetl, the predominantly Jewish small town of eastern Europe. Eastern European hazanuth crossed the ocean with the great cantors of the day. By the early twentieth century, melodies that had originated in Hungary, Russia, Poland, and Romania rang in the golden age of the cantorate. Cantors cultivated a liturgical music that favored their solo role over communal participation. They also became full-fledged artists for recording companies, appearing regularly on radio programs devoted to liturgical music and Yiddish folk songs, and performed in concert halls and vaudeville theaters. With this, cantorial music expanded its liturgical function to be also heard as entertainment.

Two major styles of cantorial music dominated the Ashkenazic synagogue in the United States in the nineteenth and early twentieth centuries: the orderly and more structured repertoires first imported from central Europe and from the late nineteenth century on newly conceived in the United States by Moritz (Morris) Goldstein, Edward Stark, Alois Kaiser, William Sparger, and Sigmund Schlesinger, who wrote for cantor, choir, and organ, and the freely inspirational styles rooted in eastern Europe and brought over by towering figures who initiated and represented the golden age of the cantorate, among them Zavel Kwartin, Adolph (Aaron) Katchko, and Samuel Vigoda. Louis "Leibele" Waldman was one of the first of that circle to be born in America. The greatest of them all, however, was Josef Rosenblatt (1882–1933), who until the late 1910s dominated the world of hazanuth in America.

Born in Bila Tserkva (near Kiev) in 1882, Rosenblatt exerted a very strong influence on hazanuth, first throughout Europe and later in the United States. At the age of seven, he was already touring Hungary, Bukovina, and Galicia with his baal tefilah father and after his death with his brother Levi. During that time, he absorbed Hasidic music and different styles of hazanuth and studied the Talmud. By the age of nine, he was somewhat of a celebrity, able to sing whole passages from the liturgy by heart. At the age of eighteen after much traveling, he settled in Mukacheve (then in Carpathian Ruthenia, now Ukraine), winning his position as cantor in that city's synagogue by beating more than forty other candidates in what amounted to a sing-off. After eleven months, in the spring of 1901, the Bratislava community "kidnapped" him. In truth, Mukacheve was dominated by two Hasidic dynasties that were strictly opposed to changes of any kind—even if kept within faithful frameworks. In 1865, rabbis had gathered in nearby Michalovce to render a *psak din* (formal ruling). Signed by seventy-two rabbis, it strictly prohibited any modification of synagogue service to avoid any resemblance to Christian worship. A choir was unacceptable.

Rosenblatt identified as Orthodox and continued to do so throughout his life, but he must have found the narrow perspectives of Mukacheve stifling. He seized on a dispute with his congregation over monetary support for the choir as an occasion to resign his post and assume the position of Obercantor in Pressburg (now Bratislava) at the Orthodox synagogue at Zámocká Street. The five years he spent there constitute Rosenblatt's first productive period in terms of composition. During that time, he produced his first major collection of cantorial recitatives and liturgical choral music for four voices. His choir, consisting of students from the local yeshiva, might have served as a testing ground for some of these settings. The untitled manuscripts of nine pieces on sixty pages, known as *Shirei Yosef*, bear approbations signed between December 1904 and March 1905 by other influential cantors. Approbations were necessary since Rosenblatt was largely self-taught as a composer and arranger. During his time in Bratislava, he acquired the nickname "Yossele Pressburger" and thereafter was known as Yossele rather than Josef. Word of his high vocal abilities spread to Western Europe. He made his first phonograph recordings between March and September 1905. Manufactured by the Edison Record Company in Vienna, the *Herrengesang* featured four cantorial pieces on phonograph and is one of the earliest recorded examples of hazanuth.

In 1906, Rosenblatt accepted an appointment in the Kohlhöfen Synagogue in Hamburg, thus making a cultural leap into Western European Orthodoxy. In Hamburg, he became acquainted with classical music and adapted some of his eastern European stylistic approaches. Rather than reject other influences, he absorbed and melded them into his clearly Eastern style of hazanuth.

In 1911, the venerable Yeshiah Meisels resigned as cantor from the First Hungarian Congregation Ohab Zedek, one of New York's wealthiest Orthodox synagogues, which by then had moved to its new building in the then upscale Jewish enclave of Harlem. It had a vested choir with thirty voices. The congregation engaged Rosenblatt in June 1912. His reputation had preceded him through his recordings. During a mere three years of service at Ohab Zedek, he established himself as one of the most venerable cantors of all time and as a vocal celebrity also recognized by non-Jewish audiences. His *El Mole Rachmin (für Titanik)* of 1913 and other recordings, as well as concert tours across the country and overseas, made him famous. In 1918 he received the offer to sing Eleazar in Chicago Opera Company's production of Jacques Fromenthal Halévy's *La Juive* (The Jewess). He was offered the extraordinary fee of $1,000 (today $25,000) per performance—quite high even by today's standards. Rosenblatt famously declined, most likely because such a venture was at odds with his sacred calling. Thereafter, he did, however, appear in public recitals on the stages of Carnegie Hall and the Metropolitan Opera House and elsewhere.

In August 1926, he left his position at Ohab Zedek (his bankruptcy earlier that year and the need for better-paying work might have played a role). Two months later, *The Jazz Singer*, a film about the son of a cantor who turns to secular music and that featured him singing "Yohrzeit," premiered (the film and its music are discussed in chapter 4). Until Moshe Koussevitzky's immigration after World War II and his recitals combining classical repertoire and hazanuth, no other cantor apart from Rosenblatt succeeded in attracting non-Jewish audiences and admirers to the extent that he did. As a cantorial public figure, he was virtually in a class of his own.

After a period of traveling and serving as a guest cantor for Orthodox congregations throughout the United States as well as appearing in vaudeville performances, he signed a ten-year contract with the Hasidic First Congregation Anshe Sfard in Borough Park, Brooklyn, for an annual record salary of $12,000 (today $170,000). He began serving in October 1927, but after the stock market crash almost exactly two years later, Anshe Sfard was unable to pay him, and he returned to Ohab Zedek, which had just moved to its new home on West 95th Street. During a concert tour in 1933, Rosenblatt died in Jerusalem of a heart attack at the young age of fifty-one. His remains are buried on the Mount of Olives.

Small in stature (he was only five feet two inches tall), Rosenblatt used his grand tenor voice (some called him a baritone) with supreme artistry. He possessed an extraordinary technique and flexibility; he intoned fast passages remarkably accurately and accomplished florid embellishment of melodic lines with perfection. The timbre of his voice varied with impressive contrasts from tender and hearty to regal, adapting to the meaning and soul of the text, from adoration to pathos. He possessed a unique ability to transition from normal voice to soprano falsetto with hardly any noticeable break at all (the falsetto used as a method of easing the strain on his overworked voice). He continued and pioneered techniques that have subsequently been adopted by cantors around the world. These include *krekhts* (sobs or sighs), in which he would deliberately allow his voice to crack or break to convey the emotion of what he was singing. With a voice of rare beauty, he is the quintessential virtuoso exponent of hazanuth of all time.

Hazanuth, which is based on the principle of improvising, can follow a well-ordered fashion (*hazanut ha-seder*) or can depend almost exclusively on the immediate inspiration of the hazan during his recitation. The latter, a spontaneous outpouring of the soul known as *hazanut ha-regesh* and sometimes referred to as "free improvisation," was the creation of later virtuoso hazanim, such as Rosenblatt. In the course of time, certain motives and melodic curves, modulations, and coloratura passages within given modes became distinctive in the improvisation of the virtuoso hazanim. And Rosenblatt, who fused the free approach prevalent before his era with the more structured, metered style, was certainly distinct. His early improvisational style formed the basis for his formally constructed solo pieces. These frequently employed a recurring motive or theme, some reminiscent of Hasidic melodies, which provided the congregants with an opportunity to participate by singing along.

Preserving his style for eternity, Rosenblatt wrote down many of his cantorial solos. Some of those original melodies reflect Rosenblatt's love of Italian and French opera, yet they never seem inappropriate and misplaced because he skillfully integrated these passages into a larger melodic framework. With Adolph Katchko, Rosenblatt was also one of the very few Orthodox émigré hazanim of his time who composed liturgical music for choir. The harmonic vocabulary of these choral settings is rather basic, having simple harmonies.

His setting of Tal, the prayer for dew recited only once a year, on the first day of Passover, exemplifies all of this. The liturgical poem was written by Rabbi Eleazar Ha-Kallir in the seventh century. In six verses with end rhymes, it asks for the blessing of dew, but it is also a prayer concerning the end of exile and the rebuilding of the city of Jerusalem. It is not accidental that this plea for redemption is found in a prayer recited on the holiday that celebrates freedom and redemption. Each paragraph begins and ends with the Hebrew word for "dew." Rosenblatt's rendition of the first four verses is dramatic, with a unique interpretation yet dignified rendering of the text. In his studio recording of 1923, he is accompanied by a small instrumental ensemble and his brother-in-law Cantor Meilech Kaufman, also a tenor, with whom he sings at times in dialogue splitting lines, in unison, and occasionally in harmony, recalling the art of the *meshorerim*, who would assist the cantor as vocal accompanists. The instrumental parts may have been separately arranged, as Rosenblatt would have rendered the prayer a cappella during service.

The recording begins with an instrumental prelude that provides a distinct rhythm. Rosenblatt opens the first verse by stating the word "tal" (dew) three times consecutively, each beginning on a higher pitch. With that, he establishes the main motive of his melody: a large upward leap. The third reiteration is stretched out with a mini-melisma. Rosenblatt heightens the inherent repetition of "dew" in the prayer. Such word repetition, although generally opposed by Orthodox Jews, is idiomatic to his style.

But this is not where repetition ends. Rosenblatt repeats the first two lines to practically the exact same melody, which contains a few of his signature sobs. With tear-like grace notes (recalling dew dripping off a leaf), the influence of opera is easily recognizable. Through repetition, he emphasizes the concern for needing dew in order for agriculture to prosper in the Land of Israel. In the last two lines of the verse, Kaufman joins in a call-and-response style whenever a word is repeated ("ko-mem," here meaning "chosen," appears four times, the last one sung in harmony). With the repeats and the ornamentation, the first verse is given profound impassioned expression to underline its greater meaning: a plea for messianic redemption (raise up the city of your desire, i.e., Jerusalem). It exhibits Rosenblatt's highly sophisticated style, which emphasizes lyrical melody, and introduces a recurring motive found at the beginning of each line: an upward leap spanning the interval of a fifth.

While the first verse adheres to an overall strict rhythm, the second verse takes a different course with extensively florid melodies. It begins with the upward leaping interval over the word "tal" but then departs into a long cadenza-like melisma that destroys any sense of rhythmic regularity and adds a heightened sense of improvisation. When Rosenblatt sings it the second time, it features his impressive falsetto, so smoothly approached that one barely notices the transition. Then he reiterates "tal" twice more and smoothly finishes the rest of the line. Elements introduced in the first verse return: word repetition and with that the establishment of short motives, upward leaps, and the dialogue with Kaufman to evoke call-and-response between cantor and congregation. By the end of the verse, Rosenblatt reaches his highest note over "ka-sukah" (the city is compared to a sukah, a temporary shelter) with very fast and yearning notes, underlining the meaning of the line—a cry for the city once so desolate. Pauses are filled with instrumental interludes that imitate the cantor's line. And because the penultimate line is so essential, Rosenblatt sings it several times with variations. The third verse is similar in the sense of having a more improvisatory and free-flowing approach, but it emphasizes less Rosenblatt's virtuosity than his gift to interpret text in so many different ways and his very poignant use of embellishment. He juxtaposes a more florid melody to express "giving light from amidst the darkness" with a declamatory, almost speech-like passage for the last line that speaks of the nation. In the fourth verse, Rosenblatt returns to the measured rhythm that began "Tal." It is upbeat and hymnic and reverts to duets on passages that emphasize community, "the chosen people," and "we will sing and raise our voice." The prayer calls for strongly supplicate expression, which Rosenblatt highlights with the power and sweetness of his voice. His rendition is structured with transitions from free-flowing solos to conclusions with a metric tune called *lidl*. In its sheer variedness, Rosenblatt's rendition is melodically forward looking while in essence remaining rooted in familiar structures. His "Tal" is in a mode known variously as *Ahavah rabah* or *freygish*, which means that it relies on notes and a step called augmented second, creating an expressive hallmark sound of Jewish music (think of "Hava nagila" or "If I Were a Rich Man")—an instantly recognizable wailing or yearning with a hint of the Middle East. It is Rosenblatt's unique approach and inimitable voice that made his cantorial style famous and exerted great influence on contemporary and subsequent generations of cantors. Indeed, Yossele Rosenblatt opened up his hazanuth in and for America.

As we can discern from the various repertoires discussed, synagogue music in America does not necessarily represent American synagogue music. Waves of immigrants brought varied musical repertoires to the New World, and it took more than a century to meld them into something new and distinctive. Some synagogue musicians had already synthesized Jewish melos with Western musical expressions to different degrees before entering the New World.

What constitutes liturgical music in American synagogues is the preservation of music from a prior location and the parallel slow process of synthesizing these sounds into something completely new. In this process, certain discourses prevailed, such as tensions between participation and performance, between congregational singing and choir music, between the demands of organized religion and the allure of modernity. To date, they have never fully been resolved.

2

SEASONED WITH SONG

At Home and at the Jewish Table

Friday night at a traditional Jewish home. Just prior to sunset, the woman of the household has lit the two Sabbath candles and recited a blessing. The family might have begun the evening in the synagogue at a service where they sang the "Lekhah Dodi" and with it welcomed the Sabbath bride, as its symbolic presence is known. On arrival home, it is customary for the father to bless his children. Once the family gathers at the table, just before kiddush, they sing "Shalom Aleikhem" (Peace Be Upon You) to inaugurate the Sabbath in the home for the entire household and any invited guests.

The text is rooted in a legend: When people are returning from synagogue on Friday night, two angels follow them—one good, the other evil. If the house is well prepared for the Sabbath, then the good angel blesses the home, and the evil angel is divinely compelled to give his assent by responding with Amen. If the home is not prepared, then the evil angel proclaims that the next Sabbath will be the same, and the good angel is forced to say Amen. The text responds to this legend by greeting, blessing, and seeking the blessing of these angels. It is ascribed to the kabbalists of Safed and believed to have been written in the late sixteenth or early seventeenth century.

Countless melodies exist for "Shalom Aleikhem." As one of her last acts, Debbie Friedman created a beautiful and haunting version in 2010. Among the more recent ones is the fast and rhythmic melody

composed by Rabbi Shmuel Brazil in the mid-1980s. The most well
known melody, however, was conceived by Galician-born Israel Goldfarb (1879–1967). In his dual calling as rabbi and cantor of Kane Street
Synagogue in Brooklyn, Goldfarb became known as the father of congregational singing. Many of his compositions, especially his High Holiday melodies, have been so widely chanted that they have come to be
regarded as traditional. He first introduced his compositions in his synagogue and at his Sabbath table. After they were published, they quickly spread throughout the Jewish world. Today, his melodies are heard in
nearly every Ashkenazi synagogue in North America and in many
homes, with many being unaware of who actually created them.

The conception of Goldfarb's melody for Shalom Aleikhem is
uniquely tied to New York. Goldfarb conceived it on May 10, 1918,
while sitting near the Alma Mater statue in front of the Low Memorial
Library at Columbia University. Later that year, he published the melody as "Sholom Alechem—שָׁלוֹם עֲלֵיכֶם" in the song anthology *Friday
Evening Melodies* and *The Jewish Songster*, a kind of modernized version of sacred songs for Jewish Americans, which he issued together
with his brother Samuel E. Goldfarb. These collections of Jewish liturgical and secular songs in Hebrew, Yiddish, and English became a staple of every synagogue and Jewish school in America. In 1953, Israel
Goldfarb published it again in the collection *Sabbath in the Home*.
Often presumed to be an old Hasidic melody, he wrote in 1963, "The
popularity of the melody traveled not only throughout this country but
throughout the world, so that many people came to believe that the
song was handed down from Mt. Sinai by Moses." Over time, the melody dispersed widely and gained standard acceptance and currency
abroad. "Sholom Alechem" has been arranged to be performed in concerts and recorded by musicians such as Celtic guitarist Tony McManus
and violinist Itzhak Perlman and in a modern, exuberantly joyful version
popularized by Israeli singer Idan Yaniv and Kinderlach, a group of
seven preteen boys who have become a worldwide musical sensation—
and these are just a few.

In its essence, Goldfarb's tune is slow and based on the repetition of
two equally long phrases over four stanzas: ABBA. The first phrase is
calm in wave form and serves to introduce (and end with) a serene
mood. The second phrase is similarly wavy in its melodic contour but
employs higher notes, thereby being more vitalizing. The whole melody

relies on the yearning mode that Yossele Rosenblatt employed in "Tal," known as Ahavah rabah or freygish. Overall, the piece is rather simple, with little vocal ornamentation and a moderate pitch range. This allows everyone to sing along, even those with little musical background.

It is a mitzvah, a religious commandment and good deed, to eat three meals on the Sabbath: one on Friday night, one on Saturday after the morning service, and one late Saturday afternoon before Sabbath ends. The Sabbath meals and their songs are repeatedly cited as being among the chief pleasures and obligations, codified with the Talmudic injunction that on the Sabbath Jews should eat, drink, discuss Torah, and sing songs. Two notions connect the Sabbath songs with food: the belief that the songs themselves are nourishment and the mystical idea that food is itself a form of worship.

"Shalom Aleikhem" opens the Sabbath as a singing festival par excellence. It is the first in the prescribed order of hymns. Although many American congregations already sing it during the Friday evening service, it is one of many quasi-liturgical Sabbath table songs or table hymns, known as *zemirot shel Shabat*, that are sung before, during, and after the meal when the family sits around the table. Although the tunes vary widely from locale to locale and from family to family, many of the *zemirot* have metrical hymn-like melodies for the (para)liturgical poetic texts in Hebrew or Aramaic. Some may be found in the siddur, the Jewish prayer book. Some directly relate to the three Sabbath meals, others reflect the mood and feeling of the Sabbath. As singing *zemirot* is as old as any Jewish practice, it might be unsurprising that two dozen of them go back to the sixth and seventh centuries CE, though some communities might sing other songs in Hebrew, Yiddish, or English if they fit in and contribute to the Sabbath mood. Indeed, today there is a wide variety of melodies for singing at the Sabbath table, ranging from specific local tunes to contemporary settings, notably of the popular neo-Hasidic genre à la Shlomo Carlebach. In Hasidic communities, which largely reject modern secular life, singing at the table takes yet another turn. Let us travel farther east to Crown Heights in Brooklyn to learn more about the rebbe's *tish*.

A *tish* (literally, table) is the quintessential Hasidic male gathering for prayer, study, and celebration around the spiritual leader, the rebbe. For Hasidim, the *tish* is a moment of great holiness. During a *tish*, the rebbe sits at the head of the table, and the Hasidim gather around it.

The nature of the *tish* can differ. A *tish* may consist of speeches on Torah subjects, Hasidic stories, and parables; religious commentary on current events and politics; and singing of *zemirot* and melodies known as *nigunim*, with kosher refreshments such as *cholent* (stew) and *kugel* (casserole) being served. The time at which a *tish* can be held also differs. During the early years of Hasidism, the *tish* took place on the occasion of the third Sabbath meal, but today some Hasidic dynasties hold a *tish* on Friday evening, others do so only on Jewish holidays, and some take place on specific occasions. A *tish* can vary in size from a handful to thousands of people. Small *tishn* are often conducted in private homes. Some are public events that are open to non-Hasidim as well. Women do not sit with the men, but they are present to observe from the women's section (provided that the *tish* takes place in the main sanctuary) and may quietly hum along.

Specific customs vary from dynasty to dynasty, and there are many ever since Israel ben Eliezer (Baal Shem Tov) initiated the movement in eighteenth-century eastern Europe as a reaction against overly legalistic Judaism. Although many groups became extinct during the Holocaust, a good number resettled in the United States, among them the Bobov, Modzitz, Satmar, Skver, Spinka, Vizhnitz, and Lubavitch (all named after the places they originated in). All promote spirituality through the popularization and internalization of Jewish mysticism as the fundamental aspect of the faith. All sing with great gusto.

Music plays an especially important role at the *tish* of the Lubavitcher, a dynasty founded in 1755 by Rabbi Schneur Zalman of Liadi (Polish Lithuania). Lubavitch is the Yiddish name for the originally Belorussian (now Russian) village of Lyubavichi, where the movement's leaders lived for more than 100 years. Today, the dynasty is also known by the name Chabad, the acronym of *ḥokhmah*, *binah*, *da'at*, that is, wisdom, understanding, and knowledge—the intellectual underpinnings of the movement. From the 1940s until the present day, the movement's center has been in the Crown Heights neighborhood of Brooklyn. Under Rabbi Menachem M. Schneerson (1902–1994), the seventh and last rebbe, Chabad-Lubavitch transformed from a small Hasidic group into one of the largest Jewish movements and religious organizations in the world.

For the Lubavitcher, music is a spiritual process. It is the most powerful form of human expression and as such maintains a special place. Believed to be closest to the divine source, music is part of prayer, celebration, and teaching. Lubavitcher stress the ability of *benoni* (the average Jew) to achieve *devekut* (devotion or unity) with the divine. Music, in performance and prayer, is a crucial step toward *devekut*.

The primary vehicle of musical communication at the *tish* are the so-called nigunim, melodies commonly sung on syllables such as "bim-bam," "oy, oy, oy," or "ya-ba-bam." The Lubavitcher have preserved their nigunim in the three-volume collection *Sefer ha-nigunim*, which contains 347 melodies written down beginning in the 1940s. They range in mood from solemnly meditative to joyously festive. The nigunim are organized from divine/bright light (earliest original nigunim) to animal/dim light (derived from groups Lubavitcher interacted with). Regarding the latter, it is not unusual to borrow, adapt, and incorporate musical (but not textual) materials from outside sources (such as folk songs or the melodies of Simon and Garfunkel) unless they are derived from *explicitly* non-Jewish sources. Before being adopted into Lubavitcher ritual, they have to undergo the spiritual process of *tikun* (healing or restoration), that is, perceiving a divine spark in the melody that evokes joy and enthusiasm, claiming the material, releasing its holy spark by removing text to find a pure melody, and returning it to its proper place. In this way, some nigunim are adaptations, reinterpreted and changed significantly to bring the melody close to the divine source.

The oldest and most important nigun is "Daled bavos" (Melody of Four Stanzas or Gates), also known as "Rav's nigun" and "Alter rebbe's nigun." While nigunim are generally not attributed, this one is believed to be by the first rebbe, Schneur Zalman (1745–1812), though note that he was not a composer or creator in today's sense but rather someone who adapted or adopted a melody into Lubavitch. Due to its holiness, it is sung only on special occasions and specific dates, such as the beginning of Elul (the last and holiest month of the Hebrew calendar).

Solemn and serious in nature, "Daled bavos" consists of four stanzas, each of which is intended to elevate the singer and listener to the next spiritual level to ultimately achieve *devekut*. Each ends with a signature step that introduces a yearning quality. This quality is enhanced by the rather slow tempo in common time. "Daled bavos" reiterates the same four notes before moving stepwise; only occasionally is there a leap. The melodic contour exhibits a specific pattern: the melody rises upward and peaks (resonating with the Lubavitcher core metaphor "from the heart to the head") and then falls again. As such, it reflects creation, restoration, and adherence to the divine as a continuous process in Lubavitcher thinking. The slow tempo allows for ornamentation and invites to linger on high notes to emphasize the peak. Like most nigunim, "Daled bavos" is not sung on text (only some use psalm text in Hebrew) but employs various vocables phonemically consistent with Hebrew, Russian, and Yiddish. These are not meaningless syllables but are understood to create a deeper connection with the divine. Wordless equates limitless. In "Daled bavos," the syllables symbolize YHWH, the tetragrammaton of God's name. Indeed, the pervasive four-ness of this nigun has many meanings, and its presence is not arbitrary. It is an important number in Judaism, signifying completion and fullness. It corresponds and lifts those at the *tish* to each of the four spiritual worlds in the descending chain of existence in which the ten attributes of the divine manifest themselves, as outlined in the kabbalah. It also corresponds to the four-stage process of *deveḳut*: closeness to God through awakening (choosing the correct nigun), self-evaluation (expressive musical gestures, such as accenting, ornamenting, and repetition), work (extraordinary musical gestures, such as wild bodily movements, screaming, and drinking), and union (spiritual ecstasy with the divine through swooning and unconsciousness). Because of its inherent four-ness, "Daled bavos" is also referred to as nigun of the four corners and thus evokes Genesis 28:14, also known as *ufaratzta* (And you shall spread out):

> Your descendants shall be as the dust of the earth; you shall spread out to the west and to the east, to the north and to the south. All the families of the earth shall bless themselves by you and your descendants.

The inner meaning of this verse is to disseminate the wellsprings of Judaism—one of the core ideals of Lubavitcher Hasidim as evident in their extensive outreach (think of mitzvah truck and soup kitchen and visit http://www.chabad.org).

Listening to Hasidim singing nigunim might startle. Reggae star Matisyahu has compared the sounds to the film music for *Star Wars* scenes "when the bad guy's ship is arriving." Indeed, the aesthetics of the nigun have little to do with Western classical musicianship. The "greatness of voice" is relative. Singing together is relative as well. The temporary disregard of strict tempo to allow an expressive quickening or slowing (known in music as rubato), usually without altering the overall pace, differs among the participants. There is a cacophony of voices as individuals proceed at varying speeds, rarely chanting exactly the same syllables at exactly the same time. With that, pitch might vary as well. Thus, there are simultaneous variations of a single melodic line, a texture referred to as heterophony.

The predominant purpose of "Daled bavos" is spiritual. But it is also a group signifier communicating Lubavitcher values. Like other nigunim, it is not merely a melody but also a melody to the self that reveals the root of the heart and unfolds divine knowledge. As a "pure" melody, it is very close to the divine. Hasidim consider nigunim a supreme vehicle of communication and a facilitator for a spiritual union with previous generations. They are also an expression of joy and enthusiasm. They reinforce Hasidic belief in the mystical communion with God and contemplation into the soul and thus become a religious act. But more than anything, the nigun is the language of the heart.

The Jewish table provides many other occasions to celebrate with song. Looking at the Hebrew calendar to mind spring the feast after the twenty-four-hour fast on Yom Kippur, the Day of Atonement; the meal Jew and guests (*ushpizin*) consume in the sukkah during the harvest festival of Sukkot; eating a festive food on Purim in accordance with Esther 9:22; and Shavuot, which in origin was an agricultural festival and is also known as the Festival of the First Fruits. Two of the most table-prone feasts are Hanukkah and Passover with its seder (literally, order or arrangement), a ritual with a festive meal in the spring that marks the beginning of the holiday.

The seder involves the retelling of the Book of Exodus—the liberation of the Israelites from slavery in ancient Egypt—and is rooted in its biblical verse 8, which commands Jews to retell the story. Families and friends gather in the evening to read the text of the Haggadah, which contains the narrative of the Israelites' exodus from Egypt, blessings and rituals, commentaries from the Talmud, and special Passover songs. Indeed, aside from telling the story and discussing it and drinking four cups of wine and eating unleavened bread known as matzah, song is an integral part of the ritual. From the setting of the table (with the symbolic foods placed on the seder plate) to the evening's conclusion, the seder is full of opportunities to celebrate Passover in song. Songs are essential to enhancing the meal while supporting a structure that leads from one part of the seder to the next.

The first group of songs consists of those accompanying the ritual before the actual meal. Among them is "Ma nishtanah" (Why is this night different from all the other nights), sung by the youngest child at the table who is able to render it. Through four questions, the song explains some of the Passover rituals and the story of the Exodus. There is a kiddush (a blessing over wine) and a song praising God for giving the Torah to the Jewish people ("Barukh ha-makom"). And there is "Dayenu."

The earliest full text of "Dayenu" goes back to the Middle Ages. Its fifteen verses list all good things God has bestowed on the Jewish people from the time of Exodus on. The first five reference the freeing of the Jews from slavery, the next group describes the miracles from splitting the sea to the feeding of manna, and the last five give thanks for making life as a Jew possible through Sabbath, Torah and Temple, and the Land of Israel. After each item on the list, the refrain emphasizes "Dayenu," which means something along the lines of "it would have been enough for us," affirming gratefulness. The number of verses is not random. The seder consists of fifteen sections. As a biblical number, fifteen represents the number of steps leading up to the main hall of the Temple, the fifteen Psalms of Ascents (nos. 120–134, each of which begins with "Shir hama'alot" or "Song of the Ascents"), and the fifteen stages that are said to lead the righteous to perfection. In addition, the gematria (the numerical value) of the letters of one of the Hebrew names of God is fifteen.

There are numerous musical settings of "Dayenu." Among the recent contemporary versions are those by American singer Eric Komar, independent Israeli guitarist and singer Udi Davidi, and the Fountainheads, a group of young Israeli dancers, singers, actors, and artists. The Maccabeats, an all-male a cappella group founded in 2007 at Yeshiva University, released their version in 2015. It renders the commonly known "Dayenu" melody in different popular styles—a kind of genre hopscotch. The opening presents the familiar tune first in unison and with a harmonized refrain. It is a simple repetitive melody with a lot of pitch repetition within a small range. The melody of the verses with their fast-paced, almost speech-like rhythms almost resembles chant.

The refrain, in contrast, takes some leaps with longer notes over "Daye-nu." The overall simplicity of the melody underscores the fact that everybody ought to sing along. After the opening, the Maccabeats skip to verse 6, which they perform in the soulfully relaxed doo-wop style, only slightly departing from the familiar tune. Set in a slow tempo in swing time, it features vocal harmony for four singers a cappella throughout. Different singers carry the main melody, variously accompanied by basic instrumental imitation with "bum" in the bass, "doo" for very simple chord progressions, and "ahh" for embellishments, as well as finger snapping and foot tapping. This way the focus clearly remains on the main melody. Next comes verse 10, rendered in the style of a polka with a very fast oompah rhythm in duple meter and with some yodeling in the refrain. Then follows a funk version to the words of verse 11; it slightly deemphasizes melody and chord progression to bring out a strong rhythmic groove of the bass line produced by beat-boxing (a form of vocal percussion that mimics drum machines). The subsequent heavy metal version of the tune to the lyrics of verse 12 is the starkest departure yet from the original melody. It offers a thick, massive sound, characterized by highly amplified distortion and emphatic beats. It also includes percussion and an electric guitar, a key instrument in heavy metal. The next verse goes for a vaguely "tropical" vibe. It sounds like a Latin preset on a Casio keyboard but rendered all vocal. The underlying Habanera rhythm is associated with Cuban music and became a signifier for all Caribbean music. Verse 14 is presented in the style of electronic dance music known as dubstep. It features a wobble bass, often referred to as the "wub," where an extended bass note is manipulated rhythmically. The resulting sound creates a timbre that is punctuated by rhythmic variations, volume, filter cutoff, and distortion. This, as well as its fast tempo, off-beat rhythms, and percussiveness, provides stark contrast to the preceding and subsequent arrangements. Indeed, the following refrain brings the listener back to the very first arrangement in the style of doo-wop. It is rendered in a quite similar style known as barbershop (doo-wop has been popular among barbershoppers). While the similarity can be found in the vocal harmony a cappella, there are noticeable differences. The lead sings the main melody, and the other voices harmonize—the tenor above the melody, the bass sings the lowest notes, and the baritone completes the chord—accompanied by finger snapping. Barbershop focuses on complex harmonies and exhibits an overall ringing timbre. After verse 15, there is a short break during which one hears kids opening the door for Elijah, who plays a symbolic part in the Passover seder in that the fifth ceremonial cup of wine is filled for him—an honorary remembrance of the prophet who will come one day as an unknown guest to herald the arrival of the Messiah and solve the legal question of four versus five cups. It is not Elijah we hear entering but the Maccabeats with a last rendition of the refrain "Dayenu." If thus far each verse has featured an arrangement of the same underlying "Dayenu" tune, we now hear the words of the refrain one last time but to the melody of Whitney Houston's "I Will Always Love You." Poking fun at stories and customs—and here specifically of a widely known holiday melody—certainly receives attention and triggers interest and also encourages Jewish learning. The fun nature of the Maccabeats' version, with its diversity of styles, certainly serves as inspiration to make the seder an exciting experience for different generations. In nature a parody, it encourages all ages to make musical traditions their own, instilling their tastes into established tunes.

After the "Dayenu" has been sung—in whatever style—the "Al aḥat" immediately ensues as a kind of follow-up song that stresses gratitude once again. After two more songs, the meal begins, and singing gives way to eating. But this is only temporary. After the meal, many families pick up folk tunes to honor the lessons from Jewish history and sing songs of praise. Among them is a song praising Elijah and asking for his arrival, "Eliyahu ha-navi." Then follow the songs of the *nirtsah*, the last of the fifteen sections of the seder, devoted almost exclusively to singing. This includes the famous hymn "Adir hu" (God of Might), which names God's virtues and is sung to a bouncy, uplifting melody, and ends with the song "Ḥasal sidur pesaḥ," which literally means "The seder has ended." No doubt, in this jungle of songs, the "Dayenu" is one of the most memorable and central melodies of the seder if not the most popular Passover song in the world. Its popularity is heightened in the Maccabeats' rendition, although their idea of arranging and popularizing a widely known melody is not entirely new.

In 1998 and 1999, Rounder Records released *A Taste of Passover* and *A Taste of Chanukah*, two live recordings of popular songs and stories featuring more than 150 outstanding musicians and singers in a celebration of the joys and rituals of both holidays at the New England

Conservatory's historic Jordan Hall in Boston, Massachusetts. Humorous, entertaining, and uplifting, these recordings capture the flavor of a large extended family enjoying the holidays. *A Taste of Passover* offers five different arrangements of the commonly known "Dayenu" melody (including one that is polka-ish with oompah rhythm and another in the style of swing). They convey the humor and parody associated with its star performer, Theodore Bikel (1924–2015).

Bikel is yet another of the many immigrants who shaped Jewish song in America. Born in Vienna and named after the founder of modern Zionism, Theodor Herzl (with whom he shares the same birthday on May 2), Bikel fled with his family to Palestine just after Austria's annexation by Germany. Before Bikel stepped on American soil, he had lived on a kibbutz, where he learned Hebrew songs and began acting. He studied at the Royal Academy of Dramatic Art and pursued a career in London's theaters and frequently visited Paris, where he connected more deeply with folk songs. Shortly after arriving in New York in 1954, he performed in the Broadway play *Tonight in Samarkand*. He also became acquainted with singer and social activist Pete Seeger, who was a central figure in the folk revival of the 1950s and 1960s.

While Jewish repertoire was never central to the revival, Jews certainly were. They owned and managed clubs and record companies. They were agents and managers. They were writers and critics. Moses Asch, son of novelist Sholem Asch, established Folkways Records. Jac Holzman and Leonard Ripley ran the Elektra record label. Kenneth S. Goldstein issued innumerable recordings of songs from the field. Israel Young ran the Folklore Center on Macdougal Street. Aliza Greenblatt, the mother of Woody Guthrie's former wife Marjorie, was a published Yiddish poet; she wrote "Der fisher," which has become a staple in the Yiddish song repertoire. The list goes on. But it was Bikel who made sure that folk songs in Hebrew, Ladino, and Yiddish became part of the revival. His first recording, *Folksongs of Israel*, appeared in 1955. His 1958 recording *Theodore Bikel Sings Jewish Folk Songs*, which exclusively features Yiddish songs, seemed to be in every Jewish household in the United States at the time.

But Bikel was more than a folksinger. A highly versatile and charismatic performer, he was a character actor, slick cabaret artist, and gifted impersonator; he was a musician, composer, and activist. Known for his unforgettable rendition of Tevyje in *Fiddler on the Roof* and for his concerts and recordings of Yiddish song, he could be discussed in the context of many venues and genres. For sure, he was also part of the club and pub scene. Together with business partner Herb Cohen, he opened the first folk music coffeehouse in Los Angeles, the Unicorn. Its popularity led to the two opening a second club, Cosmo Alley, which in addition to folk music presented poets and comics. Given his celebrity, what Jewish family would not want Bikel at their table, bringing song and cheer on Passover and Hanukkah? He would render holiday songs with his unembellished voice and lightly accompany himself on the guitar—all with much entertainment. Indeed, musical virtuosity was not Bikel's point. Bikel approached song as folk instilled with show biz. In this way, he leaned more toward continental cuisine than local cooking. While Bikel's unvarnished voice is eternalized on many recordings, his musical approach is especially manifest on *A Taste of Chanukah.*

A large number of songs have been written on Hanukkah themes, perhaps more so than for any other Jewish holiday, which is easily justifiable by its sheer length of eight days (paralleled only by Sukkot). Hanukkah remembers the rededication of the Jerusalem Temple after it was defiled by King Antiochus III of Syria in the second century BCE. Among its chief observances is lighting oil or candles of a nine-armed candelabrum each evening after sunset. One candle is lit on the first evening, two on the second evening, and so on, with one additional candle kindled each night so that the number corresponds to the day in the festival (the ninth candle is used to light the others). This is to celebrate the triumph of light over darkness and to remember the miracle of the oil: when the royal Hasmonean family, also known as the Maccabees, overpowered the Greeks to liberate parts of the Land of Israel from the Seleucid Empire, they searched and found only a small cruse of pure oil, enough to light the menorah for a day, though miraculously it would burn for eight days. The Festival of Lights, as it is also known, features specific customs, such as the consumption of fried food (immortalized in the Yiddish song "Latkele latkele" about cooking potato pancakes), playing games with the dreidel (one of the most conspicuous symbols of the holiday), and the singing of joyful songs. By the 1920s, American Jews added gift giving to their Hanukkah festivities and began to embrace this holiday as a celebration of family.

Some of the best-known Hanukkah songs are featured on Bikel's recording, among them "I Have a Little Dreidel" and "Oy Chanukah";

most noteworthy is the universal and central "Ma'oz Tsur" (Rock of Ages). According to the Talmud, the main song should be Psalm 30. But for most Jews, the medieval Ashkenazi hymn "Ma'oz Tsur" is the musical pièce de résistance. It was originally sung only in the home but has been used in the synagogue since the nineteenth century or earlier. It is now sung each night when igniting the candles or oil—the key ritual of Hanukkah. Its title derives from Isaiah 17:10, but it is named for its Hebrew incipit, which means "Stronghold of Rock," an epithet for God. The text originated in the thirteenth century, written by a poet known only through the acrostic found in the first letters of the original five stanzas of the song: Mordechai (perhaps the same who authored the Sabbath table hymn "Mah Yafit"). "Ma'oz Tsur" consists of six stanzas (the final verse is generally believed to have been composed around the turn of the sixteenth century). The first and last deal with general themes of divine salvation and exile, and the middle four focus on events of persecution in Jewish history and praise God for survival of the exodus from Egypt, the end of Babylonian captivity, the miracle of the holiday of Purim, and especially the Hasmonean victory that is commemorated during Hanukkah. Like much of medieval liturgical poetry, "Ma'oz Tsur" is full of allusions to biblical literature and rabbinic interpretation.

Countless tunes have been written for the poem. An Italian version can be found in Benedetto Marcello's setting of Psalm 16, published in *Estro poetico-armonico: Parafrasi sopra li primi [e secondi] venticinque salmi* (Venice, 1724–1726). There is a Hasidic version from Lithuania that strings together several motives; there are Moroccan and Bukharan renditions as well as several modern melodies. The most widespread and universal tune, however, that Bikel uses in his sing-along recording is the bright and stirring melody that originated in Germany. It has become so popular that it serves as the "representative theme" in musical references to the feast (as do "Adir Hu" for Passover and "Aḵdamut" for Sukkot), four other Hebrew hymns for the occasion being also sung to it. The melody is an adaptation from an old German folk song notated in Franz Böhme's *Altdeutsches Liederbuch* of 1877, "So weiß ich eins, das mich erfreut das plümlein auff preyter heyde." The tune was widespread among German Jews as early as 1450. Martin Luther used this melody for his German chorale, known in English as "Dear Christians, One and All Rejoice." The earliest transcription of the tune in a

Jewish context can be found in a setting of George Gordon Byron's poem "On Jordan's Banks" (*Hebrew Melodies*, 1815) by the Anglo-Australian composer Isaac Nathan (1790–1864). From that time on, the melody has been included in countless anthologies in two versions. Julian Lazarus Mombach (1813–1880), a German-born synagogue composer who held the position of musical director of the Great Synagogue of London from the mid-nineteenth century on, introduced a modified version in his adaptation for four voices. It features a slight change in melodic contour along with a bridge passage (a modulation to the dominant) at the end of the repetition of the first phrase; the closing phrase of each verse is not sung a second time. The German original repeats the first phrase exactly and the last phrase with a small change, thus following the structure AABCC'. It is this version that Bikel chose for *A Taste of Chanukah*. Donning his self-taught guitar accompaniment, he leads a large chorus in unison, accompanied by an orchestra that includes festive brass instruments. It is noteworthy that he sings only the first verse, initially in Hebrew and then again in English:

> Rock of Ages, let our song, praise Thy saving power;
> Thou, amidst the raging foes, wast our sheltering tower.
> Furious they assailed us, but Thine arm availed us,
> And Thy Word broke their sword, when our own strength failed us.
> And Thy Word broke their sword, when our own strength failed us.

The bilingual rendition allows audiences on all levels of observance to understand the text and to participate. When sung in the Jewish home, "Ma'oz Tsur" accompanies the lighting of the candles. The singing of other Hanukkah songs ensues. Some Hasidic and Sephardi Jews recite Psalms 30, 67, and 91.

A Taste of Chanukah features two other popular tunes sung during the festivities and widely known in America. The first is "Oh Chanukah," which is based on the Yiddish "Oy Chanukah," originally written by Mordkhe Rivesman (1868–1924), who was born in Vilnius, Lithuania (there is also a Hebrew version). It is an upbeat playful children's song whose multilingual lyrics exist in slightly alternating versions. Inversing how he approaches language in "Ma'oz Tsur," Bikel sings the tune first in English, then in Yiddish. The translation does not exactly match the original, though both speak of the fun of the secular trappings of the holiday, with slight reference to the religious aspects. The first line names the holiday, the third calls for joy and happiness, and the next point to the core activities on Hanukkah: spinning dreidels all night, eating latkes, and lighting the candles. The second verse in the Yiddish rendition references another Hanukkah key prayer, Al Hanisim (For the Miracles), and praises God for the miracles he performed. The tune is possibly Hasidic in origin. Its lively rhythm supports a melody that can be easily sung. It features quite a bit of repetition, both of pitches and of phrases, with only minimal variation.

The true table song of the feast is a song known under various titles and casually called the dreidel song. It is the first Hanukkah song that preschoolers learn and refers to a game played with the dreidel, a square top marked with the four Hebrew letters—nun, gimel, hei, and shin—that stand for the Hebrew phrase "Nes gadol hayah sham" (A great miracle happened there), referring to the miracle of the oil. The four Hebrew letters also stand for the Yiddish words *nit* (nothing), *gants* (everything), *halb* (half), and *shtell* (put), which constitute the rules of the game. Some scholars maintain that the four letters point to the four Jewish exiles under Babylonian, Persian, Greek, and Roman rule. There are some variations in the way people play the game, but I learned that everyone puts in one coin. One of the players spins the dreidel. If it lands on nun, nothing happens; on gimel, he gets the whole amount; on hei, he gets half; and on shin, he puts one coin into the game. The game is over once one player is in possession of all coins, but to be fair, the amount should be redivided, as nobody likes a poor winner. In essence rooted in folklore, the game has historical roots. During the time of Antiochus's oppression, those who wanted to study Torah (then an illegal activity) would conceal their activity by playing gambling with a top (a common and legal activity) whenever an official or inspector was within sight.

The lyrics of the dreidel song do not allude to this history, however. The song is about making a dreidel and playing with it. While the Yiddish and English versions are largely the same, there are subtle differences: the English adaptation by lyricist and playwright Samuel S. Grossman (1893–1930) sings about a dreidel, whereas in the Yiddish the singer *is* the dreidel; in the Yiddish version, the dreidel is made out of *blay* (lead), which is historically accurate, and in the English version it is made out of clay in order to preserve the rhyme.

Samuel E. Goldfarb (1912–1981) set the lyrics in the 1920s when a variant of dreidel spinning had swept America in the course of a gambling craze of Put and Take. At the time, he worked as music director for the progressive Bureau of Jewish Education of New York. Having gained experience in collaborating with his older brother Israel Gold-farb on Jewish song anthologies and having just worked together with Grossman on the operetta *The Jews in Egypt* (1926), as well as many other children's songs, the dreidel song reflects his pursuit to help Jewish children learn more about their heritage through contemporary re-imagined versions in English. The song was first recorded in 1927 with Goldfarb at the piano and Arthur Fields, one of the most popular singers of the day, as vocalist. Composer Michael (Mikhl) Gelbart (1889–1962) was also involved, but it is unclear to what extent—he might have crafted the Yiddish text and also helped in shaping the melody, which has the same twisting and turning quality as the dreidel.

On the Bikel recording, the Yiddish version "Ikh Bin a Kleyner Dreydl" is sung by a children's chorus with piano accompaniment; the English version "I Have A Little Dreydl" is sung by a mixed adult choir, also accompanied by piano but rendered in a jazzy swing arrangement, that takes away the key musical features of the song: the melody moves in a stepwise motion with many repeated notes, a few pitches altogether, and a simple rhythm with little variation, all sung in a moderate tempo. Its nostalgic minor key brings universal sound into a Jewish context. No list of Hanukkah songs would be complete without a mention of the Maccabeats' music video "Candlelight" (a parody of Taio Cruz's "Dynamite") or, for an earlier generation, the Yiddish song parodies by Mickey Katz and his Kosher Kittens. These push the boundaries of the Jewish table.

The tunes sung in the Jewish homes are both particular to the specific table and universal in that some of them seem to have always existed, passed down from one generation to the next, and extant beyond the shores of America. They represent a mosaic of different languages and versions, often bridging the sacred and the secular. Some songs inscribe food and drink and other customs. Some are filled with humor, others are devout. Some fulfill a pedagogic function with lyrics and melody serving religious teaching. The diversity of song in the Jewish home—from folk songs and nigunim to *zemirot*—all serve to reinforce memories not only of Jewish history and practice but also of celebration throughout the years with relatives and friends, as hosts or as guests, and at communal gatherings. Whether you are young, old, or somewhere in between, there is always a melody for you to enjoy in the privacy of your home.

3

THE YIDDISH STAGE

In November 1881, the fifteen-year-old Boris Thomashefsky (ca. 1866–1939) arrived in New York City on the SS *Egypt*. Far from the shtetl near Kiev in which he grew up, he worked as a cigarette maker in a sweatshop on the Lower East Side. It was there that he heard fellow immigrants singing excerpts from the Yiddish theater they had enjoyed in their homelands. Although Boris had never attended such performances, he fell in love with what he heard. A year later, he would be involved in the first performance of Yiddish theater on the Lower East Side. According to his memoirs, he managed to convince a local saloon owner, Frank Wolf, who was also president of the Henry Street Synagogue, where the boy served as chorister, to rent Turn Hall on Fourth Street for a performance of Abraham Goldfaden's popular Yiddish operetta known by a multitude of titles, including *Di kishef-makherin*, *Di makhsheyfe*, *Di tsoyberin*, and Koldunye. It was one of the final plays of Goldfaden's early cycle of Jewish Enlightenment satires. A Ukrainian-born Jewish poet, playwright, stage director, and actor, Goldfaden (1840–1908) is generally considered the father of modern Yiddish theater, an umbrella term for spoken drama, operetta, musical comedy, and satiric or nostalgic revues that are written and performed in Yiddish, the historic language of the Ashkenazi Jews. This dramatic genre emerged only in the nineteenth century.

Since ancient times, rabbinic Judaism had disapproved of theater. It was considered especially immodest for women to perform and inconceivable for men to cross-dress and sing. Only during Purim, one of the most joyous and fun holidays on the Jewish calendar, lively amateur entertainment took place with Jewish men permitted to dress as women for merrymaking. It is in the course of this carnivalesque holiday that the roots of theatrical expression in Jewish life can be found, in the often satiric plays known as Purim plays. There were also Jewish minstrels dating back to the Middle Ages who presented stories along with folk songs, mime, jokes, dances, and pageantry. Religious practices, especially forms of call-and-response, as well as Jewish secular and sacred songs informed dramatic presentations in refined form.

With the societal changes in the course of the nineteenth century, the Jewish population gained access to the theaters of their hometowns, and a Jewish literary and theater culture began to grow. Some Yiddish plays were written during the nineteenth century to be read at home as literary entertainment. Formally staged Yiddish theater with continuity came to exist when in 1876, Abraham Goldfaden formed a troupe in Iaşi (Romania). Its establishment was possible because of a general relaxation of governmental restrictions on Jewish culture from the outside as well as a loosening of rabbinic restrictions. Goldfaden's troupe was small and initially consisted of men only, who played female roles as needed. Later, the troupe grew to include female actors as well. It traveled throughout Romania and Russia, disseminating the art and initiating its wide reception.

Goldfaden was a playwright first and an actor and composer second. In the course of his career, he penned some sixty stage works in Hebrew and Yiddish, among them *Shmendrik* (1877), *Di tsvey Kuni-lemels* (1880), and *Bar Kokhba* (1883 or 1885), all of which, along with *Shulamis* (1881), Joseph Rumshinsky would later arrange for performances during the so-called second golden age of Yiddish theater. A prolific songwriter, Goldfaden's "Rozhinkes mit mandlen" (Raisins and Almonds), which he first introduced in *Shulamis*, is his most famous song and has come to stand on its own. But his musical skills were not enough to outfit his operettas with original music. He adapted and arranged largely existing pieces, drew melodies from the synagogue, and outfitted them with simple orchestral accompaniment. Ultimately, it is because of his multiple abilities that modern Yiddish theater would become above all *musical* theater. Indeed, productions, whether advertised as operas, operettas, melodramas, comedies, or dramas, offered music as an integral part of the performance. Although the different types of Yiddish theater were not clearly defined and its different designations were used interchangeably, they all integrated elements of Eastern European Jewish culture and non-Jewish elements, sacred and secular music, and folk and art music for unique theatrical expressions.

Goldfaden's *Di kishef-makherin* or *The Sorceress* (as it is widely known in English translation), first staged in 1878, was one such work. In five acts and eight scenes, it tells the story of the seventeen-year-old Mirele while interweaving different aspects of the shtetl and its inhabitants, romantic love, and an exotic setting. The plot is complicated. The central story line tells how Mirele's stepmother has plotted with sorceress Bobe Yakhne to have full access to the family's wealth. Mirele's father is wrongfully arrested and the girl is sold off to Turkey, where she has to entertain guests at a café. After many reversals of fortune, the unlikely team of fiancé Markus, an "enlightened" Jew (*maskil*), and Hotsmakh, a Hasidic peddler, rescue her and return her home. After further tribulations, father and daughter are united, and a happy ending is in sight. With this work, Goldfaden's concept of Yiddish theater had truly come into its own: a regular theater stage with scenery and costumes; a scenario with fixed dialogue, solos, choruses, dances, and musical interludes; and versatile and trained male as well as female performers (the role of Bobe Yakhne is commonly played by a male, a remnant of the early male-only performances).

The New York performance of *Di kishef-makherin*, on August 12, 1882, is the first documented full-length Yiddish musical theater production in America. Unfortunately, we do not know what it sounded like. The score is lost; only a few excerpts of the music have survived, among them partial arrangements and an orchestration of a production in Odessa in 1916.

There is, however, much lore about the 1882 performance's reception. According to Thomashefsky's highly questionable if self-serving account, the event was tumultuous and had to overcome obstacles. Many in the established Jewish community wanted to stop the performance, believing that Yiddish theater was not dignified. The "uptown" German Jews tried to buy unsold tickets and pay off those who already held tickets not to attend by offering them beer in exchange. They even bribed the Romanian female lead into faking a sore throat at the last minute. If the story is true, the ploy backfired. Thomashefsky went on in her place and with that launched a long and successful career in

Yiddish theater as performer and impresario. In the decades to come, he would largely be responsible for building a Yiddish theater culture in New York and beyond. Following Goldfaden's example, Thomashefsky took Yiddish theater on the road, performing a wide repertoire of Yiddish plays in cities with a substantial population of Eastern European Jewish immigrants, such as Baltimore, Boston, Chicago, Philadelphia, Pittsburgh, and Washington, D.C.

The 1880s were a pivotal period for Yiddish theater in America. The Russian ban of the art in 1883, one of the many suppressions of civil liberties following the assassination of Czar Alexander II, effectively pushed performers and producers to different parts of Europe and to the New World. With the arrival of more professional companies the subsequent year, the evolution of Yiddish theater in America took its course. The ban was lifted in 1904, but in the meantime successive waves of immigrants had arrived on America's shores, some as artists seeking an audience but many as a result of persecutions, pogroms, and economic crises in Eastern Europe. Goldfaden was one of them. In 1887, he left his temporary residence in Warsaw and took on the job of director of the new Romanian Opera Company, the home of one of the first professional Yiddish theater troupes in New York. After the failure of the first production, Goldfaden (unsuccessfully) attempted to found a theater school, then headed to Paris in 1889 but returned once more to New York in October 1903. His plays continued to be performed in the New World during a time when Yiddish theater existed almost entirely onstage rather than in print.

Most of the productions during the 1880s and 1890s had to rely on amateur companies, of which there were many. Regular weekend performances took place in New York City at the Bowery Garden, the National, and the Thalia and elsewhere on the continent. But the early phase of Yiddish theater in America did not produce any memorable songs, with the striking paradoxical exception of "Eili, Eili" from Moyshe Hurwitz's operetta *Brokhe, oder der yidisher kenig fun poyln oyfeyn nakht* (Bracha or the Jewish King of Poland for a Night). Directed by Boris Thomashefsky, it played for a number of weeks during the Passover season in 1896 at the Windsor Theatre in New York. The operetta featured a bizarre but effective scene in which the young woman Bracha (then played by the Romanian-born actress Sophie Karp) hangs from the cross, refusing to repudiate her Jewish faith. "Eili, Eili" is her dying song.

The melody, not the plot of this scene, would become one of the most popular pieces in the Western Hemisphere and an all-time classic. Although in the Yiddish operetta sung by a female, noted cantors such as Yossele Rosenblatt rendered interpretations of the melancholy song, possibly identifying with its musical features. Lore has it that the great opera star Enrico Caruso, a fan of Rosenblatt, stepped forward and kissed him after hearing his rendition. During the 1910s and 1920s, it was performed and recorded by folk and opera singers and famously sung by Judy Garland during an audition. The song made its way into the African American community, which identified with the theme of racial despair. Arrangements for violin and other instruments appeared. In 1910 and 1917, the text and melody were included in published anthologies of Jewish religious and folk songs. The music made its way into other genres, too. Played by an orchestra, it accompanied screenings of the silent horror film *The Golem* during its run at the Criterion Theatre in New York. By 1920, the melody had become so omnipresent that it was the subject of a playful parody in Leo Wood and Archie Gottler's number "That Eili Eili Melody," whose chorus began, "That melody called 'Eili, Eili,' is always haunting me." It gained nearly universal renown after vaudeville superstar Belle Baker recorded it in 1921.

To be sure, "Eili, Eili" has biblical ties. Its Hebrew opening line is an adaptation of Psalm 22:1, which begins with the words "My God, my God, why have You abandoned me?" As such, it references Jesus Christ's "Seven Last Words." The subsequent Yiddish verses are attributed to Boris Thomashefsky. The song closes in Hebrew with the words of Shema (Hear, O Israel), a prayer that serves as a centerpiece of the morning and evening services; it is an affirmation of Judaism and a declaration of faith in one God. If Yiddish theater spans high and low culture, this very piece uniquely combines religion and entertainment, possibly to convey the larger message of strength of faith through a lighter medium. It inadvertently references Yiddish theater's religious roots, and so does the music.

The plaintive tune is rendered in the wailing freygish mode with its expressive hallmark step. Its alternating rhythmic units, long associated with Eastern European Jewish song, further emulate hazanuth, as do the ornamental notes, all of which evoke an improvisational feeling. Its solemn mood, slow tempo, and leaping melody are evocative of Kol Nidre. The melody reminds us that early entertainers were rooted in the music of the synagogue and that liturgical motives and religious hymns would often find their way into entertainment music. In this vein, the tune has been variously labeled as "a traditional Jewish melody," "Hebrew prayer," and "religious prayer." Even the copyright issues associated with "Eili, Eili" tie into this. When in 1919 the M. Richmond Music Company in New York published a rendition for voice and piano, the song was attributed to Jacob Koppel Sandler (ca. 1856–1931), a choral conductor from Bila Tserkva, who had emigrated to the United States in 1888. In 1925, Sandler sued music publisher Joseph P. Katz for violating his copyright by continuing to publish arrangements of the music. Simply put, the infringement case posed the question of whether the melody was an original composition, a folk song from eastern Europe, or a melody for the selihot, the Jewish penitential prayers said in the period leading up to the High Holidays. Although the controversy could not be fully resolved, the judge ultimately decided in favor of the publisher.

In the meantime, Yiddish theater had risen to be a major cultural establishment. The first outward sign of this had been the establishment of the Grand Street Theatre in 1903 at the south corner of Grand and Chrystie Streets as the first purpose-built Yiddish theater (previously there had been only temporary and rented spaces). In the first decades of the twentieth century, a dozen groups performed in more than twenty Yiddish theaters and two vaudeville houses in New York City alone. Another 200 or so traveled to other cities and towns throughout the United States, though the center of Yiddish theatrical production remained in New York. By World War I, the Yiddish Theater District on the Lower East Side was a rival of Broadway in scale and quality, cited by critics and others as the best entertainment district in the city and known as the Jewish Rialto (a nod to the 2,000-seat theater on 42nd Street). As such, it had become the leading such district in the world, with twenty to thirty shows a night. Almost outshining what was being played in English on the other Broadway, there were performances in Yiddish of vaudeville acts and movies, original plays, musicals, and adaptations of Sholem Aleichem (though he never landed a real hit). There were performances of translations and adaptations of

Goethe's *Faust*, Henrik Ibsen's *Hedda Gabler*, William Shakespeare's *King Lear* and *Hamlet*, and *Uncle Tom's Cabin*. The stories were often tweaked to make them more accessible to the audience. Some of these works appeared on the "Yiddish Broadway" long before they premiered on the actual Broadway. Even Richard Wagner's *Parsifal*, which was the sensation of fin de siècle New York and the *Game of Thrones* of its day, was performed to make high culture accessible to an audience whose primary language was Yiddish. Some critics viewed it as a step away from immigrant acculturation, others as one step further toward common ground between the new residents and their American neighbors. For sure, through Yiddish theater, the Jewish population entered into dialogue with the outside world both by putting itself on display and by importing theatrical pieces from other cultures. These were performed by high-caliber actors such as Bertha Kalich (1874–1939) and later Jacob and Stella Adler, who began to cross over to Broadway or moved back and forth between New York's leading Yiddish and English stages.

The rise of Yiddish theater correlated with large numbers of Yiddish-speaking immigrants entering the country. Some 2 million Jewish refugees came to America between the 1880s and the early 1920s, fleeing persecution. Just when the first golden age of Yiddish theater had begun to fade, another half a million Jewish immigrants entered the country between 1905 and 1908 alone. Many of them settled on the Lower East Side, which also became the home for a second, American-born generation who later would leave their imprint on light entertainment music. Composer and pianist George Gershwin (born Jacob Gershowitz, 1898–1937) and his brother, lyricist Ira Gershwin (born Israel Gershowitz, 1896–1983), grew up on the second floor on 91 Second Avenue between East 5th Street and East 6th Street. They frequented the local Yiddish theaters, with George running errands for members and appearing onstage as an extra. Irving Berlin (born Israel Baline, 1888–1989) grew up on the Lower East Side in a Yiddish-speaking home. And of course, there were the shining stars of Yiddish theater, Molly Picon (1898–1992) and the Warsaw-born Menasha Skulnik (1890–1970), who are memorialized on the corner of Second Avenue and East 10th Street, the Yiddish Walk of Fame.

For inhabitants of the Lower East Side, the broad comedy, vaudeville, and light operettas of Yiddish theater surely offered respite from daily hardship. Like most immigrants, they faced homesickness, deprivation, and language difficulties. The Yiddish theater aided them in coming to terms with their environment by reminding them of the old home while highlighting the benefits of the New World, thus bringing onstage past and present struggles of the audiences. The theater helped put their incongruities into perspective. Political oppression, poverty, and limited educational opportunities were some of the subjects entering the art. Broader themes, such as the New World, immigration, and acculturation, and family ties, can be found in many new Yiddish theater productions of that period.

Some of these themes are aptly immortalized in Solomon Smulewitz's song "A brivele der mamen" (A Little Letter to Mama), composed and first published in 1907. It is one of the most noteworthy examples of sentimental popular song in Yiddish. Although it was not composed in connection with any operetta or other theatrical piece, it spawned subsequent full-length productions of the same title that built around or incorporated it, such as Samuel H. Kohn's four-act comedy-drama with the parallel English title *The Golden Dream*.

The song presents a story in itself, though only the first of its three stanzas is generally sung. Conceived as a ballad (a form of verse featuring a narrative), it takes the perspective of a mother whose only request to her departing son is that he remember to write a little letter from America to ease her bitter pain of separation. He never does despite "a hundred letters" from her. And by the final strophe, which renders this a lesson song, it is too late: the son, now an exceedingly prosperous New Yorker with a lavish lifestyle and a beautiful family, receives word that she has died while waiting for his letter. But she had one last wish: that at least he remember her in death by reciting Kaddish for her—the obligation of Jewish children to recite that doxology in memory of parents during the eleven-month mourning period as well as annually on the *yortsayt*, the anniversary of death: "Your mother will hear your Kaddish / In her grave gladly / You'll heal her pain and her bitter heart." Unlike "Eili, Eili," which weaves together Hebrew prayer with references to the Russian homeland, persecution, and exile ("Like once you saved our fathers from an angry czar"), "A brivele" praises the new home ("In New York City, a wealthy home / Full of hearts without pity / There lives her child in luxury / With his happy family"). But it does not entirely abandon religious references as evident in the twice-mentioned Kaddish in the third stanza. At their core, the lyrics resonate with the internal challenges the immigrants faced. Coming to America, many of them had left their parents behind, knowing that they would probably never see them again and that letters would be their only form of communication.

The sentimental music supports the tone of the verses. Take the 1908 recording of Smulewitz himself singing "A brivele." A small orchestra with some string instruments softly sets the slow and steady tempo and then accompanies him. Small in range, the vocal melody moves stepwise. It features a repeated downward motion that sounds like a sigh. The simple rhythmic patterns repeat as well. The melody is in a darker mode, underlining the pervading sadness of the song. The overall simplicity manifests itself also in the form of the song, which is very structured, with clear phrasing adhering to the verse. The melody repeats over the first two stanzas, separated by the refrain (only in the third verse is the melody slightly different). If "Eili, Eili" sounds close to a prayer song, "A brivele" sounds close to a folk song or, more concretely, a street ballad. What both have in common is the lamenting over the tragedies of the Jewish experience—anti-Semitism, Diaspora, and dislocation.

The reception of "A brivele" was broad. It was heard in music halls and variétés and in vaudeville shows. It was recorded in many different arrangements. The melody became popular on its own, beginning with Smulewitz's publication of a version without text, for violin or mandolin. "A brivele" achieved immense popularity beyond the shores of America, serving as the basis for a 1911 silent film in Russia, where it was also recorded. It served as title of the last Yiddish film made in Poland in 1938, about the reunification of a Jewish family. Abraham Ellstein composed the score, but Smulewitz's song returns throughout the film, and strains from its melody are used as a recurring motive. In 1973, the melody outfitted the Hebrew song "Mikhtav me'ima" (A Letter from Mother). Credited exclusively to Natan Alterman and Sarah Fershko, it circulated in Israel and became tied to the Yom Kippur War. The lyrics tell the story of an Israeli mother worrying about her son who had joined the Israel Defense Forces. The Jewish mother, associated with home, family, tradition, and religion, for sure, represents all that is familiar and loved (and therefore missed).

In this vein, the original Yiddish text of "A brivele" inspired composers to create similar songs, and a category of mother-related and letter-based songs emerged. One of the best-known ones might be "My Yid-dishe Momme" of 1924 with lyrics by Jack Yellen and music by Lew Pollack. Belle Baker and Sophie Tucker made it famous, and later the Barry Sisters popularized it. It was written at a very crucial time when the vast immigration of Yiddish speakers came to a halt. In May 1921, the United States passed a law that greatly limited the immigration of Jews from eastern and southern Europe, and another federal legislation in 1924 reduced it to a trickle.

By then, a new generation of composers for the Yiddish stage had established themselves, among them the "big four of Second Avenue," a group of Yiddish theater composers who succeeded Goldfaden: Joseph Rumshinsky (1881–1956), Alexander Olshanetsky (1892–1946), Sholom Secunda (1894–1974), and Abraham Ellstein (1907–1963). Among the writers and managers who collaborated with these composers were Bor-is Thomashefsky, Anshl Shor (1871–1942), Moyshe Shor (1872–1949), and Jacob Kalich (1891–1975). Their works focused on themes such as conflict between "old country" immigrants and their American-born children and the tension between Hasidim and maskilim ("enlightened" Jews) and were often influenced by contemporary American musical styles. A September 1925 *New York Times* article confirms that "the Yiddish theatre has been thoroughly Americanized . . . it is now a stable American institution and no longer dependent on immigration from Eastern Europe. People who can neither speak nor write Yiddish attend Yiddish stage performances and pay Broadway prices on Second Ave-nue." The other side of the coin was that Americanization eroded Yid-dish culture during a time when the language itself faced several pres-sures: its association with poverty and provincialism, the emergence of Zionism and with it a new nationalist advocacy for and embrace of modern Hebrew, as well as the immigrants' full acculturation into America through the adoption of their new language, English. With momentous changes in social norms, and Jewish audiences drifting to Broadway and motion pictures, Yiddish theaters were forced to close midseason in 1929. The next year, Yiddish theater was on the verge of collapse. What was left of it during this period of decline that coincided with the bitter Depression that gripped the American nation in the early 1930s brought new topics to the stage. Indeed, Yiddish theater was no longer straddling the Old World and the New. The effects of

Americanization on Yiddish culture began to become more pronounced also in terms of attendance and audience profile.

The influence of American mainstream is evident in Sholom Secunda's hit song "Bei mir bistu shein" for the 1932 Yiddish comedy musical *M'ken lebn nor m'lost nit* (One Could Live, but They Won't Let You—officially subtitled in English *I Would If I Could*). The musical closed after one season. "Bei mir bistu shein" was published in 1933 and survived the ages.

As one of the big four of Second Avenue, Secunda had still absorbed the best of both worlds. Born in Ukraine, Secunda was known as a brilliant choirboy in his youth. At age twelve, he played in Goldfaden's *Akeydes Yitskhok* (The Sacrifice of Isaac) and *Di kishef-makherin*. After emigrating with his family to America in 1907, he continued to sing in the synagogue while composing songs, musicals, and sacred works. He received solid training at the Institute for Musical Arts in New York City (predecessor of the Juilliard School) and later studied orchestration with Ernest Bloch. His 1915 song "Heym, zise heym" (Home, Sweet Home) brought him first fame in the Yiddish world. But he never lost touch with his religious roots, composing and arranging liturgical music for Cantor Reuben Ticker, who became known as the Metropolitan Opera tenor Richard Tucker. In the course of a long, successful career, Secunda wrote the music for more than eighty shows, but it is "Bei mir bistu shein" for which he is remembered best.

Secunda conceived "Bei mir bistu shein" in collaboration with lyricist Jacob Jacobs, whose original Yiddish version is, in essence, a dialogue between lovers who share lines of the song, tossing back and forth their virtues and nonvirtues, leading to the refrain "Bei mir bistu shein" (By me, you are beautiful) with its triple entendre of "to me, you are beautiful"; "standing with me, you are beautiful"; or "compared to me, you are beautiful"—a playful way of courtship. References to the Jewish experience are virtually absent with the exception of one subtle manifestation in the first verse: "When you are wild as an Indian / Even if you were a Galitzyaner, / I say: It doesn't bother me." Hollywood's stereotype of Native Americans as wild is joined by a reference to the people of the easternmost Polish province of the old Austro-Hungarian Empire. At the time, acculturated American Jews perceived Galicia as the breeding ground of everything that was clannish, corrupt, deceitful, and low-class eastern European (undeniably, Jews from Galicia were smart, resourceful, and determined). But in the context of the song, these stereotypes serve to humorously reaffirm that no matter who you are, "Bei mir bistu shein."

In spite of humor and positive affirmation, Secunda's original version of the melody is set in a darker mode. American influence is evident in a few swinging rhythms in the chorus. The melody of the verse exhibits speech-like aspects that are reminiscent of American musical theater. In early recordings, its catchy melody is occasionally interrupted by instrumental interludes by brass and percussion that hint at jazz, and there is a distinct second vocal line occasionally accompanying the main melody. This is unsurprising given that it is a Yiddish song of the Jazz Age and, as such, a cross-cultural mediator between Yiddish stage and mainstream culture.

"Bei mir bistu shein" is also an example of a Yiddish song that was recast as an English hit. By 1937, the partners had sold the rights to the song (in 1961, the copyright on the song expired, and the ownership reverted to Secunda and Jacobs). What has happened depends on who tells the story. Apparently, Sammy Cahn heard the Yiddish song at the Apollo Theater in Harlem, New York City, sung by African American performers Johnnie and George, and convinced the still-unknown Andrews Sisters to perform and record it. With that, it evolved from shtetl to stage door. To be sure, Warner Brothers had purchased the song. With new English words by Sammy Cahn (Samuel Cohen), a Germanized title ("Bei mir bist Du schön" [Means That You're Grand]), and a musical adaptation by Saul Chaplin (Saul Kaplan), the song became a megahit indeed. While the melody has remained largely the same (it was lowered to make it easier to sing, square rhythms were made groovy throughout the verse and chorus, and a thudding "oom-cha" accompaniment was turned into a jazz beat), the song took off. After Decca released the new version in December 1937 sung by the Andrews Sisters, it earned them a gold record and became one of the best-selling records of the late 1930s. This set off the song's worldwide reception. Adaptations in other languages and arrangements for many different instruments and ensemble configurations ensued. After the enormous success of the reworked version, many other Yiddish tunes were successfully subjected to swing treatment in recordings and on the radio in the 1940s. This success, however, paralleled the beginning of the near obliteration of Yiddish culture.

The success of "Bei mir bistu shein" remains unequaled. It gained prominence among Jewish and non-Jewish audiences worldwide, finding its way into various contexts. One is Judy Garland's cantor-ish rendition in a scene deleted from the 1938 film *Love Finds Andy Hardy*. Another is the French film *The Last Metro*, about the Holocaust in Paris. A 1967 recording by The Temples, "Bei Mir Twist Du Schoen," offers a double pun, referring both to the dance craze of the 1960s and, clearly with a tinge of Jewish humor, to the braided (twisted) Sabbath bread known as challah. Ultimately, the evolution of "Bei mir bistu shein" demonstrates the lasting reception and influence of Yiddish theater music in Jewish and general audiences' lives during a time it had begun to die out. By 1945, only four Yiddish theaters remained in New York City, and following the zeitgeist they actually produced musicals. As the Yiddish-speaking population declined, Yiddish theater productions became rare and had nearly disappeared if not for the National Yiddish Theatre Folksbiene, New York's oldest-surviving theater company. Its continuous presence under changing and difficult circumstances was instrumental in yet another turning period for Yiddish culture in America.

The dawn of the twenty-first century marked a turn for Yiddish culture. The first and second generations of Yiddish-speaking immigrants were gone. What was left of Yiddish was its persistence as the language of daily life and commerce in Hasidic communities (rather than, as it once was, the shared primary language of millions of secular, religious, and, above all, socialist Jews) and its academic study. But eventually, Yiddish culture enjoyed a renaissance. In the late twentieth century and increasingly so during the early years of the twenty-first, a younger generation had begun to reengage with the language, its culture, and its music. A steady stream of new songbook publications and recordings in Yiddish flooded the market. The repertoires included both well-known singers performing nostalgic favorites and newly composed songs, American songs translated into Yiddish (think of the most recent adaptation of Leonard Cohen's "Hallelujah" by Daniel Kahn), and even forays into Yiddish hip-hop. After its earlier ebbs and flows, Yiddish theater has not lost its relevance either. In 2015, the Folksbiene revived *Di goldene kale* in a lavish production that ran over the course of several months in New York.

Di goldene kale (The Golden Bride) had premiered in February 1923 with music by Joseph Rumshinsky, lyrics by Louis Gilrod, and a book by Frieda Freiman at Kessler's Second Avenue Theater. After its eighteen-week run, it had toured many American cities and traveled to Europe and South America. Regularly performed until World War II, it had dropped out of the repertoire after 1948, in parallel with the decline of the Yiddish stage.

The success of *Di goldene kale* is reflective of its composer's stardom. Of the mighty four, Rumshinsky was undoubtedly the one who ruled the Yiddish Broadway in the early twentieth century. A prolific composer, his creative output consists of more than 150 stage works as well as hundreds of songs, sacred choral music, music for two movies, and an opera in Hebrew.

Di goldene kale was written at a critical time of transition when the United States passed stringent immigration laws and arrivals from eastern Europe peaked. Russia was in the final stages of a civil war that would end in October 1922. But ties between the Old World and the New World remained hopeful. The story is typical for the time of its conception. An abandoned village girl in a shtetl in the Old Country by the name of Goldele, raised by innkeepers and in love with their son Misha, suddenly receives visitors from her New York family and learns that she has inherited a fortune from her father. Pursued by eager young men from her village, Goldele announces that she will marry whoever can find her long-lost mother. Among her suitors are Yankl, the shoemaker; Berel, the tailor; Motl, the cantor's choir singer; and Misha, all of whom take off to find the mother, traveling as far as Japan and Palestine. The second act takes place in New York, where Goldele now lives the American Dream. When her suitors show up at a lavish masked ball, a happy ending is in sight. *Di goldene kale* brings up many social themes relevant to an early twentieth-century audience: the Russian Revolution, poverty, families separated by an ocean, pain at leaving loved ones behind, husbands abandoning wives to start fresh, and the universal theme of love. But Gilrod's Yiddish lyrics, on occasion interspersed with some English and Russian words for added drama, also caution. When the townspeople rejoice in the opening chorus about the American visitors who "swim in money as in a bathtub," it comes with a warning about the dangers of the almighty dollar, which can buy off anything or anyone, thus foreshadowing the conflicting feelings expressed in the show about capitalism versus communism, America versus Russia, new home versus old.

Rumskinsky's views on Yiddish musical theater—namely, that it feeds on two main influences: cantorial music as its oldest and jazz as its most recent—is insightful for understanding his compositional approach. The finale of the first act begins with the customary Sabbath eve meal, at which Misha chants the blessing over the wine. We hear ragtime when the American uncle tries to woo Goldele with the razzle-dazzle of the new world "Over there, over there in the golden land." Musical references to the Old World are prevalent in quasi-European folk songs and simple tunes sung by the local village girls ("A tree stands deep in the woods"). The overall catchy tunes are accompanied by a brilliant and bright-sounding orchestra. There is also a comic synthesis of old and new, as in the matchmaker's fast and almost jazzy patter song, with its rapid succession of notes, each of which corresponds to one syllable of text: "You Are a Beauty" infuses the traditional idea of matchmaking with references to the Roaring Twenties. The masked ball is a scene worthy of Italian opera at its grandest. But the definite hit is the love duet between Goldele and Misha, "Mayn Goldele," which first appears in act I and gets an encore in act II during the masked ball scene, there leading to a climactic moment. The simple lyrics of the refrain, shot through with diminutives, are outfitted with a melody that one can hardly get out of one's head:

> My Goldele, my dear bride,
> My beautiful, sweet little angel,
> My only desire is to be with you,
> With you forever and ever, I swear.

The refrain's melody is the signature tune of the operetta, though with its waltz rhythm it is closer to Viennese operetta than Yiddish song. It draws neither on any Jewish material nor on any continuum of melody type associated historically with Jewish experience, sacred or secular. Like "Bei mir bistu shein," "Mayn Goldele" is a demonstration of the Yiddish language in terms of its purely aural parameters and of its context to create the perception of a Yiddish theater song regardless of actual musical content. But this did not limit its success. On the contrary, it was recorded three times during the initial run of the show; it was one of only two pieces published and was undoubtedly what audience members sang as they left the theater, having heard it repeatedly throughout the performance. Certainly, this is what I did after seeing *Di goldene kale* in the fall of 2015, when the Museum of Jewish Heritage in Lower Manhattan offered the revival run.

That *Di goldene kale* is timeless and can be appreciated even a century after its conception, after all the ups and downs of Yiddish culture, is evident from the record-breaking 25,000 attendees who came to see it during that run. Given the absence of Yiddish speakers (and performers!), the production featured supertitles in English and Russian. It received six Critics Picks and accolades in publications including the *New York Times*, *The New Yorker*, *Time Out New York*, and *New York* magazine. The show was also nominated for two Drama Desk Awards, for Outstanding Revival of a Musical and Outstanding Director of a Musical, the only off-Broadway production nominated in these categories. In early 2018, the show went on a national tour. Rumshinsky would have been proud. Although the latest success of *Di goldene kale* is rooted in Yiddish theater being a historical artifact, it remains relevant as an archetype of every immigrant group integrating into the American mainstream.

While no single work can embody the wealth of diversity found in the Yiddish theater music during its flourishing years in America, the songs introduced here offer a sampling of its different traits. The evolution of Yiddish theater and song on American stages shows a convergence of Yiddishkeit and American popular styles by way of song. The progression from "Eili, Eili" to "Bei mir bistu shein" reflects the Americanization process that Yiddish theater underwent, with its different stages that began humbly, culminating in its first golden age, whose end coincided with Goldfaden's death, to its second golden age, which lasted from the 1920s to the 1940s. In the course of this, Yiddish theater became more and more assimilated into musical theater found outside the enclave of the Lower East Side, slowly losing its original almost liturgical-folkloristic qualities. Part of this shift may have been due to the acculturation of the American-born generations who wanted to move away from the culture their immigrant parents embodied. Indeed, Yiddish theater in America can best be understood as a product of its time and its people. It is imbued with the history of the Yiddish-speaking Jews living in the shtetls of eastern Europe, their persecution and emigration to the United States, their struggles to adapt to a new life and language, while first maintaining and then losing ties to their former homeland. It thus charts the evolution of a community in its acculturation to and influence on America.

The diversity prevalent in the different songs attests to the musical style of the Yiddish stage being a world of its own. Just as other genres of music—think of pop and classical—have many subgenres, music for the Yiddish theater does as well—from solemn ballads like "Eili, Eili" to energetic swing-prone tunes like "Bei mir bistu shein." Indeed, we find songs that are folkloric, reminiscent of liturgical music and dance tunes, but also swinging rhythms that reveal the oscillation of the repertoires between the American influence and Jewish heritage. This diversity correlates with the evolution of Yiddish theater, which has absorbed themes of both early and contemporary Jewish history to produce a culture that is sometimes light, sometimes nostalgic and mournful.

In many ways, Yiddish theater, both in story and in song, helped bridge the shtetl and America. As a contested site of Americanization in terms of aesthetic principles, moral concerns, commercial interests, and the social pressures of acculturation, it also exerted its own influence. Yiddish theater broadly informed Jewish humor and found its way into the American idiom; it left traces in the music of Tin Pan Alley and, as you will read next, in Hollywood and on Broadway.

4

ON THE SILVER SCREEN

On April 25, 1917, the young Samuel Raphaelson (1894–1983), a native of New York City's Lower East Side and a recent graduate of the University of Illinois, attended a performance of the musical *Robinson Crusoe, Jr.* in Champaign, Illinois. The star of the show was thirty-year-old singer Al Jolson, a Russian-born Jew, already famous at the time for his blackface acts. In an interview ten years later, Raphaelson would recall the cathartic experience of watching Jolson perform: "I shall never forget the first five minutes of Jolson—his velocity, the amazing fluidity with which he shifted from a tremendous absorption in his audience to a tremendous absorption in his song. . . . My god, this isn't a jazz singer. This is a cantor!" The emotional intensity that Raphaelson perceived in Jolson and that he associated with a cantor and the image of the blackface actor inspired the short story "Day of Atonement" of 1922. He later fleshed it out to a successful play, titled *The Jazz Singer*, which premiered in Times Square in 1925. The plot demanded music, and there was singing offstage.

A mere two years later, Warner Brothers turned the play into a feature-length motion picture with synchronized dialogue sequences and Al Jolson in the title role. For the song scenes, Warner had erected the first soundstages. Directed by Alan Crosland, *The Jazz Singer* would become widely but wrongly celebrated as the first talkie. In actuality, it is a hybrid between silent and sound film. Dialogue is presented through caption cards or intertitles, which are standard in silent movies. There is barely two minutes' worth of synchronized talking, much or all of it improvised. Still, *The Jazz Singer* heralded the commercial ascendance of the talkies and the decline of the silent-film era as the first megahit of the new genre. *The Jazz Singer* represents a pioneering achievement of another kind in that it was the first Hollywood film with a Jewish subject.

The plot takes place largely in New York (the Lower East Side and Broadway) and was partly shot there and in Hollywood for interior scenes. As in the play, the film details the conflict between a devout cantor and his son, Jakie (short for "Jacob," the prodigal son) Rabinowitz. After singing popular tunes in a beer garden, Jakie is punished by his father, prompting the youngster to run away from home. Some years later, now going by the name of Jack Robin, he becomes a talented jazz singer. Although he continues to pursue a career in show business, his professional ambitions ultimately conflict with his Jewish heritage. Promoted as fiction, the plot suggests parallels to Al Jolson's real-life story.

Born in the Lithuanian shtetl of Srednik (now known as Seredžius), Asa Yoelson (1886–1950) came to the United States in 1894 when his father, a rabbi and cantor, brought the family to secure a better life. On being introduced to show business in 1895 by entertainer Al Reeves, Asa and his brother Hirsch became fascinated by the industry, and by 1897 they were singing for coins on local street corners, using the names Al and Harry. After a stint as a singer with a circus, Jolson performed in burlesque and vaudeville shows. While performing in a Brooklyn theater in 1904, he decided on a new approach and began applying blackface makeup, which boosted his career. He then continued wearing blackface in all of his shows and remained successful nationwide as a vaudeville singer. His role in the musical comedy *La Belle Paree* at New York's Winter Garden in 1911 propelled him to stardom, accompanied by an unbroken series of smash hits (at age thirty-five, Jolson would become the youngest man in American history to have a theater named after him). At the peak of his career as singer, film actor, and comedian, he was dubbed "The World's Greatest Entertainer." His success aside, he never lost touch with his Jewish roots, neither as a man nor as performer. In March 1922, for example, he gave a special benefit performance to aid injured Jewish veterans of World War I.

The Jazz Singer was Al Jolson's second film. The first was the ten-minute short *A Plantation Act* of 1926, in which Jolson, in blackface, sings three of his hit songs: "April Showers," "Rock-a-Bye Your Baby with a Dixie Melody," and "When the Red, Red Robin (Comes Bob, Bob, Bobbin' Along)." In *The Jazz Singer*, Jolson's use of blackface is more complex given the story line. Blackface as a form of theatrical makeup had been used by performers to represent a black person. The practice gained popularity during nineteenth-century minstrel shows. As such, blackface was a double-edged sword. On the one hand, it created stereotypes embodied in the stock characters of blacks and thus played a significant role in cementing and proliferating racist images, attitudes, and perceptions worldwide. On the other hand, it popularized black culture. Indeed, blackface performances were the conduit through which African American music, comedy, and dance first reached the white American mainstream. They played a seminal role in the introduction of African American culture to world audiences. To be sure, Jolson was not the only entertainer to perform in blackface make-up. It was a theatrical convention of many entertainers at the beginning of the twentieth century. Working behind a blackface mask gave the performer "a sense of freedom and spontaneity he had never known." According to Eric Lott in his 1993 book *Love and Theft: Blackface Minstrelsy and the American Working Class*, for the white minstrel man "to put on the cultural forms of blackness was to engage in a complex affair of manly mimicry. . . . To wear or even enjoy blackface was literally, for a time, to become black, to inherit the cool, virility, humility, abandon, or *gaité de coeur* that were the prime components of white ideologies of black manhood." By the mid-twentieth century, changing attitudes about race and racism effectively ended the prominence of blackface makeup used in performance in the United States and elsewhere. There are more than seventy examples of blackface in early sound film, that is, between 1927 and 1953, including Jolson's nine subsequent blackface appearances. *The Jazz Singer*, however, is unique in that it is the only film where blackface is central to the narrative development and thematic expression.

Following the trend at the time, the score of *The Jazz Singer* fuses preexisting music with very few original arrangements by the highly experienced Louis Silvers (1889–1954), who also conducted the orchestra for the film's music. Matching music to the visuals frame by frame in the blend of silent film and synchronized sound, the score features a wide variety of musical styles: original melodies; snippets of classical music that trademark emotions (and are part of Jewish acculturation, too) by greats such as Claude Debussy, Peter Tchaikovsky, and Édouard Lalo; and Jewish-titled tunes, such as "Chassidic Dance" and "Bar Kochba." Jewish liturgical music, Yiddish song, and popular Tin Pan Alley tunes appear in their respective contexts. Bobby Gordon, who played the young Jakie, and Al Jolson would be dubbed and synchronized performing popular songs in saloons, nightclubs, and vaudeville. Yossele Rosenblatt played himself on the concert stage, and Warner Oland would be dubbed by Hungarian-born cantor Joseph Diskay in synagogue. Presenting the well-known songs purely as performance numbers within the film supported the completely silent version of *The Jazz Singer*, released to theaters not yet equipped with sound. They took the place of the spoken word and made music and the moving image equally prominent.

The Jazz Singer starts out the way so many silent films had begun, with an overture based on a synchronized orchestral score made up of a tapestry of melodies that recur throughout the score; these include original themes and short snippets from borrowed melodies, such as the pseudo-Irish sentimental song "Mother O Mine" composed by Louis Silvers. The overture serves as both a musical introduction and a summary of the main themes of the film. The opening titles follow to the theme composed by Silvers already heard in the overture. With its slow tempo, the leaping intervals (though initially upward rather than downward), and darker mode, it is reminiscent of and perhaps is meant to foreshadow Kol Nidre, an Aramaic prayer annulling vows made before God, sung by Jews at the opening of the Day of Atonement service on the eve of Yom Kippur; it will play an important role in the course of the plot. A nostalgic melody borrowed from the Russian cradle song, op. 39, no. 1 by Alexander Krein, a Russian Jewish composer, alludes to the cultural roots of young Jakie/Al. It accompanies the written prologue: "In every living soul, a spirit cries for expression—perhaps this plaintive, wailing song of Jazz is, after all, the misunderstood utterance of a prayer." But this song and the featured solo clarinet are all but jazz. For those familiar with it, it might reference the Jewish immigrant experience or the protagonist's young age at the beginning of the film. The following frames provide a period view of the Lower East Side to the sounds of "The Sidewalks of New York" (also known as "East Side, West Side" after the opening words of the chorus), a popular song with a slow and deliberate waltz rhythm that tells about life in New York City during the 1890s. The tune was composed by Charles B. Lawlor, an Irish immigrant, in 1894. Those who watched *The Jazz Singer* in 1927 would know the tune very well and with its quotation in the film would be sonically brought to New York, the immigrant haven not only for Jews but also for the Irish and many others. Visually and sonically, this opening sequence sets the stage for the whole film. It is particular in referencing Jewishness and the universal by presenting a diverse cultural fabric that sets the location and period; it also insinuates the general themes of heritage, immigration, and integration—these themes will continue throughout. As such, the whole opening sequence does not necessarily convey the Jewish experience per se but rather suggests a variety of immigrant experiences.

If the film begins as a silent picture with background music, it continues in that vein, at least for a while. Music creates reference, and the next sound is that of the opening bars of the Kol Nidre melody, accompanying a frame that depicts Cantor Rabinowitz's house and referencing "the ancient traditions of his race" and that Jakie "is to sing Kol Nidre." Mood music ensues: nine bars of an excerpt from Édouard Lalo's *Symphonie espagnole* of 1874. With its Spanish motifs, the symphony suggests exoticism and thus seems to broaden the sonic story to create a general immigrant experience. But Silver does not take just any excerpt. He extrapolates the solo string part from the fourth movement, which greatly resembles the opening of Kol Nidre. An excerpt from the *Sérénade mélancolique* by Peter Tchaikovsky transitions to the first synchronized sound. Music is not merely background to the drama but also a central element in conveying the plot. It comments on the film and adds to scenes. As we shall see, many of the songs are striking because they have a realistic source on-screen, such as in the next scene.

Announced as "Ragtime Jakie," Bobby Gordon, playing Jolson as the thirteen-year-old son of the cantor, is dubbed by an unknown singer to perform "My Gal Sal" (1905) in an East Side saloon. Written by one of the great songwriters of the early days of Tin Pan Alley, Paul Dresser, "My Gal Sal" was typical of the kind of song formula Tin Pan Alley relied on at the turn of the century. With its portrait of a small-town girl who has gone astray in the big city but is still fondly remembered by her first sweetheart, "My Gal Sal" is a ballad that tells a story in verses that alternate with a more lyrical chorus in contrasting waltz time, and it is this chorus that is heard in the film's sequence:

> They called her frivolous Sal
> A peculiar sort of a gal
> With a heart that was mellow
> An all 'round good fellow, was my old pal
> Your troubles, sorrow, and care
> She was always willing to share
> A wild sort of devil, but dead on the level
> Was my gal Sal.

While the lyrics, in diction and sentiment, would have been deemed proper by middle-class standards, that a cantor's son was singing them in a saloon would have been shocking in the dramatic context of the film. And shock it does. When Cantor Rabinowitz and his wife fretfully wonder why Jakie is not home as the Sabbath draws nigh, the film cuts to a man having a beer in a tavern. Beguiled by a sweet voice emanating from the adjoining saloon, he enters through the swinging doors to find Jakie singing "My Gal Sal." Aghast, the man, who turns out to be a neighbor of the Rabinowitz family, rushes to their home and, as the film reverts to silence, "tells" them (through title cards) what their son is doing.

The film then cuts back to the saloon—and to sound—where Jakie sings a very different kind of early Tin Pan Alley song with ragtime influence, "Waiting for the Robert E. Lee" (1912) by L. Wolfe Gilbert and Lewis F. Muir. Although it has the same form with verses and refrain as "My Gal Sal," with its overt references to black culture (dubbed, in the parlance of the day, a "coon" song), it would have been even more reprehensible for a cantor's son to sing. Its verses narrate a story about blacks rejoicing at the arrival of the "good ship Robert E. Lee that's come / To carry the cotton away" and alternate with a chorus, of which a short excerpt is heard in the film, that punctuates the narrative with vernacular exclamations. Musically, it introduces sprightly offbeat rhythms that set it apart from the nostalgic three-quarter-time waltz chorus of "My Gal Sal," foreshadowing the kind of songs Jolson will later sing in nightclubs and vaudeville. To add to his performance, Jakie moves rhythmically and sensuously while singing the chorus until suddenly his father enters the saloon. Over the protests of the accompanying piano player, the father drags his son home for a whipping despite the fervent pleas of his wife, played by Eugenie Besserer. After tearfully taking leave of his mother, Jakie runs away from home to pursue his singing career.

These first two songs, as American as they might seem, introduce a different facet of Jewish culture, namely, that of Tin Pan Alley, a nickname given to 28th Street in Manhattan, where many music publishers and songwriters worked between 1880 and 1953. When immigrants from the Lower East Side began to dominate Tin Pan Alley in the first half of the twentieth century, it essentially became a Jewish industry, one that greatly contributed to the golden age of American song. Although the music of Tin Pan Alley itself cannot be regarded as innately Jewish, many of the main players were, among them George Gershwin and Irving Berlin. With Tin Pan Alley, Jewish affiliation entered the American mainstream. Berlin would bridge the two worlds in 1909 with his first hit, "Yiddle, on Your Fiddle, Play Some Ragtime."

While the stylistic differences of the two songs foreshadow the boy's evolution from Jewish boy to jazz singer, the father's rendition of Kol Nidre, with an extra layer of seriousness, adds stark contrast. The fact that the cantor's son is rebelling against his father and his belief system on the most serious day of the Jewish year takes this already earnest prayer to the next level. The cry in the cantor's voice can be heard here for his almost estranged son. Two Jewish worlds consecutively encounter each other in sound: the secular-assimilated and the religious-traditional.

In the ensuing scene, "Coffee Dan's" sequence, the Jewish boy Jakie has become the American adult now known as Jack Robin performing at a San Francisco nightclub for amateurs. The first shot opens with switching between the "Hop Skip," a tune by Henry R. Cohen that accompanies couples dancing the Charleston in the scene, and—while shifting the frame to Jolson—a brief excerpt of the vaudeville song "My Mammy" (1920), which references the southern archetype for a black woman who works as a nanny, often for a white family, nursing the children. This was one of Jolson's signature songs, and here it foreshadows the sonic end of the movie. It also accompanies a moment when Jack is depicted eating ham and eggs, that is, food not satisfying the requirements of the Jewish law. The music might have been conceived to support an internal monologue: the unkosher, *trayf* transgression makes him think of his caring and providing mother, perhaps as a *Jewish* mother. The song, however, that would make this scene one of the most famous in movie history would be "Dirty Hands, Dirty Face," with music by James V. Monaco and lyrics by Edgar Leslie and Grant Clarke. It is the first synchronized song in the film. In contrast to "My Gal Sal" and "Waiting for the Robert E. Lee," this and the following exemplify the kind of songs that would dominate American popular music in the 1920s.

"Dirty Hands, Dirty Face" is about a boy who gets soiled in the yard; when his father returns home from work, he runs to greet him and is embraced as "an angel of joy." The song foreshadows what would become of Jack, as "dirty face" insinuates blackface, an analogy that by today's standards would be considered blatantly offensive. It also foreshadows reconciliation with his father—multiple associations in the songs parallel the multiple associations of the film. Immediately thereafter, we hear the first synchronized speech. When the audience of extras breaks into applause, Jolson, seemingly forgetting he is in a movie, tells them, "Wait a minute, wait a minute. You ain't heard nothin' yet. Wait a minute I tell ya, you ain't heard nothing.' You want to hear 'Toot, Toot, Tootsie'?" These were well-established lines that Jolson would tell the audience during his time at New York's Winter Garden before performing additional songs. They had become something of an in-joke. In 1919, Jolson recorded the song "You Ain't Heard Nothin' Yet" and spoke very similar lines in the 1926 short *A Plantation Act*. In *The Jazz Singer*, those words became a metaphor for the birth of "talking" pictures. Jolson's signature song "Toot, Toot, Tootsie" follows.

The Jazz Singer was a star-studded affair. Aside from Al Jolson, there was tenor Richard Tucker in the supporting role of impresario Harry Lee and the renowned cantor Yossele Rosenblatt, whose heavenly voice, by then also known through his appearances on the vaudeville stage, secured him a role. There is much myth about what role he was actually offered to play and what piece to sing. In truth, he appeared in one scene as himself, singing in his distinct Orthodox appearance a Yiddish song about reciting the Kaddish on the anniversary of a relative's death—"Yohrzeit" (In Memoriam) by Rhéa Silberta, composed in 1920. Although it is a Yiddish song, he renders it in cantorial fashion, with improvised ornamentation on the Hebrew parts, such as the opening and closing phrase "Yiskadal, v'yiskadash sh'mai raboh," and with an occasional cry in his voice. He merges the secular and sacred (as does the song in language and lyrics). Here, as in Cantor Rabinowitz's Kol

Nidre, the cantor is both a visual and a sonic icon. When Jack hears Rosenblatt in concert, he is faced with a role model of a cantor, who managed to preserve his honor between bimah and stage. When the face of his praying father blends into the frame, the song's meaning becomes more implicit: Jack thinks that his father has declared him dead. This scene also blurs fiction and reality, as the reconciliation of religion and entertainment in performance is an autobiographical narrative. It depicts the truth of partial integration.

The pivotal moment in the main character's evolution from Jewish boy Jakie to jazz singer Jack comes when he visits his family on the occasion of his father's sixtieth birthday. In the film's second sound sequence, Jack talks with his mother, then plays the piano and sings the chorus from "Blue Skies," the famous popular song Irving Berlin had composed in 1926 as a last-minute addition to the Rodgers and Hart musical *Betsy*, with the Jewish musical star Belle Baker in the title role. At the time, Berlin stood out as the most successful and prominent of the Jewish songwriters on Broadway and Tin Pan Alley. This is the first song in the film that Jack does not perform onstage but rather in his family home to prove to his mother that after running away from home, he is in the process of finally attaining stardom. Before he sings, the scene is silent. Jack enters his parents' apartment, surprising his mother, and we see his father giving Hebrew lessons in another room. After a few moments of title-card dialogue, Jack offers to demonstrate one of the songs from his new Broadway show. As synchronized sound returns, Jack strides to the parlor piano and launches into "Blue Skies." While he renders the song as a performance, his hammy, flourishing rendition portrays him as a kid showing off to his mother.

After one chorus of "Blue Skies," however, Jack did the then extraordinary—he talked, telling his mother about the possibilities that would come with being a well-earning jazz singer: he will buy an apartment in the Bronx (at the time considered a social rise), deck her out in a new pink dress, and take her to Coney Island, where he will kiss her in the Shoot the Chutes, an amusement ride. The expression on Eugenie Besserer's face reveals the same surprise that the audience at that time must have felt when they saw the scene. The mother has only a few words of her own, muttering, "Oh, no, Jakie" as he goes on. At some point, she leans over and grabs him as if she wants him to stop talking but then stoically resigns herself to waiting him out. Finally, he sings a second chorus of "Blue Skies" and claims it to be in a jazzy style. It amounts, however, to little more than a faster tempo, a few scats (already rendered when he sang it the first time), and a flamboyant pianistic performance style.

It may be that the vaudevillian interlude between the two renditions of "Blue Skies" was an attempt to make the song more integral to the dramatic context of his performance. Jack's banter turns the song from a demonstration of his talent to an expression of his happiness at being reunited with his mother. However, Jack's irate father interrupts the jazzy repetition. Just at the moment when the end of the chorus wants to shift from a darker to a brighter mode, promising a happy ending, the father pronounces one very conclusive word: "Stop!" Not only does the father bring to a halt the song, but he also turns sound into silence. To add to the Freudian overtones of the whole scene, we hear the sound track, which tellingly introduces the love theme from Peter Tchaikovsky's *Romeo and Juliet* for added melodrama. Title cards reappear as the father angrily dissents that his son has brought "jazz" into his house. For the father (and the son), redefining a Tin Pan Alley song as jazz is assigning value to it. Jazz becomes a metaphor for subversion. And subversion it was for many, Jewish or not, especially for an older generation who thought jazz corrupted the morals of the youth. However, by 1926, when Berlin wrote "Blue Skies," the American audience did not hear it as jazz but rather as a product of Jewish sensibility. In this way, "Blue Skies" can be seen as a musical expression of secularization and acculturation, which is unacceptable for the father, who is representing the unassimilated Old World.

The movie's finale does not completely dissolve the conflicts presented throughout, and nowhere is this more apparent than in the music. As Jack prepares for the opening of *April Follies*, he learns that his father is gravely ill. Jack must once more decide between bimah and stage. Will he stand in for his father on Yom Kippur or appear in blackface? The father dies after reconciling with his son, and Jack subsequently cancels the show to sing Kol Nidre. But how he sings it! The rendition his father delivered earlier in the film was a cappella, slow and solemn with much melisma, demure and full of dignity, with the congregation singing along. We saw and heard cantorial pathos.

Jack's version starts out similarly; he maintains the cry in the voice but begins to accelerate the tempo and adds ornamentation. His interpretation emulates a sentimental popular style. Jack atones in singing Kol Nidre, but he atones as a jazz singer. The two Kol Nidre renditions could not be more different in their actual delivery. One is prayed, the other one performed. That Jack is ultimately a stage performer and will remain exactly that is confirmed in the final moments when he appears in blackface onstage singing Walter Donaldson's "My Mammy" (Jolson's signature song) directed toward his mother, who sits in the audience. As the Jewish mother blends with the southern mammy, the immigrant experience runs its course. Americanization wins out in the final scene. There is no going back to the Lower East Side. Such an ending, however, is unique to the film. While for some there was and still is no reconciliation between Jewishness and Americanness, both coexist and can influence one another. In other words, a Jew in America can have a truly dual identity rather than having to choose between Jewishness and Americanness.

Jack's blackface at the end only masks his Jewishness. It also distracts from the fact that no blacks are seen or heard in the film and that there is no actual jazz, though there are plenty of references to black (musical) culture, which relates to the merger of Jewish and black self-representation beginning in the 1910s. By the 1920s, blackface entertainment was dominated by Jews, who perhaps felt solidarity with the pariah group and mirror other and sought a Jewish interpretation of a black idiom. In *The Jazz Singer*, Jolson escapes his Old World heritage through blackface and American popular songs designated as jazz. They become a means to express a new kind of Jewishness, that of the modern American Jew. *The Jazz Singer* implicitly celebrates the ambition and drive needed to escape the shtetls of Europe and the ghettos of New York and the attendant hunger for recognition. Thus, in the context of this film, they also become a metaphor for social rise and for integration, for independence and self-fulfillment.

The film strategically premiered on Yom Kippur of 1927. As an emblem of the generational revolt against established social orders in the Jazz Age, it received favorable reviews both in the Jewish press and in African American newspapers. The Jewish press noted with pride that Jewish performers were adopting aspects of African American music. African Americans had long seen Jolson as an ally of the black community, and many welcomed *The Jazz Singer* and saw it as a vehicle to gain access to the stage. Harlem's newspaper, *Amsterdam News*, called it "one of the greatest pictures ever produced." For Jolson, it noted, "Every colored performer is proud of him." Reviewers also recognized the symbolism and metaphors inherent in the film. The Yiddish *Der morgn zhurnal* (Morning Journal) wrote, in a language deemed acceptable at the time, "Is there any incongruity in this Jewish boy with his face painted like a Southern Negro singing in the Negro dialect? No, there is not. Indeed, I detected again and again the minor key of Jewish music, the wail of the Chazan, the cry of anguish of a people who had suffered. The son of a line of rabbis well knows how to sing the songs of the most cruelly wronged people in the world's history." For sure, *The Jazz Singer* also had universal appeal. It aptly reflected the symbolic struggle between Old and New World, parent and child, tradition and modernity, religious devotion and secular entertainment, communal obligation and individual desire.

The Jazz Singer's importance in movie history and in the history of film music received recognition at the first Academy Awards presentation in May 1929. Warner Brothers was awarded a statuette (not yet called an Oscar) for producing the film. For sure, *The Jazz Singer* holds a unique position in film history in the way it thematicized Jews in America. Its social fabric and musical approach gave impetus to the development of Jewish-themed films in which music plays a major role. It gave way to Yiddish cinema beginning in the 1930s, such as the successful film musical *Yidl mitn fidl* (The Little Jew and His Fiddle), *A brivele der mamen* (A Little Letter to Mama), and *Der vilner balebesl* (The Little Vilna Householder). It also gave way to noted cantors appearing in Hollywood cinematic productions (sometimes even catching the main role)—among them Louis "Leibele" Waldman in *Cantor on Trial* (1931), with music by Sholom Secunda and Moishe Oysher in *Overture to Glory* (1940)—and in documentaries.

Today, *The Jazz Singer* gives audiences the chance to hear and see the musical superstars of the day in the biggest movie blockbuster of that decade. A blog post at *OyChicago*, an online community created by the Jewish United Fund/Jewish Federation of Metropolitan Chicago, deems *The Jazz Singer* as the number one Jewish music sound track. "The Top 18 Jewish Movie Soundtracks" lists a diverse conglomerate of other noteworthy films, from the epic *The Ten Commandments* (1956), with music by Elmer Bernstein, to *Defiance* (2008), about the Bielski partisans, a group led by Jewish brothers from Poland who recruited and saved Jews in Belarus during World War II. James Newton Howard composed the moody, almost haunting sound track, with violin solos played by Joshua Bell. In fifteenth place is Steven Spielberg's *Schindler's List* (1993), with film music by John Williams (b. 1932), one of the most successful film music composers of the past decades (he is also a noted composer of concert works and a sought-after conductor).

Williams has been involved in more than 100 films and over a period of forty years collaborated many times with Spielberg. He had exposure to Jewish music as arranger of the score for the 1971 film version of *Fiddler on the Roof*. But *Schindler's List* was different. At a 2009 concert at Boston's Symphony Hall (at which Spielberg was also in attendance), Williams told the audience that he was flabbergasted when he first saw a rough cut of the film: "I had to walk around the room for four or five minutes to catch my breath. I said to Steven, 'I really think you need a better composer than I am for this film.' And he very sweetly said, 'I know, but they're all dead.'" Williams's gift for composing music that perfectly fits a film led to a striking sound track for this three-hour historical drama. It won the Academy Award and the BAFTA Award for Best Original Score and the Grammy Award for Best Score Soundtrack for Visual Media.

Here is the story in a nutshell. In September 1939, businessman Oskar Schindler (Liam Neeson) arrives in Krakow on the heels of the German invasion, ready to make his fortune from World War II, which had just begun. As a member of the Nazi party and an agent of the German military intelligence, he appropriates a factory originally set up by Jewish businessmen and staffs it with Jewish workers for pragmatic reasons. When the SS begins the extermination of Jews, Schindler protects his workers to keep his factory in operation but soon realizes that in so doing he is also saving innocent lives.

At the very core of the film's music is "Theme from Schindler's List." It is one of the most recognized contemporary melodies. Ever since the film's release, it has been performed in concert and used by many high-level figure skaters in their programs. It is most famous in the sound track rendition with solo violin and orchestra. The instrument of choice is self-evident. The violin has been the most widespread musical instrument in Jewish culture. Throughout the ages, disproportionate numbers of performers were Jewish. In the film's sound track, the solo is performed by the world-famous classical violinist Itzhak Perlman, who signed on to the task because of the subject of the film.

The theme is four minutes long and adheres to the form AABAA'. The first part is introduced by a sober orchestral opening (recalling the ending of "Afn pripetshik"). After about fifteen seconds, the solo violin joins in, introducing the main melody. Like the nigun, a song without words, the melody rises and falls and lingers on the higher notes. Its looping gestures repeat. It features a sigh motive and a repeating larger leap, both of which emphasize the overall downward motion. At the end of phrases, it does not seek resolution. It is delicate and tender, with an inward feeling that suggests yearning. Some might perceive it as haunting, melancholic, somber, or sorrowful, which is underscored by its darker mode and its overall slow tempo. But its extended phrasing suggests hopefulness as well. It also bears an air of dignity and sweetness, which is brought out by Perlman's deeply expressive singing vibrato and rubato. The repetition of the A section, which occurs after one minute (and before slowing down), is in a higher range and sounds even more expressive. A new musical idea is introduced shortly after the second minute, easily recognizable as it plays out in the lower registers and has a more animated rhythm. It winds up in another loop and returns to the opening idea at two minutes, thirty-eight seconds, which is repeated with some slight variation during which the orchestra retreats into the background, becoming barely noticeable. The ending is ever so soft, with the violin lingering on the last cathartic high note. Quiet resignation? The repetitions of the first part not only help one easily remember the theme but also emphasize its meaning. Brilliant in its overall simplicity, it is the type of melody that does not tell a one-dimensional story. The music is all and everything at the same time, a mini tone poem.

The theme occurs several times throughout the film in the manner of a leitmotif, a popular film-scoring technique where prominent characters in the drama have their own musical theme, heard in some form throughout the score in conjunction with their appearances. As such, the theme appears with modifications at important junctures when the characters deal with or move on from tragedy. Its first manifestation is about seventeen minutes into the film when the mass entry into the Krakow ghetto takes place and its borders are sealed off on March 20, 1941. Its opening gesture is played in unison by the horns, evoking a call to the ghetto and depicting the Jews as a persecuted group. The theme eventually fades out and remains unresolved.

Next, it appears about one hour into the film at around fifty-seven minutes, accompanying the liquidation of the ghetto—a long sequence that also weaves in a well-known Yiddish song, Mark Varshavski's "Afn pripetshik" (The Alphabet or On the Hearth), which tells about a rabbi teaching his students the Hebrew alphabet. Its fourth stanza introduces tragic pathos into the song: "When, children, you will grow older / You will understand / How many tears lie in these letters / And how much crying." These lyrics hint at the Yiddish saying that the history of the Jews is written in tears. But in the film, only the refrain and first stanza are heard. Sung off-screen by the Li-Ron Choir, an Israeli children's choir, and accompanied by solo piano, the song gives voice to a scene that embodies the terror and helplessness (the music competes with sounds of chaos and gunshots) of the youngest victims of the Holocaust: a girl in a red coat governs the picture, standing out in the overall black-and-white movie. "Afn pripetshik" and the child in red contribute to one of the starkest dramatic counterpoints in the film, contrasting innocence with cruelty and bloodshed. This macabre contrast could be surpassed only by the well-known and very sentimental German song about an unhappy mother, "Mamatschi, schenk' mir ein Pferdchen" (Mother Give Me a Hobby Horse), which is played on loudspeakers in the camp when the children are taken away on trucks.

When the main theme returns at 137 minutes, it accompanies a sequence that focuses on saving the Jews. This time, it is played by a solo guitar (its first plucked sounds evoke the plucking at the heartstrings). It is rendered significantly slower, and its tempo only slightly picks up when the string section of the orchestra joins the solo guitar. The variability of the theme during this sequence is striking; dramaturgically, it suggests a shift from desperation to hopefulness. Orchestration plays a major role in the manifestations and transformations of the theme, as evident when it recurs right after "Immolation," a Requiem-evoking song composed by Williams on the Hebrew text *"Im ḥayeinu, anu notnim ḥayim"* (With our lives we give life), which proposes a mysterious spiritual fruitfulness of the victims' deaths. The film shots show the horrors of the concentration camp: the ashes of cremated bodies, the pyres, the mass graves, all of which are leading to a new stage of Schindler's awareness, underscored by the appearance of the now deceased child in red. The theme then returns with the flute taking the solo. Phrases are extended, conveying hopefulness, fragilely accompanying a sequence in which Itzhak Stern, Schindler's accountant, is being saved from deportation.

Later, when Schindler aims to save more than 100 Jews, the theme is played by the whole orchestra—a fullness that might reflect the hope of survival by so many. But it is also rendered very slowly and conveys a somber timbre, thus balancing hopefulness and sorrow. By the end of the film, Schindler has saved 1,200 Jews. Between his saying good-bye to the survivors and before the arrival of the Soviet army, the theme returns. It dominates the whole final sequence, sounding softly in variation, featuring different instruments, among them the sweetest solo violin passage of the whole film, reserved for the moment when Schindler exits. But there is no irony here. As a parting gift, Schindler receives a gold band with the inscription "Whoever saves one life, saves the world."

The film's epilogue, which traces the image of the workers walking away from the factory, points to the Jewish future on Israeli soil with Naomi Shemer's Hebrew song "Yerushalaim Shel Zahav" (Jerusalem of Gold), which describes the Jewish people's 2,000-year longing to return to Jerusalem and is the unofficial national anthem of the state. It is sung largely in unison to soft guitar accompaniment while the film transitions to color. The theme played by the sweet solo violin returns one last time in a frame that shows the actual Schindler Jews and their descendants returning to Schindler's grave and, following Jewish custom, placing stones on it. It ends on a very high soft note that sounds as the legend reads, "In memory of the more than six million Jews murdered."

Apart from Williams's original compositions, the film's music features noteworthy quotations of preexisting material: there is the famous Argentine tango "Por una cabeza" (which Williams had adapted before for *Scent of a Woman*) and the Hungarian song known as "Gloomy Sunday." There are German schlager and folk songs, Polish songs, and Johann Sebastian Bach's English Suite No. 2—some are used for dramatic counterpoint, others to support scenes. The music creates a tapestry of sonic worlds associated with the cultures of Germans, Poles, Hungarians, and Jews. But more poignantly, the score depicts a specific Jewish experience in sound. We hear eastern European Yiddishkeit, Israeli pathos, Jewish popular music as evoked in the clarinet parts played by klezmer virtuoso Giora Feidman, and prayer chant, which appears prominently in a number of key moments and frames the film: the very first scene of the movie shows the blessing over the wine on Sabbath eve after the candle lighting to the sounds of the prayer chant beginning with "Savri maranan . . . ," a phrase that assures everybody at the table that this wine is to be enjoyed. The celebration of the Sabbath returns at the end of the film, thus creating a cycle or frame that ultimately emphasizes the indestructibility of Jewish custom. But the chant at the end changes to the Aramaic prayer Yisgadal (May His Name Be Praised), an excerpt from the Kaddish. It is a painful reminder that albeit surviving, so many Jewish lives have been lost in the Holocaust.

The Jazz Singer and Schindler's List are only two examples for the Jewish sound worlds that Hollywood has produced. Jewish culture and film have been tightly interwoven in America in several respects. Many producers have been of Jewish descent, and, as a book title asserts, Jews Invented Hollywood. Jewish composers have dominated the industry ever since its inception, from the songs of Irving Berlin of the early talkie era to the orchestral scores of Jerry Goldsmith. From the mid-twentieth century on, many of the composers who left Nazi Europe settled in Los Angeles—one may think of Erich Wolfgang Korngold and Franz Waxman, Eric Zeisl, and Ernst Toch—and became active as composers of film music. They were among the first to write original music for motion pictures. The significance of the Jewish contribution to film music in America is most evident in composers who received nomination for the Academy Award for Best Original Score: Jerome Kern (Can't Help Singing, 1945) and Dimitri Tiomkin (The High and the Mighty, 1954) are only two, though it is important to note that notwithstanding their heritage, many of them wrote not for Jewish-themed films but rather for all-time classics, such as Casablanca and Gone with the Wind (Max Steiner) and Psycho (Bernard Herrmann). Exceptions are movie musicals such as Samuel Goldwyn's film Porgy and Bess (1959), which is based on George Gershwin's 1935 opera; Fiddler on the Roof (1971), with a score adapted by John Williams; and Barbra Streisand's Funny Girl (1968) and Yentl (1983). But nowhere is the intersection of music and Jewish identity more evident than in iconic movies of the past fifty years, such as Sophie's Choice, Radio Days, and The Pianist—though their composers were not Jewish. Melodies by John Williams, Marvin Hamlisch, Dick Hyman, Wojciech Kilar, and countless others have appeared in popular films with Jewish subjects. That many composers who wrote the music to Jewish-themed films were not Jewish did not affect the integrity of their scores. It has rather contributed to the intricate puzzle of how to define American Jewish music culture. As a medium involving multiple agents, films and their music connect the Jewish and the non-Jewish, thus contributing to universal stories through a specific cultural heritage.

5

FIDDLING ON BROADWAY

Since it first opened on Broadway in September 1964, *Fiddler on the Roof* has constantly been onstage somewhere. To date, it counts six Broadway productions as well as performances in countries from Argentina to Japan, in thousands of schools, community centers, and even army bases. For almost ten years, it held the record for the longest-running Broadway musical and the first musical theater run in history to surpass 3,000 performances. Originally planned as its fiftieth-anniversary production, *Fiddler on the Roof* returned to Broadway in November 2015, and I was lucky enough to get tickets for the third evening of previews. I had been wondering what to expect from the show. After all, the revival was long in the making. I had seen so many times the acclaimed 1971 film version, which won three Academy Awards, including one for the score arranged by John Williams. It was nominated for several more, including Best Picture, Best Actor for Chaim Topol as Tevye, and Best Supporting Actor for Leonard Frey, who played the tailor Motel Kamzoil (both had previously acted in the musical: Topol as Tevye in the London production and Frey in a minor part as Mendel, the rabbi's son).

But not all productions had been celebrated. In February 2004, critic Thane Rosenbaum of the *Los Angeles Times* had accused David Leveaux's previous Broadway production of lacking "Jewish soul." He opined, "The sensation is as if you're sampling something that tastes great and looks Jewish but isn't entirely kosher." Rosenbaum's criticism, including his implicit condemnation of the lack of Jews in the musical's

mately cannot accept Chava's and Fyedka's. Only at the very end is he willing to acknowledge her again as she and her husband leave the shtetl. To be sure, the rule-bending marriages cause anxieties about the role that tradition plays in the Judaism of the next generation. But Tevye's reactions show his ability to balance tradition and progress. At each juncture, he recites, "On the one hand . . . but on the other hand . . . ," weighing the terms of his difficult decision. In this way, Tevye embodies the inner nature of tradition—while some rules are malleable, others are truly unbreakable. In order for a community, such as the shtetl, to remain intact, the breaking with some practices is unacceptable, while others can be stretched. In *Fiddler*, the bending of traditions is a family affair, dependent on Tevye and his children, who are willing to even abandon them (and with it their family) for a new lifestyle. Such generational conflicts are universal. Thus, while the story takes place in a shtetl, in essence it applies to all families who encounter a changing world or society. Harnick himself described the musical as being "about the disintegration of a whole way of life."

There are many other characters and side plots that add to the story of *Fiddler* and contribute to a full shtetl picture. While respecting Tevye's status as head of the family, the sharp-tongued Golde tries to hold the family together. Yente, the gossipy village matchmaker, involves herself in Tzeitel's life. There is a village rabbi and a constable who reminds us that Anatevka is under Russian authority. But the core of the story centers on Tevye's attempts to maintain his family and Jewish practices while new influences encroach on their lives that move his daughters farther away from the customs of his faith—and in the very end, with the edict of the czar, from their village by eviction.

To be sure, the story departs from Sholem Aleichem's original. It adds a pogrom, which closes act 1, following the celebration of the eldest daughter's wedding. It omits the dark destiny of the remaining daughters (one commits suicide, the other separates from her husband) and sets Tevye's final destination in the United States, not Palestine—a twist on the Promised Land. With these and many other changes, *Fiddler* balances dark and humorous moments, nostalgic Yiddish stories of shtetl life and American fiction. This balancing act and the adaptability in the face of challenge and even catastrophe are captured in the show's icon—the fiddler.

The musical's central symbolic image was partly inspired by Marc Chagall's series of surreal paintings that depict fiddlers as larger than life standing on top of a roof (this iconography inspired many set designs and the 1971 film version). Violinists have been central figures in Yiddish literature as well. In 1888, Sholem Aleichem wrote the novel *Stempenyu*, whose title character is an exceptionally talented itinerant fiddler who seduces women in every town he visits. The novel was adapted multiple times into Yiddish theatrical productions. With the almost complete decline of New York's Yiddish theater after World War II, the shtetl fiddler ultimately reappeared in what would become its best-known and most enduring form—the Broadway musical.

And it is the fiddler who opens the show, and he does so in the most unorthodox way possible. Instead of an overture by the twenty-two-member orchestra, an essential component of many Broadway musicals, the iconic fiddler plays his tune solo onstage. With the exception of its first notes, which feature an initial upward leap, it sounds a little bit like a children's tune, as it revolves around just a few notes with many repetitions. After a few bars, another solo violin joins in from the pit but with a different theme, later sung by the papas. Although both melodies are equal in importance and act in competition to each other, they come from different corners of the theater: one from the stage, the other one out of the pit. The fiddler's theme is a happy tune that only in its final downward steps suggests folksy difference. The "papa theme" has some freygish inflections. It is thus not the fiddler who introduces the Jewishly sounding melody but rather the violin in the pit—an interesting juxtaposition that creates a visual and sonic balance between the Jewish and Broadway sounds. The prologue continues with Tevye making an introduction while the strings retreat into the background. Turning toward the audience, he explains the significance of the fiddler:

> A fiddler on the roof. Sounds crazy, no? But in our little village of Anatevka, you might say every one of us is a fiddler on the roof, trying to scratch out a pleasant, simple tune without breaking his neck. It isn't easy. You may ask, why do we stay here if it's so dangerous? We stay because Anatevka is our home. And how do we keep our balance? That I can tell you in a word—Tradition!

Aside from being the bearer of melody, the fiddler's significance is open to interpretation. He is a nameless and imaginary figure who accompa-

nies the characters at important junctures (though depending on director's choice). In the 2015 Broadway production, the fiddler flies over
the stage and the roofs of Anatevka when Tevye concludes the prologue
with the words "Without our tradition, our lives would be as shaky as . . .
as . . . as a fiddler on the roof!" He reappears at crucial junctions: during
"Sabbath Prayer," after Tevye arranges his daughter's marriage with
Lazar Wolf, and during the wedding scene. These are all moments that
revolve around tradition. As an icon of shtetl life, the fiddler might
symbolize the Old Country but with a measure of ambivalence given
the vulnerability of the shtetl in the face of modernization and anti-
Semitism. That the fiddler does not carry an identifiably Jewish melody
suggests acculturation, adaptability, and the departure from tradition.
The fiddler appears also in scenes less expected. When Tevye learns
that Chava has married Fyedka, he sits in the background, not playing
the fiddle but holding it closely and eventually striking a mournful tune;
at the very end of the show, when the Jews leave the shtetl, the fiddler
joins them playing his famous tune. Here, the fiddler becomes a metaphor for Jewish survival in a world of uncertainty and imbalance. Overall, he accompanies scenes where transition and adaptation play a greater role. In this way, he represents continuity.

But back to the prologue. After Tevye's monologue, the musical
narration of the chorus of shtetl residents begins, introducing the people of Anataveka and their values, accompanied by a folksy oompah
rhythm. There are four groups: the papas, the mamas, the sons, and the
daughters. Initially, they all sing together, loudly belting out the word
"tradition" in unison, thus setting off Tevye's spoken words, which explain the roles of each social class in the village. Then each group sings a
little about themselves, each having their melody. We hear the papa
theme again, this time with the descriptive, introductory text sung by
Tevye and the papas:

> Who, day and night must scramble for a living,
> Feed a wife and children,
> Say his daily prayers?
> And who has the right
> As master of the house
> To have the final word at home.

All chime in to confirm "The papa, the papas." Everyone starts dancing
and affirmatively singing "tradition" to the oompah rhythm. Then the

mamas introduce a new melody, whose rhythm stretches over lyrics that highlight their core responsibility: making a good and kosher home. All chime in to confirm "The mama, the mamas," followed by the echoing "tradition." The subsequent melodies sung by the sons and daughters recall the fiddler tune. They both feature the initial upward leap, which the sons maintain throughout, while the daughters continue with repeating notes. After each respective group has introduced itself, the chorus returns in unison. (It returns many more times in this number.)

With small variations, these four themes are all based on the same chord progressions and similar orderly rhythms. This identical foundation of the themes makes it possible to present them stacked on top of each other, and that is exactly what happens after all four groups have been introduced with their unique melody. However, the papas enter earlier than the other groups and thus throw off what would normally be a smooth alignment of the melodies. The melodies and harmonies do not quite line up, creating a clashing, dissonant ending to a series of introductions that had previously been unfolding in a quite orderly manner. For a very brief moment when everyone is singing their melodies at the same time, we have chaos and conflict in both music and lyrics: "Say his daily prayers" clashes with "A quiet home," "To mend and tend," and "At ten I learned." The cacophony suggests that traditions are about to be challenged, bent, or even broken, giving way to change and modernity. Traditions can no longer be taken for granted and come under attack. The parts come together at the end of this number, when they repeat the song's title, "Tradition."

There are other noteworthy sonic moments in the prologue, such as the rabbi's blessing, which turns a painful historical reference into humor: "May God bless and keep the czar . . . far away from us." The orchestral melody that previously accompanied Tevye's monologue follows but is now sung by the whole ensemble on the syllable "dai," thereby recalling a nigun. When the non-Jewish inhabitants of Anatevka are introduced, the sounds of bells and organ music reference Eastern Orthodoxy—the latter is true Broadway imagination given that instruments have no presence in Russian worship. Tevye points to the others in the village and explains how one person sold him a horse but delivered a mule. A fight breaks out, implying conflict between Jews and non-Jews. The diverse sonic tapestry symbolizes the social one: the shtetl has many faces and many characters. There is diversity and discord. What unites all is the continuance of their lives in a changing world.

The numbers that follow conform to a more typical Broadway sound, though occasionally Jewish themes resurface in music and lyrics. A prime example is "If I Were a Rich Man," which Tevye sings in the stable, musing about his modest circumstances and his standing in the community. The number was inspired by Sholem Aleichem's Yiddish monologue "Ven ikh bin Rothschild" and uniquely turns a negative Jewish stereotype upside down: the money-hungry Jew. Tevye dreams of monetary splendor and the luxurious life it would afford him. But there is also faith, piety, and reverence as Tevye muses about finally having time to pray in the synagogue, engage in Torah and Talmud study, and even visit the Western Wall in Jerusalem. The song begins and ends with a direct address to God, an affirmation of Tevye's deep beliefs. The religious underpinnings are reinforced by the song beginning modestly with just a few strings (the lack of rich accompaniment also underlines Tevye's poverty) and by featuring the syllables "yubby dibby dibby dibby dibby dibby dibby dum"—another nod to nigunim. This is not arbitrary. Bock and Harnick got much inspiration from hearing Hasidic song at a benefit for the Hebrew Actors' Union. Together with Jerome Robbins, they also visited Hasidic Brooklyn and gathered ideas from observing the natives. But while "If I Were a Rich Man" was clearly inspired by the nigun, Bock removed its transcendental-spiritual purpose to create a song suitable for Broadway. He did so by standardizing the syllables, adding more instrumental accompaniment to a rustic dance rhythm in moderate tempo and uniform note values. These passages are occasionally interrupted by sections with a smooth melody in free-flowing rhythm, vaguely reminiscent of a prayer chant but ultimately supporting Tevye's dreamy musings, such as in the fifth verse, when the lyrics reference a biblical figure:

> They would ask me to advise them,
> Like a Solomon the Wise.
> "If you please, Reb Tevye . . ."
> "Pardon me, Reb Tevye . . ."
> Posing problems that would cross a rabbi's eyes!

"If I Were a Rich Man" avoids depicting Tevye as a miser, and with its humorous undertones, it breaks through the stereotype. The American actor Zero Mostel (1915–1977), who was extremely animated in his demeanor and facial expressions and over-the-top in his humor and attempts at getting the audience to laugh, made it famous. Indeed, no other actor shaped *Fiddler* more (Mostel even claimed that he sang Yiddish melodies that later found their way into *Fiddler* in altered versions). Right with him comes Theodore Bikel, who, with more than 2,000 appearances—more than any other actor in that role—was one of the greatest and most practiced Tevyes (similarly, he claimed that his recording of Jewish folk music inspired the melody and style of Bock's melodies). Claims of contribution aside, Bock asserts, "I knew I could write this score, not from any formal knowledge of ethnic forms, nor from any arduous labor of research, but rather, strictly and simply, from the heart."

Bock wrote a score that only very occasionally gestures toward the eastern European Jewish musical sensibility. Indeed, while the music remains largely in the style of Broadway, Jewishness is implied mostly in the lyrics. Among the passages that feature snippets of Hebrew text is the Sabbath scene. When Tevye prays to himself before the meal, he does so reciting the Ashrei, a prayer that praises the Lord and blesses the people of the house. But Golde keeps interrupting him, making the text of the prayer impossible to understand. When the whole family has gathered at the table, joined by Perchik and Motel, Tevye and Golde sing a prayer for the health and safety of their family, eventually joined by a chorus of other families. Although "Sabbath Prayer" is rendered in English, it is a near-literal translation of the Hebrew blessing said over children on the Sabbath. Introduced by the English horn, whose first solo notes emulate a shofar calling the faithful to prayer, the melody was initially intended as a theme for Tevye, but in the end, Harnick used it to create this solemn piece. Bock himself said about it, "It's got a certain Yiddish-Russian quality. It's overly sad, which might be a point of humor. On the other hand, it could also be legitimately sad, which might be more poignant than humorous"—in other words, a typical Broadway melody, adaptable to multiple occasions.

Occurrences of Hebrew in *Fiddler* are easily understood. Take the scene in the tavern. Tevye has been told that the butcher Lazar Wolf wants to speak with him. The two men meet in the tavern to discuss the arranged marriage of Tzeitel. When they toast to their agreement, they do so in Hebrew with the customary word "L'chaim." Not only is this toast extremely short, but it is also self-explanatory, as its translation precedes it twice: "To life, to life, l'chaim." (The same can be observed in the Hebrew word for congratulations or good luck: "A blessing on your head, mazel tov, mazel tov," which occurs throughout and especially in the dream.) There is no doubt about the meaning.

But "To Life! (L'chaim!)" also functions as an ethnic identifier. The ensuing dance sequence is accompanied by a nigun-like melody with traces of "To Life! (L'chaim!)" sung on wordless syllables. It transitions into the Russian toast "Za vashe zdorovye, Na zdorovye" (To your health), accompanied by balalaika sounds and Russian-style dancing by the non-Jewish villagers. The commonly known Hebrew and Russian toasts clearly serve to juxtapose two different cultures during an encounter of the groups they represent. When Tevye is invited to join in the Russian celebration, he hesitates. A moment of tension sets in that reminds the audience of the situation in the Pale, but this quickly dissolves when Tevye participates. On the way home, the Russian constable warns Tevye of an impending "unofficial demonstration" against the Jewish members of the community—a foreboding of the impending pogrom. The lightness of the scene turns into darkness, followed by a humorous exchange between the two men and again followed by the "If I Were a Rich Man" melody, which is first played by the fiddler solo (perhaps reflecting Tevye's inner monologue) and then taken up by the orchestra.

In the end, love prevails over money and over tradition. The finale of the first act begins with the wedding of Tzeitel and Motel. There is a recurrence of the fiddler's tune and then the famous Broadway-style number "Sunrise, Sunset," whose melody resurfaces throughout the finale. There is also klezmer-ish music, evoked by the genre's emblematic clarinet and tsimbl (the latter a portable hammer dulcimer with some 100 strings), accompanying the dance numbers, including the famous "Bottle Dance." There are "mazel tov" shouts and "dai, dai" syllables on Hasidic-inflected melodies. Motives from the opening "Tradition" number return as well, serving as a counterpoint to the traditions that had just been broken to make this marriage possible and those that are newly broken, such as women and men dancing together. In this way, "Sunrise, Sunset" is allegorical, as the sun is setting on a whole era with its unique customs.

The second act does not feature any noteworthy Jewish-themed music. Its disappearance parallels the action: the plot focuses on the other two daughters, who further distance their generation from previous traditions, and on the expulsion of all Jewish residents. It is ultimately about the dissolution of Jewish shtetl life. Motives from "Tradition" occasionally resurface, and toward the very end, there are snippets of Hebrew prayer chant. The final number "Anatevka," which accompanies the scene when the Jews are forced out of their homes, encapsulates Broadway's imagination of a changing world. "Anatevka" consists of a lot of repetition. Even the notes for the word "Anatevka" revolve around the same note with one downward step that emulates the gesture of a sigh. This cleverly conceived motive not only expresses sheer sadness but also symbolizes the inherent tension between tradition and modernity. Tradition wants to remain the same just like these first notes; modernity, in contrast, implies change. The repetitions inherent in the number extend beyond the opening motive. The melody repeats, the orderly rhythm stays the same. The lyrics reveal an even deeper message. The phrase "Soon I'll be a stranger in a strange new place" alludes to the biblical verses from Exodus 2:22 and 22:21. In the first, Moses names his son Gershon (which literally means "a sojourner there") because he was a stranger in a strange land; in the second, God commands the Israelites to not wrong or oppress a stranger, for the Israelites were also strangers in a foreign land. The concept of being a stranger and being in a strange land is thus deeply rooted in Jewish thought. Over these words, the melody changes. It takes leaps and rises upward, thus conveying consolation and hopefulness within a generally nostalgic mood. Later on, after the choir asks "Where else would Sabbath be so sweet?" the flute and oboe provide the answer with a short motive, higher in pitch, exotic in nature, and both strange and bittersweet. Compared to the energetic opening number "Tradition," "Anatevka" is overall bleak and melancholic. This framing with very different moods is a musical indicator that times have changed.

Mirroring the very opening, the final sounds stem from the fiddler, who very slowly, almost mournfully, plays his signature tune. If in the very beginning his melody has introduced and represented the pull of tradition, at the end it accompanies the Jewish inhabitants of Anatevka on their way to an uncertain future. But instead of appearing in competition with the "papa theme" to match the opening, both melodies now appear consecutively, with the "papa theme" preceding it from the pit, thereby insinuating the separation of the Jewish and non-Jewish sound worlds instead of their encounter. In the 2015 Broadway production, the fiddler's tune appeared with one significant change. Per the director's choice, the fiddler omitted the very last note, losing it after a long stretch of silence to the orchestra. He thus did not resolve the tune himself, leaving the melody unfinished and incomplete—a suspended ending, if an ending at all. His actual last lingering note might represent what the expelled Jews of Anatevka have left behind—an intangible reminiscence of home. But this silent final note still resonates strongly today. It implies that changes in society are ongoing—there is no final note to that.

Indeed, the director of the 2015 Broadway revival, Bartlett Sher, was adamant that the revival should explicitly, if briefly and quietly, connect to current events. To bring this out visually, he created a striking framing device. Danny Burstein, the rich baritone who sang Tevye with roof-raising force, opened the performance by standing on a bare stage as a contemporary character, bareheaded, in a red parka, carrying a book. He is, we assume, a descendant of one of the townspeople, coming to see what is left of the shtetl. The answer: nothing. While rendering the show's prologue words, he removed the parka, untucked the prayer shawl, and put on a cap, thereby transforming himself into Tevye. At the end of the show, the device is mirrored. When the fiddler played his final tune, Burstein returned to the stage dressed in a red parka, with a bare head and a book. While waiting for the elusive final note, he nodded to the fiddler to join the line of refugees (until that moment, the fiddler had been largely apart from the characters of Anatevka, except for Tevye), silently picked up Tevye's cart, and alongside his family joined the exodus. "You see him enter the line of refugees, making sure we place ourselves in the line of refugees, as it reflects our past and affects our present," Sher told the *New York Times*. With few exceptions, Broadway musicals are generally regarded as escapist, but this visual nod to the twenty-first-century refugee crisis makes *Fiddler* newly relevant and the worldwide issue of migration and displacement inescapable. Indeed, we face a world of torn-apart Anatevkas and thousands of immigrants and refugees seeking a better life.

But *Fiddler* addresses a broad range of other themes that are relevant in today's America, if not universally relevant through the ages: love, family and generational conflict, communal cohesion and intergroup bridge building, renewal of societies, the breakdown of traditional structures and the creation of new rules and rituals, as well as shifts in gender, class, race, and power relationships. *Fiddler's* timelessness and universality appeal to everyone. Such a conclusion is in line with the creators of *Fiddler*—particularly Robbins—who wished the musical to convey a message about tradition, change, and adaptation, not only in Jewish history but in society more generally, to make the show relevant and accessible to a broad audience.

Regardless of its universality, *Fiddler* remains one of the quintessential *Jewish* Broadway musicals. Not only does it boldly bring the Jewish experience onstage, but it also introduces the audience to many different topics that have defined this experience in general terms: the Torah and prayer, the Jewish life cycle, oppression and persecution, immigration and acculturation, and the Jewish family and home. While no other Broadway musical has ever presented these tropes in such condensed and unified form, these themes have occasionally surfaced throughout musical theater's history. Take, for example, *Joseph and the Amazing Technicolor Dreamcoat* (1968). Composed by the British Andrew Lloyd Webber, it has enjoyed runs on American stages. Rooted in the Book of Genesis, it tells the story of Joseph. Its choral number "Deliver Us," a plea to God to remember his children and save them from hunger and slavery, includes snippets of Hebrew, such as "Elohim" (God). John Cale's cover of Leonard Cohen's acclaimed song "Hallelujah," which alludes to the biblical story of David, can be heard in *Shrek* (2001). Although given that the Tanakh/Old Testament is shared by Jews and Christians, there is a universal appeal to these references, too. However, the inclusion of Jewish prayer is unequivocal, such as the chanting of the Kaddish in the number by the same name from *Rags* (1986), a musical about Russian Jewish immigrants arriving in America.

Among the Jewish life cycle events, bar mitzvahs and weddings have been eternalized in several musicals. "The Year of the Child" from *Falsettos* (1992) is about the joys and craziness when becoming a bar mitzvah and taking full responsibility of one's actions in accordance with Jewish law. The number opens with the child reciting a snippet of a blessing in Hebrew. "Shiksa Goddess" from *Last Five Years* (2001) addresses interfaith marriage, a rising concern for many Jewish families. *Milk and Honey* (1961) focuses on remarriage while indirectly dealing with death, mourning, and divorce. It takes place in Israel and follows the journey of touring widows from America and their new romantic possibilities.

Oppression and persecution of the Jewish people and anti-Semitism are perhaps the most common manifestations of the Jewish experience in the Broadway musical, from referencing Jewish slavery in Egypt in "Deliver Us" from *The Prince of Egypt* (1998) to *Fiddler*'s pogroms in the Pale to suppression at the onset of the Enlightenment, such as "In My Own Lifetime" from *The Rothschilds* (1970). The Holocaust is overtly thematicized in *Cabaret* (1966), which tells the story of a young American writer who travels to Berlin at the onset of the Nazis' rise to power. The duet between a Jewish shop owner and the German Fräulein Schneider, "It Couldn't Please Me More," is the beginning of their courtship. It also foreshadows the problematic relationship between Jews and non-Jews in Germany. *The Producers* (2001) takes a transgressive comic tone toward the events of World War II and the Holocaust. But this work also creates nostalgia for the golden age of musical theater (which roughly corresponds to Rodgers and Hammerstein's *Oklahoma!* and Bock and Harnick's *Fiddler on the Roof*) and references Yiddish theater on the Lower East Side.

Its turn-of-the-century immigrant community is a topic in *The Education of Hyman Kaplan* (1968). While focusing on the linguistic integration of immigrants in general, it is tinged with Jewish humor, playing with the bizarre logic of English through a Jewish lens ("to die" is conjugated as "die, dead, funeral"). Similarly, *Rags* focuses on the difficulty of settling in a new country. Mother and son have arrived from Russia in America, trying to find the head of the family, who had already left many years ago. Facing tough times in their new country, the mother sings "Nothing Will Hurt Us Again" to explain that they need to rely on one another in order to thrive in America. Trying to convey hope, she tells her son that they will be just like they used to be and that their family will become the same once again. As she says this, her husband finds them, and the family is reunited. *Ragtime* (1996) looks more broadly and in a larger context at immigration by telling the story of three groups in early twentieth-century America: blacks, upper-class suburbanites, and eastern European immigrants from Latvia. The latter prepare themselves for arrival while en route to their new country. In "Journey On," the father tells his daughter how their lives are going to change as they venture to a new country. But anxiety about anti-Semitism persists: the father explains that, in order to ensure a fresh start, nobody can know their Jewish name.

The stability of the Jewish home and family is the subject of *I Can Get It for You Wholesale* (1962). Set during the Great Depression, it tells the story of Harry Bogen and his family. "The Family Way" is sung in both English and Yiddish and features nigun-like melody snippets on the nonsense syllables "dye dye digga gigga dye" in an overall folksy-sounding arrangement supported by klezmer-ish instrumentation. The "Old Fashioned Husband," a number in *The Education of Hyman Kaplan* (1968), explains the patriarchal role that the head of a traditional Jewish family holds. In an inversion, "Lonely Room" from *Oklahoma!* (1943), a musical plea for American inclusiveness that also addresses anti-Semitism and the place of Jews in society, laments the loneliness of what life is like without a family.

Since Broadway is a place where a diverse group of individuals goes for entertainment, the musical has offered an opportunity for different cultures to enlighten others as to their history, practices, and values. Just like Yiddish theater, the musical aims to amuse but also to instruct. In this way, these Jewish topics are conceived as broadly as possible both in text and in sound. In both style and content, most of these musicals present Jewishness as integral to the American experience, thereby representing a theatrical acculturation in which Jewish interests are advanced while overt Jewish characters, themes, and sounds actually disappear. The musical itself helped little to convey the dramatic weight of the Jewish aspects of the drama, carrying mainly for what it is has been composed for: the Broadway stage. Indeed, there are only a few instances when Jewish music enters the score of the musical. An exception is *Soul Doctor—Journey of a Rockstar Rabbi*, which details the life of Shlomo Carlebach and includes his lyrics and settings of prayers to melodies influenced by Hasidism and folklore.

Born in Berlin, Carlebach (1925–1994) had emigrated to the United States by way of Lithuania and Great Britain in 1939. Being brought up strictly Orthodox, he eventually ventured for a secular education. Carlebach began writing songs at the end of the 1950s, based primarily on biblical verses or prayers. Similarly to Debbie Friedman, he was not literate in music, but he wrote thousands of songs. Becoming fluent in English only at the age of twenty-six, he developed an unusual grammar that became his hallmark as a songwriter. His audience broadened after he met Bob Dylan, Pete Seeger, and other folksingers who encouraged his career and helped him get a spot at the Berkeley Folk Festival in 1966. His soulful renderings of Jewish texts, his infectious music, and his charisma made him known as "The Singing Rabbi." He often just accompanied himself on the guitar, but sometimes he used a wider range of backup instrumentation. When not touring, Carlebach maintained both his late father's synagogue on the Upper West Side of Manhattan (ever since known for its musical program) and a religious communal settlement in Israel. For sure, he brought a new energy to synagogue music, as is evidenced by the continued success of the Carlebach Shul.

Many of his melodies became standards across the Jewish spectrum, including "Am Yisrael Chai" (The Nation of Israel Lives), the musical's closing song. Composed in 1965 on behalf of Soviet Jewry, it became the movement's anthem. Like most of his songs, "Am Yisrael Chai" has a relatively short, catchy melody with repetitions and a chorus and a poignant rhythm; it blends elements from folk songs and nigunim—at the time considered a revolution in the world of Jewish music. Its lyrics were borne out of Genesis 45:3: "Joseph said to his brothers, 'I am Joseph. Is my father still well?' But his brothers could not answer him, so dumbfounded were they on account of him." Carlebach modified the phrase "Ha'od avi ḥai?" (Is my father still well?) to "Am Yisrael chai" and changed the reference to Jacob's father to a reference to God—the father of the children of Israel. The lyrics create a potent image of the essence of the Jewish nation, a reaffirmation of Jewish identity and an anthem of survival. It was sung the day after the start of the Six-Day War in 1967 and at the end of the Yom Kippur War in 1975. To close the musical with this song is a powerful statement not only regarding the survival of Carlebach's legacy but also to cement the strength of the Jewish experience in general.

In the history of the Broadway musical, the topic and music of *Soul Doctor* has remained an exception. Still, as a song from the 2005 musical comedy *Spamalot* put it, "You Won't Succeed on Broadway If You Don't Have Any Jews." Created and received in good humor, the number parodies the "Bottle Dance" from *Fiddler* and weaves in snippets of "Hava nagila" to pay tribute to the Jewish contribution to Broadway. Indeed, *Spamalot* highlights Jewish songwriters' involvement from the 1930s to the present, reminding us that the genre would barely exist without Jewish composers and lyricists. Indeed, from the 1889 opening of Oscar Hammerstein's Victoria Theater to the just-closed revival of *Fiddler on the Roof*, the long-term relationship between Jews and Broadway has produced countless icons.

Just like the music for the moving image, many of Broadway's musical scores come from composers of Jewish descent. Think of Jerome Kern and Irving Berlin, Oscar Hammerstein and Lorenz Hart, George Gershwin, Frederick Loewe, Richard Rodgers, and Harold Arlen. Among them, they wrote the songs for practically all the great musicals of the 1930s and 1940s. Many of them teamed up with Jewish lyricists. Indeed, at the time, almost every successful Broadway songwriter was Jewish—except for Cole Porter. Deeply aware of Broadway's cultural fabric, he told Richard Rodgers the secret for writing hit songs: "Simplicity itself. I'll write Jewish tunes," he claimed in 1926. Porter knew little of political correctness, and his latent anti-Semitism is a point of debate. Still, Jerome Kern echoed his remark when answering Oscar Hammerstein's question of what sort of music he would be writing for a musical about the life of Marco Polo. Kern replied, "It'll be good Jewish music." Clearly, their music was not "Jewish music" as many understand it, and Porter's tunes were not "Jewish tunes." The composers were not simply adapting the songs of the Yiddish stage for an English-speaking audience. While some were bridging the Lower East Side to Tin Pan Alley and to Broadway, they were all drawing on the wider musical traditions of America. In their sound, these composers fashioned an America of their own. Many of them brought on the musical stage a unique vision of song and dance that was optimistic, meritocratic, and selectively inclusive. After all, they lived in a country in which Jews could at once lose and find themselves and enact their acculturation onstage and off.

If the Broadway musical clearly emerged as a form by which artists of Jewish descent negotiated their entrance into secular American society and constructed a vision of America that fostered self-understanding as the nation became a global power, in the 1940s, with Rodgers and Hammerstein's musicals, this overtly assimilationist phase came to an end. But the lineage of Jewish composers continued into the next era with greats such as Leonard Bernstein and Stephen Sondheim, and carried on with Marvin Hamlisch, Stephen Schwartz, and Alan Menken. In its course, the Broadway musical has absorbed the Jewish experience in more than one way: it is a product of producers, lyricists, directors, and musicians who were born Jewish. But ultimately, only a few of them incorporated the Jewish experience into their work or did so peripherally, with occasional allusions. Although Jewish music has not deeply anchored itself in the musical in spite of its creators' heritage, the Broadway musical constitutes a strong statement about the influence and universality of its Jewish creators.

6

ON THE CONCERT STAGE

Classical Music and the Jewish Experience

When pianist Daniel Schlesinger (1799–1839) arrived at the shores of the New World on October 6, 1836, nobody could have predicted that in his short life he would be instrumental in paving the way for a Jewish presence in American concert life. Not only was he America's first significant classical musician of Jewish descent, but he also played a transformative role in shaping the tastes of American audiences who previously had little opportunity to hear instrumental virtuosos. But the 1830s became a turning point, and it was Schlesinger who contributed to it. Who was Daniel Schlesinger?

Born into a large Jewish family in Hamburg (he had nine siblings), Schlesinger began to play the piano at age five and received his first lessons from the organist at Hamburg's St. Peter's Church. He also studied the violin with Andreas Romberg, among others. When his father died prematurely, Daniel had to pick a profession, and in 1814 he became a clerk at the local trade company Robinow, Goldschmidt & Co. He continued to play the piano in his spare time. At a salon, he drew the attention of Ferdinand Ries, a former student of Beethoven's. This was a pivotal moment for the young Schlesinger, one with great consequences. In 1818, he embarked on becoming a pianist by profession, first as a musical prodigy student of Ries and later studying with Ignaz Moscheles, a Jewish piano virtuoso. Schlesinger also began to compose; among his first works is an *Allegro di Bravura*, which he

dedicated to Ries, and a *Rondo brillant*. Many of his early works have
been printed in Hamburg and Leipzig. By the mid-1820s, he had performed in concert halls throughout Europe, showcasing the works of
Johann Sebastian Bach, Ludwig van Beethoven, and Johann Nepomuk
Hummel. Later, he would introduce American audiences to those
works. In search of economic opportunity, that is, new patronage, and
encouraged by one of his brothers who had settled in New York, Schlesinger embarked on his journey to the New World on August 27, 1836.

His first appearance was at the National Theater, a short-lived opera
house (1836–1841), previously home of Lorenzo Da Ponte's New York
Opera Company and, as an institution, the predecessor of the New York
Academy of Music and of the Metropolitan Opera. Schlesinger's performance of variations on the march from Gioachino Rossini's opera *Tancredi* at the benefit concert created little sensation, but it helped to
spread his name. Had he arrived a few years later with the wave of
European virtuosos who came in the mid-nineteenth century, he might
have encountered a far different reception. Music lovers would have
courted and admired him. But at the time of Schlesinger's arrival, audiences still favored fine vocal music over the mostly rudimentary instrumental performances they heard.

In the absence of concert opportunities, in the winter of 1836–1837,
Schlesinger began to teach (although his high fees by New York standards did not win him many students). He also played at the salon of a
German patron. It was there that he began to draw attention for his
"musical eloquence, poetry, and genius." The audience must have been
German, as he improvised a set of variations on Carl Maria von Weber's
patriotic song "Lützow's Wild Hunt" of 1927 and on one of the many
musical settings that the Rhine River, a symbol of German national and
cultural identity, had inspired. His improvisatory skills were at once
virtuosic and imaginative, exposing him as a skilled pianist who was able
to draw from a wide variety of melodies; he used excerpts from Rossini's *Tancredi* and melodies that were widely known in the American
world —"Yankee Doodle" and "God Save the King," "Hail Columbia,"
"The Star-Spangled Banner"—melodies of the African American popu-
lace, and even the chirp of the cricket outside the window. Contempo-
raneous accounts speak of "highest brilliancy," "hazardous modulations," and "opulent in harmony," which enhanced rather than stifled
the free flow of melody.

In April 1837, Schlesinger gave his second public concert, organized by a Mr. Russell, and in June another one that showcased Hummel's Piano Concerto in A-flat and improvised variations on an American national air (presumably "Yankee Doodle"). Its promising reception gave Schlesinger impetus to establish a chamber concert series following European models, the first of its kind in the United States. But in the long run, he did not win an audience. In the spring of 1838, Schlesinger became director of the Concordia, a society devoted to German instrumental and choral music. Under his tenure, the Concordia offered concerts in different parts of the city and served as a platform to introduce New York audiences to hitherto unknown European composers, such as Hummel and Sigismund Thalberg, and to promote the work of better-known ones, such as Beethoven. In this way, private music making came into the public realm, and European aesthetics entered the United States. Schlesinger also transplanted the postemancipation understanding that high art served Jews as a bridge from separatism to integration into society to becoming part of the middle class. He also exemplified a process in which musicians born Jewish began to lose an active connection to their heritage, musical and otherwise. Schlesinger and many of his peers evidently had no difficulty in replacing it with a new role in American musical and cultural life. For them, classical music was an artistic outlet in the secular society they were part of.

The year 1838 constituted a turning point for Schlesinger in that he established himself as a musician, admired and respected by the German immigrant community and native New Yorkers alike. His probably last performance took place in the course of a private Concordia concert at the end of May 1839; he played an arrangement of Carl Maria von Weber's *Invitation to the Dance*. On June 8, he died suddenly and unexpectedly but not in vain. Schlesinger was not only the forerunner of many successful Jewish musicians who began to frequent America's concert scene throughout the mid- to late nineteenth century and beyond; more importantly, his memorial concert had lasting consequences. On June 25, many of New York's most important musicians came together to honor him at Broadway Tabernacle, a Presbyterian church. The so-called Grand Musical Solemnity was not merely a tribute to Schlesinger but aimed at raising funds for his widow and two children. It featured an orchestra with five horns, unusually large for

that time. This gathering laid the seed for the Fourth New York Philharmonic Society. Founded in 1842, it was eventually renamed the
New York Philharmonic. In this way, Schlesinger's presence and perse-
verance as musician had been doubly important. In the mere three
years of his concert activity, he instilled a deep appreciation for chamber music in American audiences, and, even if under tragic circumstances, he ultimately launched the oldest continually operating orchestra in the United States.

A decade after Schlesinger's untimely death, Jews began to emerge
among the important promoters and patrons of the arts. Nowhere was
this more evident than with Max Maretzek (1821–1897). A Jewish violinist and composer born in Brno, Maretzek came to America in 1848
after having established himself as an opera conductor in London. He
first settled in New York as conductor of the Astor Opera House. A year
later, he formed his own opera company, which, heavily supported by
fellow Jews, quickly achieved success in New York and elsewhere in the
country with productions of Italian opera. According to the *Jewish Mes-
senger*, performances of *Rigoletto* and *La Traviata* in 1859 were "splen-
did successes." Referring to productions of the operas *La Juive* and
Nebuchadnezzar, the same paper proudly stated that "citizens of New
York at the present moment, owe their principal sources of amusement
to Israelite and Jewish subjects" and that Jews were very involved in the
management and talent of the New York opera and were among "the
most critical and sensible spectators" of "current dramatic productions."

By the end of the 1850s, much of the Jewish population had advanced in economic and social standing. In the decades to come, they
would enter opera houses and concert halls as appreciative audiences,
musicians, and conductors. Jews participated in chamber music, taught
music, and sang professionally or in amateur choruses. There were at
times whole families that fostered the arts, such as the Franko family,
who had immigrated from Germany to New Orleans (blood relatives of
the well-known composer Victor Holländer). At least eight members of
the Franko family were active as musicians throughout the United
States. The families of Leopold Damrosch (1832–1885) and Joshua
Heschel Singer (1848–?) would be another example of new Jewish immigrants melding into the Western art music scene in nineteenth- and
early twentieth-century America. Many of them were highly acculturated and made little or no effort to express their Jewish heritage in music.

In their immersion in the arts, as in business, many Jews chose to join non-Jews, sitting side by side at opera houses, music academies, and theaters. Participation in the arts offered the affluent and striving Jewish population an opportunity to mix with the non-Jewish population on equal terms. Through patronage of the arts, they could attain social acceptance in America's mainstream. Integration remained an appealing goal as Jewish life increasingly reached beyond the synagogue.

For the most part, however, these developments came at a later period, around 1900. By the turn of the century, Jewish audiences were embracing classical music to a much greater extent. As in previous decades, the concert music scene was defined largely by immigrants or guests from Europe and farther east who contributed to the shaping of musical taste in America as impresarios, performers, and composers. To provide one example, the acclaimed conductor of the Vienna Philharmonic Orchestra, Gustav Mahler (1860–1911), settled for a brief time in the United States. In 1908, he became the conductor at the Metropolitan Opera and from 1909 to 1911 served as principal conductor of the New York Philharmonic. He also conducted his own works, among them the First Symphony, whose third movement evokes associations with klezmer due to its instrumentation (the emblematic E-flat clarinet is prominent), dance-like rhythm, and melody. Its American premiere in December 1909, however, was not well received. A review in the *New York Times* mentions "mingled emotions" and details that the third movement contains "ironical traits, as of a parody or something—of what, and why?" Many decades later, Leonard Bernstein, remembered mainly as conductor of the New York Philharmonic and the composer of *West Side Story* and who headed the Mahler renaissance beginning in the 1960s, would perceive in this very symphony the "suppressed sigh" generally identified as Jewish.

The year 1908, the same time Mahler gained prominence in the United States, marked also the beginning of a Jewish national movement in art music in Russia. It was the year when a group of students and recent graduates of the St. Petersburg Conservatory formed the Society for Jewish Folk Music. By 1913, the society counted more than 1,000 members and opened subsidiaries in seven cities, including Kiev, Moscow, and Odessa, and later in Poland and Vienna. The society provided a platform for young composers and gave them an incentive to devote themselves to art music (in spite of its name). Some of these

composers became known as the Jewish National School. In the aftermath of the Russian Revolution, the Jewish National School eventually
dispersed around the globe. The group's aesthetic and intellectual lega-
cies would endure in many different forms in the cultural life of the
United States throughout the remainder of the twentieth century.

Elsewhere, too, Jewish composers began to create distinct works for
the concert stage. One of them was Ernest Bloch (1880–1959). Born
and raised in Geneva, Bloch's first musical contact came from hearing
his father sing Jewish folk songs and liturgical melodies as well as his
older sister playing opera selections and light music on the piano. He
began to compose at age six, improvising melodies on a toy flute given
to him by his mother. When he was nine, he began to study violin with
Albert Goss, and soon thereafter, he began composing music for the
violin. At age ten, he decided to become a composer, optimistically
stating, "I would compose music that would bring peace and happiness
to mankind." His grandfather (and to a lesser extent his father) had
been actively involved in the local Jewish community, and young Ernest
celebrated his bar mitzvah, but this was the end of his religious education—at least for a time. After completing his studies with the noted
Swiss composer Émile Jaques-Dalcroze, he left Switzerland in 1896 to
continue his music lessons in Brussels; he then moved on to resume his
education in Frankfurt and Munich and after that went to Paris. With
that, his aesthetics oscillated between German and French styles—
quite unusual during a time preoccupied with nationalism and race.
Bloch turned to Richard Wagner's writings for answers—an irony given
the composer's anti-Semitic stance. He agreed with Wagner that Jews
fundamentally deceived themselves by believing that they could assimilate. But contrary to Wagner, he thought that Jews should embrace
their racial identity. Indeed, Bloch became the first composer to define
his art as racially Jewish—race being a commonly accepted category at
the time.

Bloch began to explore his Jewish roots more deeply after he returned to Geneva in 1904. Trying to find a distinctively Jewish approach
to questions of language and form, he composed a series of works between 1911 and 1916, known as the "Jewish cycle," which included
Prélude and *Two Psalms* for soprano and orchestra, *Trois Poèmes Juifs*
for orchestra, the symphony *Israel*, and *Schelomo*, a rhapsody for violoncello and orchestra. As Bloch did not quote any preexisting musical

material associated with Jewish culture, the "textual" origins of these works create Jewish affiliation.

When Bloch arrived in the United States in July 1916, he closed the "Jewish cycle," but he never fully abandoned Jewish-themed compositions. In 1924, just when he became a naturalized U.S. citizen, he completed *From Jewish Life: Three Sketches* for violoncello and piano. Not long thereafter, Bloch began to conceive his artistically unequaled setting of the Hebrew liturgy, *Avodath Hakodesh* (Sacred Service). Its conception falls into a period when the ideas put forth two decades earlier in Russia began to take hold in America, with the founding of the Makhon Erets-Israeli le-Madaei ha-Muzika (MAILAMM), also known as the American-Palestine Institute of Musical Sciences and preceded by the Society for the Advancement of Music in Palestine of 1929.

On its founding in January 1932, MAILAMM was the first U.S. institution to successfully support Jewish musical causes. Initially, it was a women's group whose principal founder and driving force, Miriam Zunser, had no music background. Among the founding members were associate chairman Joseph Achron, chairman Lazare Saminsky, Solomon Rosowsky, Jacob Weinberg (all relocated exponents of the Jewish National School), and Joseph Yasser. But MAILAMM was not merely a transfer product of the Russian School; rather, it was cultural Zionism American style with a broadened idea of Jewish music in search of a new identity. That Ernest Bloch was an honorary member should come as no surprise. The self-understanding of his Jewishness as racial answered the questions raised by MAILAMM, especially the idea that Jews should embrace their own race because they cannot easily assimilate.

MAILAMM's goal was to promote political and cultural Zionism in the United States through music. In order to make this happen, the group tried to establish a network and sought exchanges with Palestine and the Diaspora. The cultivation and preservation of works by composers of Jewish heritage or works with Jewish content were important to the group. The society's leaders aspired to cultivate a new kind of Jewish cultural space by bringing such works on the concert stage and with that engaging Jewish audiences who would revalue their cultural heritage as simultaneously a national expression and a cosmopolitan, modern art. Beyond the confines of the synagogue, the political club, or the formal communal meeting, the concert hall setting offered a neutral public forum, a place in which, at least in theory, all Jews could gather to consume and affirm Jewish culture without a requirement of ideological commitment in either religious or political terms. Although the very concept of such cultural nationalism represented an implicit political statement about Jewish collective identity, the society repeatedly emphasized the open nature of the musical project.

MAILAMM organized concerts (between 1938 and 1941 specifically for the benefit of refugees), lectures, and social gatherings and collaborated with non-Jewish institutions and forums, such as WQXR for radio programs and the World's Fair in Queens in 1939–1940, whose theme "Building the World of Tomorrow" inspired MAILAMM to contribute to a "Palestine Pavilion and Temple of Religion." An intended performance of Bloch's *Avodath Hakodesh* did not materialize due to costs. The members of MAILAMM never clearly defined Jewish music in its statutes and approached it as plural as can be. In the end, however, its mission failed. It did not create a Jewish national music; it did not create a pan-U.S. network (except for a West Coast branch that opened in 1934). The upheavals of World War II affected audience numbers. The Holocaust demanded other priorities than focus on culture. Interest in Jewish music declined. By 1941, MAILAMM ceased to exist due to interorganizational problems and poor organization of programs, among other issues.

Bloch conceived *Avodath Hakodesh* before MAILAMM, when the concert repertoire was still short of works with Jewish association. The impetus came in 1930, when cantor Reuben Rinder, one of Bloch's earliest friends in San Francisco and a major force in commissioning music for Congregation Emanu-El, encouraged Bloch to accept a project writing a Saturday morning service for the synagogue. Rinder was able to obtain some funds from local donors, but the bulk of the money for the commission came from the wealthy New York violoncellist and philanthropist Gerald Warburg and his family. Freed from teaching commitments at the San Francisco Conservatory he was heading at the time, Bloch retreated to his native Switzerland to conceive what would become *Avodath Hakodesh*.

In preparation and given his limited knowledge of Hebrew, Bloch studied the Jewish liturgy and its text in great detail. His textual selections stemmed from the Reform movement's *Union Prayer Book*, but he modified them, omitting English readings and prayers that expand on the Hebrew texts. While these texts are crucial to the religious service, for him these were logical omissions. He added Hebrew texts from Deuteronomy, Exodus, Isaiah, Proverbs, and Psalms, among others. Although there is spoken dialogue in English, *Avodath Hakodesh* is mostly in Hebrew.

Just like the Saturday morning service in the *Union Prayer Book*, *Avodath Hakodesh* is divided into five parts. The first part is a meditation on the unity of nature and the unity of man—a message of faith and hope for life. The second part is about sanctification and holiness, "a dialogue between God and Man." This section speaks also of the everlasting power of the Almighty. The third part begins with silent devotion and response. Then the choir sings a cappella the words of Psalm 19:14, "Yihyu leratzon" (Let the words of my mouth). The remainder of the third part and the fourth part center on the Torah. (Bloch reverses the established structure of the Saturday morning service, where the Torah is read in the last of the five sections of the service, a clear indicator that the work does not easily facilitate liturgical use.) The choir sings "Etz chayim," a peace song about the tree of life. The fifth part functions as an epilogue—all people recognize that they are united in spirit and that one day the world will be one. Before ending with the benediction and right after "Tzur Yisroel" (Rock of Israel), the choir sings "Adon Olam" (Master of the Universe), a prayer whose centrality of "olam"—which means universe, space, eternity of time—particularly inspired Bloch. Toward the end of the benediction, just when the final "Amen" passage begins, the cantor interpolates the last spoken section (in the vernacular) that reiterates the last line of the benediction: "May the Lord lift up His countenance unto thee and grant thee peace." Bloch claimed that these last measures took him two years to write. Throughout, the mixed chorus in some cases repeats or comments on the texts delivered by the baritone-soloist and in others gives its own statement. There are orchestral preludes and interludes that represent periods of congregational stillness—such as during the removal of the Torah scrolls from the ark and their return or while standing in silent devotion.

The underlying idea of *Avodath Hakodesh* is unity. When Rinder shared with Bloch previous musical settings of the Jewish liturgy, Bloch was concerned by the lack of thematic unity. Individual prayer settings seemed unrelated, with little perceived musical connection. In *Avodath*

Hakodesh, he therefore employed motives that recur throughout the five parts and thereby unify the one-hour work. One such motive is presented at the very beginning. It comprises altogether six notes that go up in near-stepwise fashion only to descend and return to where it started. There is nothing distinctly Jewish about the motive. Its notes are set in a mode associated with church music, used by many composers for the setting of the Magnificat, the Song of Mary. Bloch was clearly aware of the semblance. In one of his letters to Rinder, he referred to the line "hakadosh baruch hu" (the Holy One, blessed be He) as "a kind of Jewish Magnificat." Bloch's belief that plainchant derived from the music of the Temple explains why he would make this analogy. But there is also semblance to motives in works by Mozart and Wagner.

The recurrence of such motives was common, especially in late romanticism, both in German and in French music, to provide an element of unity in longer compositions. In his operas, Wagner particularly used short, constantly recurring musical phrases in association with a specific person, place, or idea. In Bloch, however, the motive is not associated with anything in particular. It appears frequently throughout, often introducing moments of great significance in the service, but also as a framing device and a unifying structural element. For example (and to mention only a few manifestations), to mirror its first occurrence, it opens the last part of the service around thirty-four minutes as well. In the third part, after seventeen minutes, it appears in the orchestral interlude for the moment when the Torah is taken out of the ark, thus coinciding with a sacred moment. In the fourth part, it closes the Torah service after thirty minutes. Here, it coincides with the word "shalom" (peace). Aside from its semantic function, it also has structural significance: it serves as introductory music for the work as a whole, the sanctuary, the call to worship, the Torah service, and the concluding portion of the service. But whenever Bloch brings it back, he changes its appearance slightly, often using it in a looser canonic form.

Let us return for a moment to the opening of *Avodath Hakodesh*. Bloch begins the work with a symphonic prelude titled "Meditation." The motive is first played by the basses in unison. After it is stated once, the violoncellos imitate the motive, slightly altering its rhythm. Violas and violins pick it up thereafter. Snippets of the motive are played a few more times by other instruments next—in its form, the opening resembles a canon (also known as a round). With its slow tempo and soft melodic line, the opening is meditative and solemn. Following the chorus's "Mah tovu" (How Goodly), the orchestra introduces the "Borechu" (Sing His Praise), the call to worship. There, it is the soloist who picks up the motive but with an exclamatory high ending after five minutes. Structurally, Bloch's setting of this prayer simulates what is common practice in Jewish congregations. He assigns the first line, "Borechu es Adonoy hamevoroch" (Praise Adonai, the exalted), to the cantor and the congregational response of the second line, "Boruch Adonoy hamevoroch le 'olom vo 'ed" (Praise Adonai, the exalted, forever and ever), to the choir. Bloch continues to adhere to such structural conventions. Interaction between soloist and choir follows quite closely the typical alternation between cantorial call and congregational response. With the exception of Rinder's not very widely known "Tzur Yisroel" melody, which closes the first part, there are no literal quotations of preexisting synagogue melodies. Rather, Bloch pursued his own distinct musical expression, inspired by Jewish liturgy. Cantorial passages are often sung with great rhythmic freedom, especially when compared to the congregational parts. Bloch emulates this effect by frequently changing meter or through specific instruction to sing with a recitative-like freedom. The quotation of the "Tzur Yisroel" is clearly reserved for dramatic effect at the very end of the first part. Sung by the soloist at around ten minutes, it stands out for its free-flowing rhythm and its highly melismatic melody. "Tzur Yisroel" returns in the fifth part at around forty-one minutes but now sung by the chorus with call-and-response effects between male and female voices. A short cantorial solo follows, and the male voices end the section.

Many scholars have written about the "Jewishness" of Bloch's music (or lack thereof). Given its title and text, it is a valid question to ask whether *Avodath Hakodesh* is ultimately a sacred or a secular work. Does it belong in a synagogue or concert hall, that is, is it Jewish or universal? After having completed the work, Bloch himself no longer viewed the text of *Avodath Hakodesh* as exclusively liturgical but rather thought of it as a unified poem, a program, a libretto for a large-scale concert work. He described *Avodath Hakodesh* as orchestral, a choral work, and an oratorio, even the first Jewish oratorio. Further, Bloch envisioned it to be performed without interruption as an integral whole, a unity without breaks for readings from the Scripture and the sermon as would be the norm in a synagogue service. With no precise liturgical function, the one-hour work is indeed more suited for the concert stage, although Bloch conceived two versions, one richly orchestrated (in addition to the usual strings section, it included double and in some cases triple winds, two harps, and percussion), the other with a keyboard reduction. The work's early performance history underlines its dual function: *Avodath Hakodesh* premiered at the Teatro di Torino in January 1934. After subsequent performances at concert halls in Italy and London, the work debuted in America at Carnegie Hall on April 12, 1934, with Bloch himself conducting the 250 members of the Schola Cantorum and 80 members of the New York Philharmonic. Only in March 1938 was it heard at Congregation Emanu-El in San Francisco at the end of service, and rarely thereafter. While liturgy was very much part of the conceptualization of the work, *Avodath Hakodesh* is ultimately a work for the concert hall.

In his 1933 lecture notes for *Avodath Hakodesh*, Bloch stresses the work's universality. Ending the service with the Adon Olam prayer thus adheres to liturgical conventions while also conveying the universal message that he was seeking. The English rendition of the title, *Sacred Service*, hints at universality, too, as it does not refer to a specific religion—just sacredness in general. *Avodath Hakodesh* thus shares a similar fate as Ludwig van Beethoven's *Missa solemnis*—their scope is too grandiose and their message too universal for the liturgical function on which they were respectively based.

Looking back at Bloch's work in 1982, Leonard Bernstein (1918–1990) considered the aims of Bloch "programmatically and deliberately Jewish," though he saw its primary manifestation not in the music itself but rather "in the program notes." This observation came from an accomplished composer and conductor though one with a very different background from Bloch's. Only a single generation removed from the shtetl of the western Ukraine (he was the grandson and great-grandson of Hasidic rabbis), Bernstein was born in Lawrence, Massachusetts, and grew up in various Jewish neighborhoods in Boston. Thanks to his father's business, the family prospered, though music was not considered central to their middle-class values. On the contrary, his father voiced strong objections when Bernstein decided to pursue his professional musical education. Bernstein's religious education, in turn, was on solid footing. With his family, he attended Boston's Congregation Mishkan Tefila, a Conservative synagogue that used a choir and organ accompaniment for services. Solomon Gregory Braslavsky, the music director and organist of the congregation, was an important influence for the young Bernstein and introduced him to "serious music." Eventually, Bernstein moved beyond the religious boundaries of his youth and developed his own individual religious belief with man at its center. Although he often struggled with matters of faith, he was a lifelong pacifist and a champion of Israeli musical culture. His Jewish identity remained an integral part of his life and shaped his approach to musical education, composition, and artistic, social, and political commitment.

Bernstein's biographer Humphrey Burton asserts that the composer's creative achievement is "the most significant body of specifically Jewish work achieved by a Jewish composer working in the field of classical music," with Ernest Bloch and Darius Milhaud being his only rivals. This body of work began with *Psalm 148* (1932–1935) and ended with "Af Mayn Khasene" (At My Wedding) from *Arias and Barcarolles* (1988). His large-scale choral music—the *Kaddish* Symphony, the *Chichester Psalms*, and even the theatrical *Mass*—are all rooted in Hebrew or Aramaic texts. He also wrote liturgical and folkloristic music for choir in Hebrew: the *Hashkiveinu* (1945) commissioned by Park Avenue Synagogue, *Yigdal* (1950), *Simchu Na* (1947), and *Reena* (1947). A number of instrumental works lean on Jewish themes, beginning with his first symphony, *Jeremiah* (1942), through the ballet *Dybbuk* (1974), based on the play by Shloyme Zanvl Rappoport, known under the pseudonym S. Ansky (1863–1920). With the exception of a gap between 1945 and 1963, Bernstein composed some twenty works with Jewish themes or texts throughout his career.

How Bernstein's Jewish-themed works are imbued with American eclecticism can be seen both in his instrumental and in his vocal music during his early and late periods. To begin, let us turn to his first symphony, *Jeremiah*, a twenty-five-minute work we might classify as program music—instrumental music with extramusical meanings that has a story attached. Indeed, its title refers to the prophet Jeremiah, who warned the Israelites of the potential consequences of their sinful actions. His prophecy was fulfilled when Jerusalem fell to the Babylonians in 587 BCE, the First Temple was destroyed, and the Jewish people were driven into slavery. The story can be found in the book of Jeremiah and in Lamentations, a series of five poetic odes written by Jeremiah that express his deep sorrow over the resulting desolation but that give hope for the Jewish people.

Bernstein created the textual nucleus of the work when, in the summer of 1939 shortly after graduating from Harvard University, he sketched what he described as a "Hebrew song" for soprano and orchestra based on excerpts from Lamentations. He then set it aside as he plunged into his conducting studies at the Curtis Institute of Music. But a few years later, as he began to write his first large-scale orchestral work, he realized that this song would be a logical conclusion to the two movements he had planned.

In its final form, the symphony consists of three movements (Bernstein had briefly considered writing a fourth), each of which adds to the customary Italian designations for tempo—Largamente, Vivace con brio, and Lento—titles that loosely relate to chapters of Jeremiah's life and the aftermath: Prophecy, Profanation, and Lamentation. Bernstein himself comments on *Jeremiah* in the program notes for the March 1944 New York Philharmonic performances: "As for programmatic meanings . . . the intention is not one of literalness but of emotional quality." Bernstein, with the exception of the last movement, did not intend a specific story line beyond the general association with Jeremiah but rather sought to evoke emotional states. Still, the ties to the biblical story are there, and decades later, in *My Musical Childhood* (1987), Bernstein confirmed this by calling the work a "biblical symphony."

Employing a very large orchestra with strings and woodwinds, four horns, three trumpets, three trombones, tuba, piano, and a large percussion section and leaning on liturgical music, Bernstein firmly establishes the symphonic genre while imbuing it with a Jewish religious dimension. This can be heard right in the opening of the first movement, when, after a few seconds of ominous sounds, the horns very slowly present the main theme in unison. It begins with a descending leap followed by a descending step. The very same motive can be found in the conclusion of the Amidah (a standing prayer containing eighteen blessings) for the festivals. The end of the theme, which begins with an upward movement in the melody, relies on a lesser-known idea from the so-called *kerova*, the poetic expansion of the eighteen blessings by the cantor. While in liturgy these excerpts are unrelated, here they form a unified whole. This theme is introduced, after the ominous opening sounds, by the solo French horn, which evokes associations with the shofar, a call to prayer—perhaps Jeremiah's plea to his people to renew their faith? This theme sounds like a voice of reason. It dominates the movement, appearing next in the strings and then the woodwinds, appearing in variants and in combination with another motive that sounds like a sigh. It prominently occurs before harsh dissonant harmonies—Jeremiah's warning to the Israelites. It also recurs, in variation, in the subsequent movements. This theme would also resurface in other compositions and come to be persistently associated with the idea of faith.

The second movement, "Profanation," is also rooted in liturgical music. The flute, the piccolo, and the B-flat clarinet present the sweet-sounding opening theme in unison. Its melodic and rhythmic configuration relies on motives found in the chanting of the Haftarah (the selections from the Prophets read on the Sabbath and certain holidays). Notice the snippets of melody with distinct intervals, one after another played by the flute and clarinet. But then an overall sense of brazenness emerges from bombastic percussion and brass outbursts. "Profanation" quickly enters into a chaotic sound world with sudden changes in dynamics and dissonances, conveying the sense of destruction and chaos that occurred after the people have rejected Jeremiah's message. As the movement takes its course, the rhythms take a jazzy turn, showing Bernstein's familiarity with a variety of popular genres, from jazz to Afro-Cuban. The rhythmic intensity communicates the horrors of the profanation that they are rendering. The sweet and calm theme from the very beginning returns both in its entirety and in fragments. Throughout the composition, the meter fluctuates, evoking irregularity, erraticism, and chaos.

While the first two movements are instrumental, in line with conventional symphonic writing, in the third a mezzo-soprano (one of several changes from the original "Hebrew song"), sparsely accompanied by the subdued orchestra, laments the destroyed, looted, and suffering Jerusalem. The text is based on verses from the first, fourth, and fifth Lamentations, which mourn Jerusalem and beg for the return of the Jewish people to the Holy City. These are recited on Tisha-b'Ab (Ninth of Av), the fast day to commemorate the destruction of both the First Temple and the Second and the many tragedies that have befallen the Jewish people. The soloist's melody emulates the repetitive, mournful motives heard on that day. To support the chant-like melody through the sacred text, the orchestra sustains long notes so as not to overwhelm the singer. The last four verses, beginning with "Na-u ivrim bahutsot, n'go-alu" (They wander as blind men in the streets), increase in intensity with a steady fortissimo and higher notes until the very opening motive of the symphony associated with the Amidah returns again, played three times by the strings and woodwinds and culminating in the final moments of the symphony in pianissimo.

Bernstein clearly composed *Jeremiah* with Jewish prayers in mind, although he himself downplayed their centrality, claiming that "the Symphony does not make use to any great extent of actual Hebrew thematic material . . . resemblances to Hebrew liturgical music are a matter of emotional quality rather than of the notes themselves." If this statement seems at odds with the actual musical content, then this illuminates Bernstein's struggle. He often spoke about his search for and crisis of faith, of reconciling his feelings of Jewishness: "The work I have been writing all my life is about the struggle that is born of the crisis of our century, a crisis of faith. Even way back, when I wrote 'Jeremiah,' I was wrestling with that problem. The faith or peace that is found at the end of 'Jeremiah' is really more a kind of comfort, not a solution." To be sure, *Jeremiah* held a great deal of raw feeling from its composer concerning the persecution of his people: "How can I be blind to the problems of my own people? I'd give everything I have to be able to strike a death blow at Fascism." Indeed, the destruction of Jerusalem had symbolic meaning at a time when the Holocaust was in full force.

Dedicated to his father following their emotional reconciliation right after the New York Philharmonic conducting debut in November 1943 (he would be the first American-born conductor to be appointed its musical director), Bernstein premiered the work at Pittsburgh's Syria Mosque with the Pittsburgh Symphony Orchestra under Fritz Reiner and Jennie Tourel as the soloist on January 28, 1944. In May, the New York Music Critics Circle voted it the outstanding new classical work of the season. *Jeremiah* was broadcast on seventy radio stations across the country, and over the next few years, Bernstein conducted it in many American cities and abroad. Most symbolically, he would go on to lead the work in a concert by the Palestine Symphony Orchestra in 1947 in Jerusalem. With *Jeremiah*, Bernstein established himself not only as a major American symphonist but also as a Jewish composer. As critic Frederick Dorian put it right after the premiere, "*Jeremiah* is easily understood as a blend of broad American diatonicism and Hebrew melos, in its rhythmic vitality and effective instrumentation." Bernstein's creative journey would continue to draw on dramatic eclecticism though not without twists and turns.

Twenty years later, in June 1964, Bernstein was on sabbatical from the New York Philharmonic. "Officially free of chore," with "fifteen beautiful months to kill!," his original plan was to collaborate with lyricists Betty Comden and Adolph Green on a musical based on Thornton Wilder's *The Skin of Our Teeth*, to be directed by Jerome Robbins. The project did not come to fruition. However, in the meantime, Reverend Walter Hussey, dean of Chichester Cathedral, commissioned him to write a piece for the annual music festival that would involve the combined forces of the English cathedrals of Winchester, Salisbury, and Chichester.

The resulting *Chichester Psalms* is a work for mixed choir, soloist, and orchestra. Each of its three movements is based on two psalms that address universal human questions and emotions. But only in the second movement does Bernstein use the psalm texts in juxtaposition. For all three movements, Bernstein uses music originally conceived for *Skin of Our Teeth*, juxtaposing or combining it with new material to create dramatic scenes. But this is not where eclecticism and theatricality end. Although Hussey gave Bernstein artistic freedom, he expressed that "many of us would be very delighted if there was a hint of 'West Side Story' in the music." As the second movement shows, Bernstein took this "request" quite literally.

Its first part is based on Psalm 23, also known as the Psalm of David, in which God appears as a shepherd. The text is often alluded to in popular media and has already been set to music many times. Bernstein opts for a simple opening, set off by the gentle sound of the percussion instruments, followed by a solo boy alto who sings the first three lines of the psalm accompanied by two harps. In the solo, Bernstein introduces two musical ideas: a tranquil melody in conventional triple meter and a second melody that switches to a slightly lower register and a downward pulling section before the opening line, "Adonai ro-i, lo eḥsar" (The LORD is my shepherd; I lack nothing), is repeated. In spite of its simplicity, such opening suggests theatricality, evoking images of King

David, the famous harpist of the ancient Hebrews, who as a shepherd boy accompanied himself on the lyre. So as not to lose this sense of innocence and naïveté and youth, Bernstein specified that the solo is *not* to be sung by a woman. Other than in *Jeremiah*, there is no motivic material in this solo that would identify as Jewish. The melody line is simple and begs to be sung deliberately and honestly, without added vocal embellishment or prepared interpretation. It represents a proto-typical Bernstein melody: largely angular and with blue notes. This famous melody actually originated as the song "Spring Will Come Again," intended for *The Skin of Our Teeth*.

Following the opening solo, a chorus of sopranos, divided into two parts, sings almost the same melody on the text of the fourth line, but they do so in canon, one measure apart. Such close imitation is a favor-ite procedure of Bernstein's. The result of this close canon is a series of prominent dissonances. These are well placed. Along with the accom-paniment, they help depict the uneasiness of the words "Gam ki ei-lech—B'gei tsalmavet" (Though I walk through a valley of deepest dark-ness). But the canon also supports a more positive interpretation, for the section concludes with, "Lo ira ra—Ki Atah imadi" (I fear no harm, for You are with me)—this suggests that even when faced with danger, God is always close by or, in this case, literally a step behind. This is a clear moment of word painting, a technique of writing music that re-flects the literal meaning of the text. In the meantime, the boy soloist sings a sustained pitch, thus joining the soft string accompaniment. The sopranos recall the second musical idea, but imitation is used more sparingly. When the boy's alto voice returns with his solo "Adonai ro-i, lo ehsar," the orchestral accompaniment begins to swell, transitioning into the echo of the sopranos. The return to the "Adonai ro-i, lo ehsar" prepares the interruption that ensues.

Following the innocence of the opening section, the middle part provides a stark contrast both textually and musically. Bernstein sets the words of Psalm 2, which is attributed to David, and conveys the mes-sage that people can either defy the Lord and perish or submit to him and be blessed. Accordingly, Bernstein interrupts the tranquillity with "the reality of what man has inflicted upon himself" with an interrup-tion by the low strings and percussion, joined by the low, rumbling sounds of tenors and basses in a blistering tempo change to a fast *Allegro feroce*. Again using two musical ideas, he begins the section with a chorus that he had cut from *West Side Story's* "Prologue," changing the words "Mix! Make a mess of 'em! Make the sons of bitches pay!" to "Lamah rag'shu goyim—Ul'umim yeh'gu riḳ?" (Why do nations assemble, and peoples plot vain things?). The music as originally composed remained the same. Then he repeats the same material but now in canon. Unpredictable rhythms and dissonances appear over a frenzied orchestra. At the mention of the "Yit'yats'vu malchei erets" (kings of the earth take their stand), the strength of the rulers is represented by strong singing in unison with the orchestra. Just as the "V'roznim nos'du" (and regents intrigue) against the Lord and his people, a march-like melody begins with the tenors incessantly blaring out "yaḥad" (together) thirteen times, thus forming an ostinato that fights "against" the bass section's continuation of the text. This second idea is the most powerful moment of the entire work—the innocent opening melody and this violent middle section could not be more different. The return to the "Mix" idea over the text "He who is enthroned in heaven laughs; the Lord mocks at them" is very brief and is treated again in extremely close canon, depicting a mysterious "battle" between tenors and basses. This final passage of the middle section is unsettling for the listener, as the location of the beat is very unclear.

If the first part features high voices and the second low voices, the third one combines both. Here, the psalm texts also interact in a very powerful way as Bernstein uses both texts in combination, stacking them on top of each other. The third section begins almost seamlessly with the alto solo and the sopranos, who join the raging male voices. Instructed to sing "blissfully unaware of threat," they sing of the Lord preparing a table before them in the presence of enemies, a passage from Psalm 23. Musically speaking, the enemy is in fact present, not only disturbing the mood of the treble voices but also working against the triple meter. Although the male voices are mostly subdued, the listener cannot ignore their incessant and percussive continuation of Psalm 2 in the background (especially given the three moments when the dynamics suddenly turn loud) as the treble voices seek a return to the initial innocence. The innocent melody gradually quiets the menace of Psalm 2. Perhaps the soprano and alto's obliviousness to the distraction represents man's obliviousness or his denial of the problems in the world. Or, to take a more positive slant, perhaps it also represents one's ability to continue and find peace and contentment in spite of turmoil.

The second idea of the opening solo returns with a slightly thicker orchestral accompaniment, and with this the tranquil mood returns over the text "Ach, tov vaḥesed—Yird'funi kol y'mei ḥayai, V'shav'ti b'veit Adonai" (Only goodness and steadfast love shall pursue me all the days of my life, and I shall dwell in the house of the LORD for many long years), unencumbered until the final measures. In the end, the sopranos echo the alto on the words "Adonai L'orech yamim" (the LORD for many long years), but when they hold their final long note, the brass and percussion instruments recall the "Lamah ragshu" melody, playing a canon of the "Mix" motive that brings in dissonance and serves as a reminder of the previous disturbance. In Bernstein's own words, the movement ends "in unresolved fashion, with both elements, faith and fear, interlocked." The juxtaposition of two contrasting melody types, rhythms, and tempos is maintained until the very end.

Even more so than *Jeremiah*, the *Chichester Psalms* transcend the boundaries of genre, style, and cultural affiliation through an eclectic mix of classical and vernacular, Broadway, and Jewish elements unique to the concert hall—but all in the service of the text and its perceived inherent theatricality. For Bernstein, such eclecticism was not a crutch but rather a liberating and conscious agent that allowed him compositional flexibility to interpret Hebrew texts and Jewish topics. This led him to a profound conclusion—that a renewal of faith in modern times requires a return to innocence, a shedding of the trappings of dogma and orthodoxy, and a fundamental belief in our common humanity. If in *Jeremiah* he struggled with faith and all its implications by way of liturgical music, twenty years later he had arrived at a more peaceful resolution by way of Broadway. In this way, Bernstein seems to have moved into opposite directions.

The setting of Hebrew psalms and the integration of chant into art music as exemplified by Bernstein has informed another American Jewish composer of a later generation as well although with a very different sonic outcome: Steve Reich. Born in New York in 1936, Reich came from a family of Jewish immigrants from eastern Europe with roots in Budapest and Kraków and western Europe from Austria and Germany who had settled in the United States generations earlier. Following the divorce of his parents when he was only one year old, Reich's childhood was divided between New York and California, subjecting him to long rail journeys that he would recall much later in *Different Trains*. Reich was brought up Reform, with little encouragement to pursue deeper and further questions of faith. He had scant exposure to the Hebrew language. For his bar mitzvah, he pointed at words in the Hebrew Bible that he could not read, having memorized their transliteration. Similarly, boyhood piano lessons left little impression. His musical education took off only when, at the age of fourteen, he began studying drumming with Roland Kohloff.

Reich's eureka moment occurred in 1965 after he had completed his studies in philosophy and composition. At the time, he was living in San Francisco, where he taped a Pentecostal street preacher named Brother Walter shouting "It's gonna rain!" during a sermon on Noah and the Flood. He then looped those words on two tape recorders. When he pushed "Play" on both machines, he found that one was running slightly faster than the other so that the loops went out of sync. The machines began producing an electronic canon for two raging voices. One of the most famous minimalist tape compositions was born.

Critic Richard Wollheim coined the concept of minimalism in 1965, referring to art that reduces materials and form to fundamentals and does not aim to express feelings or convey the artist's mind. Composers such as La Monte Young, Terry Riley, Philip Glass, and Reich picked up on this kind of thinking and became the first masters of a new genre—minimalist music. They reduced materials to a minimum and simplified procedure as a reaction against the complexity, density, irregularity, and expressive intensity of postwar abstract expressionism. Indeed, minimalism favors simplicity, clarity, and regularity. It features a continuous formal structure, a simple and repetitive rhythmic pattern, and an overall bright tone. It uses very simple motives and harmonies that are repeated many, many times. Rock, African, and Asian music, as well as romanticism, were important influences for minimalist composers. Steve Reich, for example, embarked in 1971 on a five-week trip to study music in Ghana. He also studied Balinese gamelan in Seattle. His engagement with non-Western sounds went hand in hand with his interest in Buddhist meditation and Mexican mysticism. In 1974, he reconnected with Judaism, a process that would continue over the next decades and would influence his compositions. (Today, Reich keeps kosher, observes the Sabbath, and studies the Torah weekly.)

He took active steps in 1975 when he attended the adult education program at Lincoln Square Synagogue in New York City, taking courses in Hebrew and in the reading of the Torah. In subsequent years, Cantor Edward Berman of the Jewish Theological Seminary (a student of Solomon Rosowsky's) introduced him to biblical cantillation. In the summer of 1977, Reich went on his first trip to Israel (many would follow thereafter, with extended periods of residence). His fieldwork in Jerusalem focused on cantillation. He recorded the first five verses of Genesis as chanted by older Jewish men from Baghdad, India, Kurdistan, and Yemen. His research confirmed the generally accepted view that, aside from regional differences, the structure of the chant is always the same. Ever since, Reich's interest in Jewish musical practices has been clearly centered on cantillation. He affirmed in 1994,

> For many people, Jewish music means "Fiddler on the Roof" or Hasidic folk songs. . . . I would go back to the homeland, to the origin, and see what is particular about my tradition, independently of how it was influenced, in the Ashkenazic experience, in Germany, France and England, or, in the Sephardic experience, in Spain. . . . The center of the tradition is the chanting of the Scriptures.

What exactly is the "chanting of the Scriptures" or, more precisely, cantillation? In synagogue services, texts from the Hebrew Bible are often rendered through heightened reading. This reading follows special signs printed in the Masoretic text (the authoritative Hebrew and Aramaic text for Rabbinic Judaism) to complement the letters and vowel points. These marks hark back to the seventh to ninth centuries CE and are known in English as accents or tropes and in Hebrew as *taamei ha-mikra* or contracted just as *teamim*.

Each sign serves three functions: syntax, phonetics, and music. Classified hierarchically, they help to divide a verse into phrases and, within each phrase, all the words; they indicate how words should be connected (like a slur in music) or divided up—roughly like modern punctuation signs, such as periods, commas, or pauses. In terms of phonetics, they indicate which syllable in a word should be stressed. As quasi-musical notation, each sign is linked to a few pitches with a distinct melody and rhythm. Different melodies exist for the Torah, the Prophets known as Haftarah, and the Book of Esther. None are transmitted for the three poetic books of the Hebrew Bible—Job, Proverbs, and Psalms.

But cantillation is not music per se. It stands in between reading proper and singing. Reich was fascinated by the concept of taking the patterns and stringing them together to form a longer melody in the service of a holy text. He asserts, "If you take away the text, you're left with the idea of putting together small motives to make longer melodies—a technique I had not encountered before." Inspired by cantillation, Reich initially intended to set the Book of Jonah but for a female voice to avoid creating "a poorer version of what's done in the synagogue." But he recognized the limitations, as it would merely be a transcription of the existing cantillation.

Cantillation found its way into Reich's music and influenced his minimalist style in other ways. He broadened the relationship between words and music in his works from the 1980s to the early 1990s. Aspects of spoken language such as intonation, timbre, melodic cadences, and metric accentuation become the defining elements of musical structure, though he maintained the repetitive, pulse-driven figures so characteristic of minimalism. From *Tehillim* (1981) to *The Cave* (1993), his new artistic approach developed in parallel with a deep quest for identity, and these works also exhibit a connection to Jewish heritage.

Composed in 1981, *Tehillim* (literally, Psalms) is one of his first works from this new creative period. It fits into the mold of his earlier minimalism, as Reich continued to rely on a spectrum of compositional possibilities used in the prototypical works—in all four parts, he used standard procedures, such as canon, variation, and ostinato—but at the same time departs from it. It is the first of Reich's works to draw explicitly on Judaism, to rely on text and specifically on the Hebrew Scriptures as the textual source. Driven by its meaning and rhythm, syntax, and phonetics, he departed from preexisting notions of what Jewish music should sound like but followed principles that "may have underlain the cantillation of the Psalms in the Temple at Jerusalem."

Tehillim was initially scored for three musicians. Reich later reworked the piece for an ensemble of four women's voices (one high soprano, two lyric sopranos, and one alto), accompanied by a chamber group consisting of piccolo, flute, oboe, English horn, two clarinets, six percussion instruments (small tuned tambourines without jingles, clapper, maracas, marimba, vibraphone, and crotales), two electronic organs, two violins, viola, cello, and double bass. The string, wind, and percussion instruments were to remind the listener of the configuration of the Temple orchestra (although no details on their actual sounds are transmitted); they also relate directly to *Tehillim*'s fourth and last part, whose text, Psalm 150:4–6, suggests to praise the Lord with the timbrel, stringed instruments and the pipe, loud-sounding cymbals, and clanging cymbals. The first part employs Psalm 19:2–5, the second Psalm 34:13–15, and the third Psalm 18:26–27.

As the oral tradition of chanting the Psalms had not been transmitted, Reich's aim was to re-create its musical setting. For sure, the fact that there is no ancient historical precedence offered him greater freedom. He did not have to follow established conventions but could still lean on the concept of cantillation in its essence. Thus, Reich formulated the relation between text and music in a way that would preserve the meaning of the words. Part four of *Tehillim* is a case in point. It begins with a transition from the previous part to create a seamless connection. This accelerating passage, dominated by percussion instruments, establishes a new steady beat. What ensues is a theme followed by four variations and a coda. The theme consists of three motives, each of which opens the line of the verse: the first over "Haleluhu, betof," the second over "Haleluhu, betsiltselei," and the third, which is then repeated with variation over "Kol haneshama." The motives are disjunct and have similar rhythmic patterns of long and short notes. They are presented by two sopranos in harmony with the instruments accompanying through irregularly placed chords. The subsequent variations come in without a break, gradually intensifying. The first variation renders the theme in a two-part canon and the second variation in a four-part canon, which is repeated many times until a sort of intermezzo reminds us of the second and third motives (in each case begun by one soprano alone). Higher vocal registers ensue. Variation no. 3 features two voices accompanied by clarinet and drums. An instrumental interlude follows, based on the reiteration of the previously accompanying chords. The fourth variation leads to a climactic high note. The enthusiastic coda highlights "Hallelu-jah" once more with electric organs, bells, and vibraphone accompanying the repeated exclamations. Here, the more vital sense of motion and direction over earlier minimalism is the most obvious. The piece then comes to an abrupt halt.

For a composer whose style originates in the consummate use of repetition, the Psalm 150:4–6 text is a gold mine. The verses repeat the words "Halleluhu" (Praise Him) nearly constantly as the psalmist urges praise in the form of musical sounds. The rhythm is entirely determined by the Hebrew text. Reich perceived a metric succession of units of two and three beats in the Hebrew text. Series of twos and threes become the basis for the rhythmic structure of his vocal lines so as to form constantly changing meters. Placement of rests and accents in the music conforms to the disposition of the cantillation accents in the biblical text.

Tehillim is a departure from Reich's earlier minimalist work in that it is his first major composition to utilize the human voice in live performance. The texts he sets are several lines long rather than the fragments used in previous works. Melody becomes a substantive element. The use of variation, harmonic motion/functional harmony, and overall more varied materials and expressivity further attests to a new direction. Instead of adhering to minimalist presets, Reich's ultimate goal was to convey the meaning of the Hebrew text.

This direction (we might call it postminimalism) manifests itself also in other works that tie into Jewish history. In *Different Trains* (1988), for tape and string quartet, Reich juxtaposes his childhood memories of his train journeys between New York and California in 1939–1941 with the very different train rides that European children were being forced to take during the same time. As in earlier works, he uses recorded voices that narrate forty sentence fragments: his nanny reminiscing about their journeys, an elderly man recalling his career as a Pullman porter, and testimonies of three Holocaust survivors. These image-conjuring texts are used to add immediacy to Holocaust remembrance as a melodic rather than a rhythmic element. Reich discovered the natural melodic content suggested by the spoken phrases and out of them generated melodies for instruments that replicate the rhythm, intonation, and inflection of human speech. *Different Trains*, which Reich calls "music documentary," has been considered "the only adequate musical response to the Holocaust" and has earned Reich a place among the great composers of the twentieth century.

As in *Different Trains*, Reich uses recorded voice also in *The Cave* (1990–1993), a multimedia theater work in three acts for vocal quartet, four woodwinds, percussionists, three keyboards, and five-piece string ensemble based on the fatherhood of Abraham. Here, he asks Jews, Arabs, and Christians in the Middle East and the United States to talk about Abraham/Ibrahim and his family. The resulting work offers fascinating insights into the historical (mis)understandings between these peoples without taking sides. Reich broadens the religious issue by interweaving it with more universal considerations. With this highly innovative opera-documentary, he crowned a multifaceted Jewish trajectory, from the personal as observed in *Tehillim*, to the collective as manifested in *Different Trains*, to the universal in *The Cave*.

7

JEWS WHO ROCK THE STAGE

Imagine you are in New York. Madison Square Garden and the Barclay Center host two very different Jewish stars of our age: Matisyahu and Lipa Schmelczer. Not only are the two venues head-to-head, but they also feature these artists on the very same night. So where will you go? Who will you hear? To make an informed decision, let us start with some preliminaries.

When Matisyahu emerged in 2004 with his debut album, *Shake Off the Dust . . . Arise*, he was a novelty. Here was a Hasidic Jew—dressed in a black suit and prayer shawl fringes with a broad-brimmed black hat worn over a yarmulke and sporting a full, untrimmed beard—who sang about the glories of Judaism over reggae beats in a Jamaican dance hall style, punctuating his performance with stage diving. For some, it may have seemed like a joke in costume, but Matisyahu was serious about his craft. His style would soon garner a Grammy nomination in the category of Best Reggae Album, gold record certifications, and, above all, a broad audience. He has attracted college students, dreadlocked hippies, and Hasidim, an audience reflective of his stylistic diversity, which is rooted in reggae but with influences of hip-hop, punk rock, and psychedelia and infused with a Jewish sensibility. Matisyahu himself said in 2004 about his music, "It is not Jewish music, but it is filled with images of Judaism. I created my own internal feelings about what it meant to be Jewish and connected it to reggae music."

Matisyahu was born Matthew Paul Miller on June 30, 1979, in West Chester, Pennsylvania. Brought up in White Plains, New York, he attended Hebrew school at the local Reconstructionist synagogue, Bet Am Shalom. Back then, Judaism did not play an integral role in his life. At the age of fourteen, two events shaped his path. During a camping trip in Colorado, he had a spiritual awakening, and he discovered the music of Bob Marley. He also began to use drugs. Two years later, in the fall of 1995, his parents signed him up for a two-month program in Israel at Alexander Muss High School in Hod Hasharon, which offers students firsthand exploration of Jewish heritage. Matisyahu credits this stay as being the pre-catalyst for his feelings toward Judaism, and, as he wrote on his website, his "dormant Jewish identity stirred into consciousness."

After returning to White Plains, he dropped out of high school, lived on the street, and followed the rock band Phish on tour. With heavy drug use, his downward spiral continued. In 1997, his parents sent him to the Northstar Center, a mental health and substance abuse treatment rehabilitation center for at-risk teenagers in Bend, Oregon. During that time, he began beatboxing and rapping at open-mic competitions and performed draped in an Israeli flag with SoulForI under the alias MC Truth. After finishing high school, Matthew returned to New York in 1998, enrolled in the New School for Social Research in Manhattan, and joined the Carlebach Shul, absorbing the musical legacy of Shlomo Carlebach. He also performed at Nuyorican Poets Café's open mics and began playing with the Jewish band Pey Dalid, which was formed in 1999 by three brothers born and raised in White Plains (the band still rocks). By 2001, he had met Eli Cohen and Dov Yonah Korn, both rabbis at New York University. He felt an especially strong connection to Korn, a Lubavitcher, and eventually moved in with the family. Not long thereafter, he began identifying as Lubavitcher and changed his name to its Hebrew version (Matisyahu is known from the Hanukkah story as the father of Judah the Maccabee). By the spring of 2002, he had taken up residence in Crown Heights. He studied at Yeshiva Hadar Hatorah, prayed, and sang nigunim. He had given up his secular life but not music. Looking back at that time, he remembers a pivotal event during one of the Lubavitcher outreach efforts:

> So I went to this producer's house, and I sang him this melody. . . . And that was like the initial hook of the initial "King without a Crown," which didn't really even make it to the recording that most people know. So I sang in that, I did a little beat box thing for him,

picked out some chords and put it down, and we put a little beat together. And that was really the first song that I'd recorded in quite some time. I went and had him play the song on a loop, and I wrote all those lyrics right then and there and the chorus in maybe 20 or 30 minutes. I put them down and then went back to the Yeshiva and I burned a CD of that song. That was before iPods—I had my Discman.

Matisyahu developed the song further during a summer in the Catskills:

And the only music that I had with me was that song. And I would say maybe once a week or so I would sort of walk down into the woods, leave everybody and go listen to that song. And that song is what kept my dream alive to do music. Listen to it, I realized there was no other music like it. It was what I wanted to hear, and I wasn't hearing anything like it. I'd never heard anything mixing those genres, mixing those styles together in that way. I realized that I had created something special because it really spoke to my soul, and that's what kept my wheels turning when I was in that environment.

He eventually got permission to continue his music. Backed by guitarist Aaron Dugan, bassist Josh Werner, and drummer Jonah David, all New School classmates of his and known as Roots Tonic, he began jamming and recording. In 2004, the recently founded label JDub Records released their first album, *Shake Off the Dust . . . Arise*, whose title references the fourth verse of Lekhah Dodi. Among its tracks are "Tzama L'Cha Nafshi (Psalm 63:2–3)," a short all-but-traditional nigun, and the slow burner "Aish Tamid." By title alone, these pieces are clearly rooted in Jewish practice and belief, although all lyrics are in English. "Aish Tamid," for example, references the eternal flame that was to burn on the altar in the Temple in Jerusalem, never to be extinguished (it is symbolically kept alive through daily prayer and Torah study). Could the fire of the *aish tamid* be understood as the spark that Matisyahu perceives in reggae? "Aish Tamid" also sings of the rhythm of the Diaspora, and it addresses the divine. It incorporates a reggae beat, integrates nigunim, and has parts where Matisyahu raps, but the rhythm and overall style remain close to punk reggae of the 1980s coming out of London. The driving tempo of the song suggests a yearning for what lies ahead, not a mourning for what has been lost.

One of the most significant tracks on the debut album is "King without a Crown." It became so popular that Matisyahu recorded it twice more. He first released a shorter edited version as an official single in late 2005 in support of his second studio album, *Youth*, on which it was included. A live version of the song also appeared on the 2005 album *Live at Stubb's*. Some limited editions of *Youth* and the "King without a Crown" three-track EP also contain a bonus track of the song, remixed by Mike D of the Beastie Boys. "King without a Crown" became one of the biggest hits of Matisyahu's career, sparking a new-age resurgence of reggae. In 2006, the *Youth* version hit number 28 on the Billboard Hot 100. "King without a Crown" even made it into the film score of the 2007 romantic comedy *Knocked Up*.

Simply put, "King without a Crown" is a song about Matisyahu's longing for the ultimate deliverance of the Jewish people. The lyrics, though in English, convey his fundamental beliefs as he sings about the Messiah. Matisyahu references Judaism in many of his songs, but it is in the rhymes of the chorus that he explicates his full faith and servitude.

The concepts of feeling and love (and heart and soul as their extension in the verses) are deeply rooted in Hasidic thought. A key line of the chorus is "Givin' myself to you now from the essence of my being." Here, Matisyahu articulates his passion for the divine most clearly. The last line, "I want Moshiach now," which he keeps repeating, is probably the most significant Jewish reference in the piece. Moshiach or Messiah means "anointed one" and refers to the savior or liberator of the Jewish people who will unify them in Israel. The Messiah embodies the hope that one day the Temple and the throne of King David will be restored in Jerusalem, putting an end to the many expulsions and deliverances in the course of Jewish history. But in the lyrics, the assertive "now" forgoes the gap between desire and fulfillment of the messianic, representing the metaphysics of presence. The phrase is so poignant that Sting in his 2006 concert in Tel Aviv in front of a crowd of 25,000 to 30,000 mostly secular Jews screamed it out three times (Matisyahu was his opening act).

What makes the lyrics ultimately so compelling is their sheer variety of imagery and meaning. In the verses, Matisyahu introduces other themes, such as the mercy and the strength of God. His rhetoric of "burning up" and of "the fire gone blaze" recalls the kabbalist legend of Rabbi Baruch of Mesibos, who burned like a fire and whose ecstasy blazed to heaven when he sang the Songs of Solomon. Matisyahu taps into the Hasidic idea that transcendence occurs through the song's flammable quality, which drives the singer to spiritual ecstasy, just like a nigun. Another reference crystallizes when Matisyahu shares his reliance on the divine with the words "I lift up my eyes where does my help come from / And I've seen it circling around from the mountain." Although he does not explicitly quote it, he implicitly references the well-known Psalm 121 while maintaining the end rhymes essential to reggae. Such procedure can be observed in lyrics of other songs as well that rely on Hasidic or biblical concepts and texts while adapting the English rhymes to the rhythmical needs of reggae. This melding also extends to the music. As Matisyahu himself asserts in 2006, "The music is a spiritual music and the lyrics come mainly from actually Torah, from the Psalms and from the Old Testament. And so I was able to connect to my Judaism like in the reggae music before I was able to connect to Judaism in like a religious way."

In the *Youth* version, the electric bass guitar and drums begin the piece in freestyle, introducing a short, slow rhythm. A backup singer enters with wordless syllables. But this is not a nigun. In fact, one of the syllables references "Jah," a short form of "Yahweh" and commonly used by the Rastafarians of Jamaica to designate the divine. But spiritually, Matisyahu is far from Rastafari, an Abrahamic belief connected to reggae and indebted to the Hebrew Bible. At the time, his messianic ideas were deeply rooted in Lubavitch messianism, not the Rastafarian belief in the Ethiopian sovereign Haile Selassie (Ras Tafari Makonnen) as the Second Coming of Christ or as God incarnate.

The slow introduction allows the listener to delve into the song and prepare for the excitement that ensues. Listen for the upbeat emphasis on the second and forth pulses of the four-beat phrase, established by bass guitar, drums, and the synthesizer, which is commonly used among contemporary reggae artists. When Matisyahu renders the first line of the verse in rap style, "Zee you're all that I have and you're all that I need," the tempo immediately accelerates, creating a high level of energy. Matisyahu sings with a Jamaican accent. As the verse continues, he blends reggae and hip-hop (in the *Shake Off the Dust . . . Arise* version, he also beatboxes). Just before the last verse, something unexpected and unique happens: a lengthy screaming guitar solo but more in the spirit of rock than of reggae. It intensifies the song's dynamism and clearly functions to set off the last verse, which differs from the previous one. Melodically, it emulates rap, and lyrically, it is elevating: "And see, I lift up my eyes where my help come from."

"King without a Crown" is particularly multivalent in its reach to different popular genres: as in most of his songs, bass and guitar establish the reggae beat; some of the melodic lines are styled à la rap; the guitar solo signals alternative rock; there is beatboxing; and the text is rooted in Judaism. Matisyahu clearly produced a piece of fusion anchored in his Jewish faith. This melding of worlds is also evident in his routine before going onstage, as he shares in an interview with the *Miami New Times*: "I try to have 15 minutes of quiet time, and I pray and meditate on God and what being Jewish means to me. But once I get that down, then I turn on Jay-Z and drink a glass of wine, and I turn into Brooklyn and I do my thing. To some it seems like a huge split, but for me, that's always what I've been. I've always had these two sides of myself."

Onstage, Matisyahu is living this as well, as is documented in the *Live at Stubb's* video version of "King without a Crown." It was taped in February 2005 when Matisyahu toured to promote the *Youth* album. Issued in April as courtesy of Or Music, it got picked up for national distribution by Epic Records. Matisyahu's transcendent energy is noteworthy. Dressed in a long black frock coat, with a black brimmed hat and glasses, swinging and swaying back and forth, one could well imagine him at a yeshiva. But there he was at the unlikely place of Stubb's Bar-B-Q in Austin, Texas, in front of a huge crowd, rapping, "With these demons surround all around to bring me down to negativity." During the guitar solo, he stage dived into the crowd. Of all the artists to emerge in 2005, Matisyahu was perhaps the most unique, and his "King without a Crown" a nearly unheard-of feat for a reggae track and a highly unique musical celebration of faith. In January 2006, he sold out Madison Square Garden; he began to tour around the world and appeared on TV. But turns in life were just around the corner.

As of July 17, 2007, Matisyahu no longer "necessarily" identifies with the Lubavitch movement, stating that "the more I'm learning about other types of Jews, I don't want to exclude myself. I felt boxed in." That fall, after spending time in Jerusalem, he began praying at a synagogue of the Karlin Hasidim, who are known for ecstatically screaming. In 2009, Matisyahu began touring for almost two years, together with his band, the Brooklyn-based Dub Trio, promoting his album *Light*. His songs began to oscillate between somber and lighter sentiments, spiritual references became more subtle, and the style moved closer to pop. He maintained the beat of reggae and the Jamaican accent. Matisyahu himself asserts, "I think it's not so much about genres or styles of music as it is about expressing the emotion or the idea. . . . Whatever allows you to do that, whatever style, as long as it's authentic." In fact, the album foreshadows further transformations.

By the end of 2011, he had shaved his beard and side locks and posted on his official website, "No more Chassidic reggae superstar." With changes in his spiritual life came changes in his music. His 2012 effort *Spark Seeker* ventured into the direction of secular pop. In 2014, Matisyahu released his fifth LP, *Akeda*, whose title refers to the biblical story of the Binding of Isaac. With the Dub Trio, he explored a new diversity of sounds while maintaining key features of his style. Although constantly evolving as an artist (in 2017, he kicked off his sixth studio album with "Step Out into the Light," a "musical reframing of Jewish philosophical differences between the constant of faith and the immediacy of trust"), Matisyahu continues to embody the melding of cultures that usually coexist but rarely intertwine as gracefully, successfully, and confidently as he aims to. Matisyahu continues to sing mostly in English, with occasional use of Hebrew and Yiddish. He remains rooted in reggae and still incorporates hip-hop and beatboxing, jazzy scats, and moments reminiscent of cantorial singing. Relying on these elements, Matisyahu's style adapts in line with his changing belief. His music has since evolved from incorporating Jewish themes to more universal themes. In this way, he parallels reggae artists such as Benny Bwoy but nonetheless remains unsurpassed.

Lipa Schmelczer, too, is a celebrity and one of a kind. While Matisyahu eventually forwent his Hasidic garb and moved toward a universality rooted in Judaism, Lipa negotiated his stance in the Hasidic community and onstage. To understand his presence onstage, one must understand the man who at the turn of the century emerged out of one of the strictest Hasidic sects in America. Born in New Square, since 1954 the insular enclave of the Skverer Hasidim in Rockland County, New York, Lazar (Lipa) Schmelczer (b. 1978), along with his eleven siblings, was raised in this modern-day shtetl. Not to invoke any sort of romanticism, for a creative individualist New Square is not at all idyllic. Recall the

news reports on the firebomb attack or read Shulem Deen's tell-all
memoir *All Who Go Will Not Return*, and you will know the reality of
Lipa's environment. For the moment, it suffices to say that Lipa grew
up without any access to the popular music of his time. And even if he
had heard it from early on, he might not have understood its lyrics
because English is not his native tongue. The Skverer Jews converse in
Yiddish in their daily lives and in Hebrew when at the synagogue. As a
musician, Lipa was largely self-taught. Music education is not part of
their core curriculum, nor is English, math, or science. This is possible
because New Square maintains its own school system. Their highest
vocation is the study of religious texts, and many men aspire to become
the head of a religious school or the rabbi of a synagogue. But Lipa was
born to be an entertainer.

Change was under way when Lipa got married in August 1998 and
needed to provide for his family. He began to work at a shoe store in
nearby Monsey and then as a delivery man for meat and fish stores. The
meat truck was equipped with a radio, and it gave Lipa access to popular music. It was then and there that he first heard "Hero" by Enrique
Iglesias and "I Need to Know" by Marc Anthony. Lipa soon found
himself devouring other pop standards by artists such as Michael Jack-
son, Ricky Martin, and Britney Spears, though his earliest influences
were the strictly Orthodox singers Avraham Fried (specifically his song
"Belz") and Mordechai Ben David, also known as MBD.

Not long after his marriage, he advertised in a small local circular,
offering his talent as a singer and *badkhn* (wedding jester). His truly
angelic voice and funny antics quickly brought him success. He began
performing at weddings and bar mitzvahs in the Orthodox Jewish communities of upstate New York and Brooklyn, singing traditional Jewish
and Yiddish songs in an upbeat fashion. He quickly earned a reputation
as a natural performer onstage and began to record the music he performed. His first LP, *Nor B'Simcha* (Only Be Happy, 1999), features
five long medleys of melodies popular in New Square, accompanied by
an orchestra and a male background chorus—musically, a humble beginning. A turning point in his career would come nine years later,
foreshadowed halfway when Lipa released *B'derech* in 2003, considered controversial among the rabbis of New Square who tried to ban it.
Among the eleven tracks is the now famous track "Gelt" (Money). Hasidic composer Yossi Green wrote the music, which features a fairly

typical pop sound—fast and upbeat, with a lot of repetition throughout the song. The brass motives are reminiscent of 1970s disco music. The arrangement is by Yisroel Lam.

"Gelt" begins with an electric guitar with a whammy and drums. Soon trumpets join in. Lipa's melody is simple and repetitive, employing a small range of pitches, supported by a steady drumbeat and at times supported by a male background chorus. During the chorus, more instruments join to heighten the excitement. A few times throughout the song, Lipa elongates strategic words ("borrowing and caring," "appreciation," and "Jewish nation"), extending the last two beats of the end rhyme, something new and slightly different from the average pop song. But overall, this piece resembles other mainstream Jewish pop music in the lineage of Avraham Fried and MBD.

The music, however, stands in stark contrast to the Yiddish lyrics, which talk about money, thereby blatantly promulgating one of the most common negative stereotypes of Jews—greed, money hunger, and unwillingness to part with money. The chorus especially pushes the envelope:

> In shul we collect money,
> In the street we talk about money,
> I come home—what do they like,
> They're begging again for money,
> Honor comes with money—wisdom comes with money,
> There is a joke—A hater of money°,
> You can hire today for enough money.

°one of the requirements to be a Jewish judge so as not to be biased by money

In contrast to *Fiddler on the Roof*'s "If I Were a Rich Man," which conveys the feelings of a poor man wishing for wealth, "Gelt" is pushing the stereotype to a new extreme, as it does not respond to the condition of poverty. But that a Jew brings such stereotypes to a heightened level also creates ambiguity. Does Lipa question the obsession and need of money, thereby offering a critique? Or does he reduce the stereotype ad absurdum?

This ambiguity dissolved when "Gelt" made its debut on the concert stage at HASC 17 in 2004 at Madison Square Garden. The HASC Concerts, also known as A Time for Music, have long been considered the ultimate pop concert experience in the Jewish music world. Always innovative, they set the standard of excellence for this niche industry. Producer Sheya Mendlowitz conceived them in 1987 as a fund-raiser for the children of Camp HASC (short for Hebrew Academy for Special Children). Located in Parksville, New York, Camp HASC is a unique summer camp serving the needs of more than 400 children and adults with intellectual and physical disabilities. The HASC Concert has long been touted as "the concert of the year," taking place annually ever since its inception and featuring many of the best-known names in Jewish music. Shlomo Carlebach, 8th Day, Avraham Fried, Matisyahu singing "King without a Crown," MBD, Yossi Piamenta, the Yeshiva Boys Choir, and many other musicians and groups made it the ultimate concert experience. Performers are usually limited to a few songs, with a stream of known and lesser-known singers taking the stage one after another. There is no question that the HASC Concert is one of the most highly anticipated Jewish musical events of the year and is a quick sellout. Given the run on tickets, HASC subsequently releases videos and CDs of their events' live performances.

Lipa's public debut was exactly on that stage—but not live. Given that HASC offers family seating, that is, men and women sitting together with their families, the Rebbe of New Square forbade Lipa to perform. After all, mixed seating is not in line with the laws and regulations of the Skverer, and many other Hasidic and Orthodox communities deem it highly inappropriate. Sheya Mendlowitz and Lipa found a solution that satisfied both sides. Instead of appearing live, they would make a video with the support of the now defunct electronics and music retailer J&R. Lipa's music video would be projected for the audience. In this way, he could adhere to the rules of his community while contributing to the fund-raiser. With the "Gelt" video, Lipa hit a mainstream Jewish audience for the very first time.

The video, although from today's perspective a humble, almost amateurish attempt, was at that time innovative in Orthodox Jewish circles and provided an example for other very observant artists. But above all, with a slightly adapted text and the added visual dimension, Lipa pushed the envelope of Jewish stereotype and created a Hasidic insularity. The video starts with Lipa explaining why he sent the video instead of performing live ("I have a wedding overseas"), and at the end of the video he returns to alluding to the circumstances of the video ("I am here but I am not here")—these were all improvised lines, said in the spur of the moment, in true badkhn fashion, but in English. Lipa closes the explanatory prelude by referencing the widely known GEICO commercial, thus introducing a secularity that none of his previous works contain. Lipa also changed the lyrics and language of the song. He incorporated references to HASC and combined English and Yiddish, sometimes even in the same phrase ("HASC needs your gelt"). Such adaptations made sense. After all, the video was intended to raise money for a charity, and the concert was frequented by Jews of all stripes, not just Yiddish speakers. Indeed, Lipa is deliberately frank about the changes, explaining in his opening, "I wrote new words for this evening." (Lipa would continue to adapt and change the lyrics of this and other songs in live performance.) His code switching between Yiddish and English asserts that Jewish languages and cultures are not immovable and, therefore, are compatible with contemporary mainstream culture. Rather, Yiddish (and Hebrew) are worthy of inclusion in pop music and are compatible with English.

The visuals introduce another component. When Lipa hails a cab, the black driver says, "Hey Lipa, is that you?," indicating that he is a widely known celebrity, which he was not at the time. In contrast to the driver, Lipa wears a black suit and proper head covering, and his side locks reveal his heritage. His Yiddish accent also alludes to his upbringing. In the course of the video, the visuals continue to emphasize money: Lipa is always shown waving cash and posing with bills. His image is even shown being on the dollar bill. Like a commercial, the video also blends in the logos of GEICO, J&R, and HASC. The latter (and also the pictures of children shown in the later part of the video) visually juxtaposes the stereotype. Still these are rare moments in a video spiked with coins, dollars, dollar signs, and other money imagery. The overall effect is that of utter humor, which leads the stereotype into absurdity. The comical approach is important here (after all, Lipa is an entertainer). Ultimately, "Gelt" showed Lipa as a Jew concerned more with humor and making fun of himself surrounded by money than with hoarding money. His humor is thus powerful in combating destructive stereotypes as it highlights the human side, which stereotypes do not allow. The use of such visual symbolism allowed "Gelt" to do much more than entertain a crowd; it allowed for "Gelt" to employ a common Jewish stereotype to create a self-controlled, contemporary image of the Jew as a benefactor.

If in his first stage performance Lipa pushed the envelope of word and image, his second appearance at HASC the following year stretched the boundaries of melody, a second turning point. Again, Lipa was not permitted to perform live at HASC 18 (he could do so only after he left New Square), and thus the same team that put the "Gelt" video together went on to produce "Abi me'leibt" (At Least I'm Alive). In essence, the song is a Yiddish cover of the melody now known as "The Lion Sleeps Tonight." The melody has a long history outside the Jewish realm. It was conceived in 1939 by the South African musician Solomon Linda as "Mbube." The Weavers recast it as "Wimoweh" in 1950; many other pop and folk artists covered it under either title. In 1961, it achieved worldwide acclaim as the immortal international chart-topper "The Lion Sleeps Tonight" by the Tokens. After many re-recordings, in 1997 it made it into the epic Broadway musical *The Lion King*. However, it did not reach its Jewish standing until Lipa's cover.

Lipa closely adheres to the original melody (apart from a short portion in which he raps and his voice is computerized) but departs from the lyrics. While he sings in Yiddish, the text itself is in essence a rather universal telling about a string of bad luck: milk without coffee, a police ticket, a closed bank, bad traffic, and a missed train. This chain is interrupted with the upbeat refrain "At least, I'm alive," a sort of King Solomon's wisdom of "Gam zeh ya'avor" (This too shall pass) that is an indication that all material conditions, positive or negative, are temporary. Noteworthy is that the lyrics give two nods to the original: the chorus "Awimbawe" (not a real word and in this way resembling the idea of a nigun) becomes the vaguely rhyming "Abi m'leibt," and the phrase "The lion sleeps tonight" makes a cameo appearance in the final verse, when Lipa waits for a train at New York's Pennsylvania Station late at night: "I should be sleeping, like the lion sleeps tonight!"

There are no specific religious references in the lyrics. This cover transforms an English song about a lion in the jungle into a Yiddish song about a Jewish man going through his own jungle of life. It transforms the lyrics into a song that subtly aligns with the notion of Judaism being a light to the world and for Jews to make the world a better place. Apart from its main actor, who retains his Hasidic garb, wearing a black suit and head covering, the video provides only subtle Jewish imagery. After the first mishap of dropped groceries, Lipa utters the Hebrew idiom "Baruch Hashem" (God bless), which can mean anything from "Great!"

to "Don't even ask." Before walking into the coffee room, he kisses the mezuzah, and he frequently stands in front of advertisements of Jewish businesses and organizations.

The Yiddish cover version did not sit well with everybody. During an interview with Zev Brenner on America's premier Jewish talk show, *Talkline*, one caller asked Lipa why he had used a non-Jewish tune. Such reaction is unsurprising given that mainstream popular music is not accepted in the Orthodox circles in which Lipa lived. The perception of specific audiences explains why other musicians, such as singer Lenny Solomon and his rock band Shlock Rock, parody popular secular songs by substituting new religious-themed lyrics without any pushback: Shlock Rock caters to a different audience. The band's aim is to preserve and heighten Jewish consciousness through music to ensure the continuity of the Jewish community. Aside from giving concerts, Solomon and Shlock Rock play at schools and Jewish events across the spectrum. Their list of parodies is long and ranges from the Beatles' "Ob-La-Di, Ob-La-Da" as "Havdalah" and Leonard Bernstein's "Maria" from *West Side Story* as "Tekiah" (the title refers to the shofar blast) to Ricky Martin's "Livin' la Vida Loca" as "Learning to Dance the Hora" and Elvis Presley's "All Shook Up" as "(It's My Lulav, It's) All Shook Up."

Regardless of Orthodox criticism, "Abi m'leibt" has become one of Lipa's signature tunes. He often uses it onstage, turning the microphone to the crowd to join in the chorus. In 2015, he even performed it with the Maccabeats at President Barack Obama's White House Hanukkah Party. And as so often, Lipa retexted the song to make it fit for the occasion (he sang it in English and Yiddish), though the chorus has always remained the same. Ultimately, Lipa's song about relinquishing control to life's unpredictability is not only his signature tune but also a wisdom he would have to embrace himself, as twists and turns were around the corner. In December 2005, the Educational Committee of Kiryas Yoel, a village in the town of Monroe in Orange County, officially banned Lipa's just released CD *Keneina Hora* for its "jazzy rock'n roll," deemed "very bad for the spirituality of those who hear it." A Yiddish one-page ad against the CD, signed by the Central Rabbinical Congress of the USA and Canada, appeared in the Williamsburg paper *Shoppers Route* on March 1, 2006. In late 2007, after many years of bullying, he moved from New Square to nearby Airmont. And with that came another turning point in early February 2008.

Lipa was scheduled to appear in the so-called Big Event, a heavily promoted charity concert for orphans living in Israel who needed financial assistance to cover wedding costs. It was geared toward strictly Orthodox Jews, and gender-segregated seating was a given. As large crowds were expected, Madison Square Garden's WaMu Theater served as the stage for a program with the major star of the scene (by that time, Lipa had already achieved celebrity status in wider Jewish circles) and an up-and-coming new singer (the just rising British singer Shloime Gertner) scheduled for March 9. Indeed, the concert was anticipated to be "the biggest event ever in Jewish music." With all but the finalized program in place, Lipa was shocked to find a *kol koreh* (a stern warning) signed by thirty-three leading rabbis from Israel and the United States, posted in *Hamodia*, a daily newspaper published in Jerusalem read by the strictly Orthodox community. The rabbis were concerned that the concert would "cause frivolity and light-headedness" and "lead to great transgression." As the only one still lined up for performance, Lipa was the only artist to be mentioned by name. The ban was extremely controversial and generated a mixed response. Some were outraged. Others believed that the rabbis who signed this decree were correct in their assessment of the situation. The ban resulted in Lipa's cancellation of the concert as well as of a show in London in April. The controversy has been widely reported in the media, and it suffices to say here that Lipa promised to discontinue performing any music of non-Jewish origin. Later that month, a full-page ad in *Hamodia* congratulated Lipa for listening to the rabbis. It bore only eight signatures, and at least one of the original signers publicly acknowledged having been misled, not having done due diligence in this matter; he no longer thought that such concerts should be banned. You do the math.

Since much of Lipa's appeal stems from unrestrained performances that often rely on freestyle rapping in Yiddish and English, the ban could easily have scuttled his career. Be it as it may, the events surrounding the concert made Lipa a household name, and he gained many fans. In fact, it created new opportunities for him. In 2008, he was named to the *Forward 50* list of most influential Jews. Three months after the controversy, Lipa released his next album, titled *A Poshiter Yid* (A Simple Jew), with cover art showing Lipa dressed as a devout

Jew studying the Torah. The semiotics of the album were masterful, proclaiming Lipa a simple Jew rather than the secularized entertainer the rabbis had accused him of being. Most impressive, thanks to Lipa's consistent good humor, the statement came across as genuine rather than cynical. The album packaging also included a bookmark featuring the album art and the prayer traditionally recited before Torah study. This put Orthodox educators in the position of either having to ban a bookmark or allowing all their students to carry advertising for a "banned" artist.

The album's songs also featured cleverly written lyrics, which, in addition to their literal meaning, provided commentary on Lipa's situation. On the title track, he sang, "Ikh fir shvere milkhomes mit sonim geferlekhe / az di yinge neshumes zol opvaksin ehrlekhe" (I fight difficult battles with awesome enemies / so that the young souls will grow correctly). Delivered in first-person Yiddish, the lyrics speak of the challenge of staying faithful to tradition while also referencing Lipa's fight with those who issued the ban. A number of the songs on the album became popular on the wedding and bar mitzvah circuit, especially the dance hit "Hentelach." Some of them ("Hentelach," "A Poshiter Yid," and "Wake Up") he sang in March 2009 at the sold-out concert at Madison Square Garden, now simply named "The Event." Lipa headlined it, singing for the first time live on the stage that facilitated his transition from badkhan to Jewish star. The Yeshiva Boys Choir came, and Shloime Gertner (he claimed to be in Spain at the time of the concert) participated with a video in Lipa style with his hit song "Schmeichel." But the program was carefully curated to not offend anyone.

After initially toning down some public appearances and pledging not to sing secular music, Lipa resumed his exuberant approach and kept going strong. Ever since that time, Lipa has maintained a heavy concert and recording schedule, finding himself on different stages in North America and Israel. He has continued to make music that draws on outside popular culture, playfully creating awareness of the divides in the strictly Orthodox community. But he has also undergone continuous style changes in terms of both music and stage presentation.

This has been noticed as of 2011 when *The Forward* titled a Lipa feature as "A Simple Jew with a Touch of Gaga," thereby inadvertently coining Lipa's dub as "the Hasidic Lady Gaga." Some assert that his

2012 music video "Hang Up the Phone" is a parody of Lady Gaga's "Telephone," but Lipa maintains that the loose similarities are entirely coincidental. If he quotes from popular songs like Lady Gaga's "Bad Romance" then only in live performance, rarely if at all on his CD recordings. If the analogy with Lady Gaga holds, then it is with regard to a chameleonic style.

Distinctly Jewish references surface in Lipa's most popular song, 2012's "Mizrach." The lyrics consist of four lines:

> East, West
> South, North
> Above, below
> And gather our exiles from the four corners of the earth.

The lines are repeated over and over again. This simplicity relates to Lipa's goal of creating a true dance tune. In fact, he conceived the song by repeatedly moving back and forth, thus creating it out of an entirely physical approach. Although not intended by Lipa, the Hebrew text with its allusions to the four corners of the earth and its poetic fourness is reminiscent of the nigun discussed in chapter 2, "Daled bavos." The last line relates to the messianic notion of Jews exiled all across the world returning again to the Holy Land. The song thus promotes a message of solidarity among all types of Jews regardless of Diaspora and denomination. The text "Le-malah, le-matah" (above, below) is also reminiscent of a passage from the Talmud, about searching for people in rubble on the Sabbath. Apparently, if you find their feet first (mi-l'matah le-malah), you need to check all the way up to their nose to see if they are still breathing, but if you find the head first (mi-l'malah le-matah) and they are definitely not breathing, you don't need to dig down any further, at least until after Sabbath. But those interpretations are subjective. What Lipa ultimately had in mind was to create a tune in line with *simcha* (joyful) dancing.

As of 2016, Lipa has released more than a dozen recordings that show his flexibility with musical styles: there are solemn prayer and folk melodies, pop and electronic music, hard-driving rock tunes and jazzy shuffles, Gangnam, techno and hip-hop, and pseudo-rap numbers with lyrics in English, Hebrew, and Yiddish that, together with his often humorous and dance-laden MTV-style videos, attest to his chameleon-like presence. Throughout, he maintains his signature look: bold eyeglasses, side locks, and head covering. Aside from his appearance, he also continues to imbue his music and the lyrics with allusions to Jewish culture.

Matisyahu and Lipa are two of a small number of emerging artists and groups who have brought the Jewish experience on to the rock and pop concert stage for different communities; among others that fill a similar niche, infusing existing styles and genres with Jewish content, but known primarily among observant audiences, are 8th Day, the Maccabeats, and the Yeshiva Boys Choir. The Canadian rapper Socalled offers one of the most successful mixes of hip-hop and traditional Jewish music for more mainstream audiences in America. To build the next generation for the strictly observant community, Yossi Soffer and his wife, Mica, had launched the short-lived singing talent competition *A Jewish Star*, the world's first *American Idol* spin-off with prominent Orthodox artists serving as judges, among them Lipa, Avraham Fried, Eli Gerstner, Yaakov Shwekey, and Yehuda Solomon, lead vocalist of the Los Angeles–based band Moshav. But the stars of the next generation catering predominantly to Orthodox Jews are only slowly emerging—among the very few are Matt Dubb and some of those mentioned in the next chapter—but none of them has yet reached the name brands of their predecessors.

Many pop and rock musicians born Jewish have rocked stages in America and beyond with great success, but most appeared with a mainstream repertoire for general audiences, from Paula Abdul to Barbra Streisand, from Judy Collins to Bob Dylan, from Carole King to Van Halen's David Lee Roth, just to name a very few. Few of them brought their Jewish identity into their work. This in itself reflects the reality of the recording and live concert business of mainstream America: Jewish-imbued music on the rock stage is likely geared toward a specific Jewish audience, though with the steady rise of world music, crossover, and fusion, the vigorous cross-pollination of musical styles allows for performers like Matisyahu to celebrate success across diverse audiences. Change has been in the air with the dissolving of American Top 40 radio's importance and growth of indie labels, reflecting the diversification of American tastes. Surely, if any of these above-named artists and groups gave a concert at Madison Square Garden and the Barclay Center on the same night, the choice would be tough and ultimately depend on the taste and devotion of the audience itself.

8

PUBS AND CLUBS

In November 2014, I walked into the Bitter End, a nightclub, coffee-house, and folk music venue on Bleecker Street, the throbbing heart of New York's Greenwich Village. There, I was surrounded by a throng of women who could not have been more diverse, of all ages, some wear-ing long, glossy wigs and pleated skirts, others in pants and sleeveless dresses, women who spoke English and women who chattered in Rus-sian. This unlikely group had come together on this night for one rea-son: Bulletproof Stockings, a Hasidic alternative-rock girl band that performs exclusively for female audiences. The band's name derives from the derogatory description of the thick, opaque hosiery tradition-ally worn by many modest Hasidic women—clearly used here tongue in cheek in opposition to the band's message of celebrating womanhood and representing femininity. Still, there is a connection between the band's name and its founders, Perl Wolfe, an amateur singer-songwriter and keyboardist, and Dalia Shusterman, the drummer. Both are Luba-vitcher women.

Perl was born into Chabad and has remained in the community except for a short period of time. Dalia was born into a modern Ortho-dox family. At age sixteen, after discovering her talent for drumming, she left home and started hitchhiking across the country and giving street performances. In 1993, Shusterman became one of the founding members of the psychedelic rock band Hopewell, which became fairly successful and released a number of albums. During a brief stay in Manhattan, Shusterman received a flyer for a Sukkot event in Crown

Heights and decided to attend. This experience motivated her to join Chabad as a *baalat teshuvah* (one who returns). She quit Hopewell, married the Hasidic rabbi she had met at the event, and subsequently moved with her husband to Los Angeles, where their four sons were born. After her husband's untimely death in the spring of 2011, Shusterman and her little boys moved back to New York. A friend introduced her to Wolfe on a rainy night in December 2011 in the Crown Heights neighborhood of Brooklyn.

Less than a month after the two women met, the duo played its first show during Lamplighters Yeshivah's "In the Glow," a fund-raiser that has provided a stage for Crown Heights' creative women—artists, musicians, and dancers. Bulletproof Stockings was born. Shortly thereafter, the group recorded its first single, "Frigid City." The song features a simple, tuneful melody. It begins with keyboard and drums that set a fast, strong rhythm. For the chorus, Perl significantly raises the pitch in her voice, emphasizing the desperation she is singing about: "Everything is so cluttered here I can't sleep / And when I do I awake on empty / Could you show your face just a little more frequently / I didn't know it was so cold in the city." For the final chorus, Perl and Dalia reduce the accompaniment to a purposeful, simple beat. To help establish a syncopated rhythm, they clap. At the Bitter End, the audience joined in clapping. If we understand communal song as metaphor for Hasidic spirituality, then by stepping aside from their instruments and simplifying the music to a level at which the audience could participate, the band was creating a forum and outlet for their spirituality.

"Frigid City" became part of the duo's debut EP album *Down to the Top*, released in the spring of 2012. Thereafter, the band expanded its lineup to include Elisheva Maister on violoncello and Dana Pestun on violin. The group began to tour clubs and pubs throughout New York (even headlining famed Arlene's Grocery on New York's Lower East Side), California, Georgia, and Maryland. By January 2015, Bulletproof Stockings reached number six on the ReverbNation Alternative charts for Brooklyn, New York. In December 2015, the band launched its debut full-length album, *Homeland Call Stomp*, and embarked on its first national tour, the Homeland Winter tour, beginning with a Hanukkah concert at Webster Hall, thereafter going south and west to San Francisco, Los Angeles, and Portland. In April 2016, Bulletproof Stockings disbanded for unknown reasons.

Bulletproof Stockings' musical style seems a long way from what is commonly understood as Hasidic music. Its sound rather parallels bands such as Radiohead, Red Hot Chili Peppers, and the White Stripes, groups whose music falls under the broad umbrella of alternative rock. Alt-rock differs greatly from classic rock in terms of its sound, its social context, and its regional roots. And Bulletproof Stockings certainly differ and not just from rock. Compare it, for example, to the nigun discussed in chapter 2. The musical output of the Lubavitcher and the songs of Bulletproof Stockings might suggest little in common between the two. But in some ways the opposite is the case. When looking at the underlying function of music in Hasidism, it becomes clear that Bulletproof Stockings are in line with the spirituality of the Lubavitch movement. The musicians' objective is to utilize music as a spiritual means to connect themselves and their audience with God. This directly follows the premise of Hasidic music: the idea that music, specifically nigunim, can help the benoni (the average Jew) attain devekut (devotion or unity) with God. The actual purpose of singing nigunim is not to produce aesthetically pleasing music; instead, its primary aim is the spirituality that is experienced with the "performance." Music as communication and prayer plays a crucial role in devekut and thus attains a special place. Bulletproof Stockings are rooted in this thinking. In the creation of the band's music and through its performance, the musicians help their audience and themselves achieve devekut.

The band is fully aware of the power that music can have in their relation to God and humankind. After a difficult divorce, Perl Wolfe was in a spiritual slump and religiously confused. Music helped her connect with God in those difficult times. The goal of her music making has always been to help individuals connect with God. "I'm trying to channel my soul," she said. "When I'm recording, I'm thinking, 'Hashem, give me the right words, the right intention, so that it comes out the right way to inspire me and the people who will hear me.'" Perl gives her entire soul during a performance. The emotion heard in her voice and the manner in which her body moves in unison with the music are a visual testimony of her communion with God and her spiritual ecstasy or *hitlahavut*. The musicians are not merely performing music; they are communicating with God and sharing this inspirational moment with their audience—a holy performance. Their songs are prayers clothed in alternative rock.

The performances of Bulletproof Stockings are another example of Jewish music's trend to borrow, to adapt, and to fuse. Even the Hasidim, widely regarded as being monolithic, are not immune to this process. Indeed, there is a practice of incorporating outsider musical materials into the nigunim repertoire provided that they undergo *tikun*, the process of healing and restoration through musical and textual manipulation, which returns the divine spark to its proper place. This process is valued and called a mitzvah, a good deed resulting from religious duty. Rebbes have regularly adapted melodies of their surrounding Hungarian, Polish, Ukrainian, Romanian, Russian, Turkish, and even Arabic cultures as nigunim. The teachings of Rebbe Nachman of Breslov suggest that there are sacred melodies in secular music, with holy sparks hidden within them, captured by evil forces in their struggle against the divine, and awaiting redemption. Spiritual masters or *tsadikim* looked for these sacred melodies in secular music in order to redeem the holy sparks. *Baalei teshuvah*, the returners, have been crucial in identifying the secular tunes that are worth redeeming. The Lubavitchers' tolerant attitude to modern sounds, presentations, and associated techniques is connected to this, especially when new materials bring nonobservant Jews to Hasidic life. In this way, the duality inherent in Lubavitcher thought between the worldly and the spiritual is blurred and provides an opportunity for Bulletproof Stockings to spawn a new creative space. While spiritually representing Hasidic music, Bulletproof Stockings clearly draw stylistically on secular sounds generally not associated with Lubavitcher tradition. But given that the adaptation of non-Jewish musical styles is a hallmark of the nigunim, the fact that Bulletproof Stockings lean on alternative rock is not alien from Hasidic thought, as long as a divine spark can be perceived in their pieces and performance. Indeed, Bulletproof Stockings perform divinely inspired music in altrock style. The musicians borrow but do not do so explicitly.

According to Hasidic spirituality, a music's aesthetics are not significant. Lubavitchers conceive music as being inherently neutral, although certain repertoires lean toward either the divine or the animal soul. While a Hasidic nigun is not necessarily pleasing to the ear, its form is closest to the divine source and hence most likely to elevate the soul. Repertoires perceived as having non-Jewish characteristics are those most likely to engage the animal soul. But these are not immutable categories. What differentiates Bulletproof Stockings' songs from the Lubavitcher nigun is that the quality of the music is an integral aspect of the performance. In order to understand and perhaps dissolve this seeming contradiction, we must understand the reason why aesthetics are an essential facet of this Hasidic band. For one, the members of the band were blessed by God with musical talents that should be acknowledged. These God-granted talents are not to be wasted. Furthermore, good music attracts a larger audience that can in turn achieve devekut. Indeed, the band members cite as their goal to inspire the audience and help it to achieve a spiritual connection with God. To do so, they embrace aesthetically pleasing music to attract and grow their public. They thus fuse good musicianship with Hasidic thought.

From a mainstream perspective, one of the unique aspects of the band is that the musicians perform only for female audiences. The band observes kol ishah, a rabbinic prohibition that forbids Jewish men from hearing women sing. But more than adhering to Jewish law, Bulletproof Stockings turn the table on the sharp social division that arises for women from kol ishah. If feminists interpret kol ishah as the silencing of women's literal and figurative voices, the band turns the potential silence into a female tish. "The deal is that it's not a women's mitzvah not to play," explained Shusterman, using the term for a religious commandment. "It's a man's mitzvah not to listen." "We could sing in the middle of the street and all the men would have to leave. But for the sake of *ahavat yisrael* [love of fellow Jews], we don't make issues for people," Wolfe said. Technically, by not performing in front of men, these female Lubavitcher musicians are helping Orthodox men adhere to Jewish law. But Wolfe also posits that "women will party and rock out in a completely different way when there's nobody there but women." The group thus represents the flip side of the gender equation by creating a forum on which women can freely express themselves without having to be concerned with a male presence. And the exclusively female context is a powerful tool appreciated by religious and nonreligious women alike. It creates an environment free of sexual tension, a relaxed atmosphere where women are not objectified. Furthermore, by playing to female-only audiences, Bulletproof Stockings are fulfilling another criterion of Hasidic music where music serves as a group signifier to connect all the individuals. By playing for an exclusively female audience, the group creates a tight connection between their listeners—a novel sonic community, at once restrictive and all-inclusive.

Maybe it was because of the dim lighting, or maybe it was truly because of the absence of men, that I felt the relaxed and cheerful atmosphere with women happily dancing and interacting in a carefree manner without concern about their looks or how men might perceive them. The expressions on their faces exuded intense enjoyment of the performance. As such, the band cannot be perceived as a suppressed group unable and unwilling to cater to men. Rather, Bulletproof Stockings are a revolution in the Hasidic world and the club scene in that they are pursuing their goals and talents in new spaces, breaking free from some of the Lubavitcher community's norms and introducing a new spirit to the clubs.

My favorite song that night was not quite alt-rock style. It was a nigun called "Ad bli dai," which translates to "Until I am forced to say enough." Before performing it, Perl briefly elucidated the nigun's message in the form of a *dvar torah*, a talk based on the weekly Torah portion. Perl explained that this nigun is a prayer asking God to send a superfluous amount of blessing. By simply providing such an introduction, Bulletproof Stockings present themselves as more than just a group of musicians. Utilizing their time onstage to share spiritual ideas and help the audience connect with God, the band members appear as spiritual leaders. They evince that one need not be at a tish in Crown Heights to achieve devekut. Instead, spirituality and godliness can enter life anywhere, even in a pub or club.

After the talk, Perl's warm voice began to rise and fall, forming sounds to "oy oy oy," a Yiddish exclamation of sorrow and lamentation that adds tremendous meaning to a melody. By starting with a deep sense of sadness, the prayer for blessing becomes so much more relevant and necessary. In nigunim, feelings are expressed in abstract syllables, not words. This is in line with the Hasidic belief that words are limiting. With a melody without words, emotion and power of the song are limitless. The use of expressive syllables creates an opportunity for the audience to identify any problem or sadness that they feel individually. Hence, by not limiting or specifying the emotion though lyrics, a wide-ranging audience can individually connect to the message of the melody. As with many nigunim, "Ad bli dai" is repetitive. At its core, it is a simple melody that moves in steps. It differs from Hasidic practice in that it was accompanied by instruments: violin, violoncello, and drums. Moreover, most nigunim are heterophonic, achieved by the gradual joining of all voices in near but not quite unison. However, Perl sang "Ad bli dai" alone. She also interspersed some Hebrew lyrics. But this aside, the piece still represents Hasidic music because of the ultimate goal to ignite spirituality in the hearts of the audience. Even when departing from slightly revamped Hasidic repertoires such as nigunim, the group conveys the essence of Hasidism—the soul.

In contrast, Perl's husky, mournful song "Easy Pray" initially conveys a universal message. The lyrics contain lines such as "Forbidden passages always tempt thee / Why you succumb is my point of intrigue," implying worldliness and seduction specifically. "If a girl hears that and that's how she connects to it, then that's what it means to her," says Perl. She thinks of "Easy Pray" as "the ballad of *yetzer hara* (evil inclination). The evil inclination is saying in this song, 'I'm looked at as this bad guy, but you have power, you have control.'" Although she sees the songs as a "conversation between the narrator and God," she and Dalia "wanted to write it in a way that people can interpret it on their own level." It connotes an underlying contrast in daily life, a balance between good and evil, dark and light—the universal message that life is full of ups and downs.

Musically, it features an unpretentious melody and clear rhythms. Wolfe's remarkably strong, unwaveringly smooth vocals and keyboard lines are layered with heavy beats and subtle guitar riffs. A unique aspect of the song is its reliance on word painting. "Easy Pray" begins with a slow, solemn tempo. Then, as Perl begins to sing about "rock bottom," the music depicts this image as the low-pitched drums begin to sound like something is hitting the "bottom." After these highly rhythmic drum sounds, Perl vocalizes "ah ah ah ah ah ah ah," and she sings each successive "ah" at a higher pitch. Again, abstract syllables are utilized in place of words. But the melodic contour depicts the forbidden passages and the ladder later referenced in the lyrics. At this point, the tempo is fast, depicting someone running up a ladder. There is a continuous switch in the song from a slow to a fast tempo, aligning with lyrics that describe "rock bottom" and the "top." The only response to "rock bottom" is to climb up your ladder and keep aiming for the top. The reason that the ladder is not described with words but rather again through syllables is clearly that words are limiting. By describing the process of growth with syllables, the message can reach the imagination of a broad audience. Whether the ladder is a metaphor for school, relationships, or anything else to be reached, achieved, or simply approached is truly dependent on the listener's association. In this way, the song is open, offering a universal message. Still, Perl Wolfe asserts that her lyrics, "while not always blatantly religious, are nevertheless inspired by Torah and by Lubavitch's version of Hasidic faith." With a simple, repetitive melody, a strong rhythm, unmistakable rock timbre, and a spiritual message, this song is characteristic of Hasidic music in alt-rock style.

Overall, the band's music is bulletproof in more than one respect: jamming unabashedly, belting out lilting lyrics while at the same time representing the Lubavitcher community in America, Bulletproof Stockings unveil radically expressive new possibilities. While the group's songs are inspired by Jewish teachings, they are nowhere close to being evangelical. "Christian music is often blatantly religious. We come from a spiritual place, but you can relate to it on many levels," says Perl. "There's no Jewish agenda," says Dalia. "We're not trying to make anyone Jewish." And in this respect, they depart from the Lubavitcher efforts to reach out to secular Jews and avoid non-Jews. Bulletproof Stockings embrace *all* women, regardless of their faith, through music.

Lubavitcher spirituality can be best understood as a set of concentric circles delineating spiritual and physical proximity to the rebbe, the spiritual leader. The most outward circles are baalei teshuvah such as Dalia, other Hasidim, and secular Jews. Non-Jews are not part of the circle. When Rebbe Menachem M. Schneerson died in 1994, the Lubavitch movement lost its central, recognized authority, an inspired and inspiring leader who had developed a small Hasidic group into a major organization in the Jewish world. The rebbe groomed no successor, and no one is openly looking for a new rebbe. But his legacy left no void; it only further opened spaces. One of them was filled by Bulletproof Stockings, whose paramount goal is to remain connected with Lubavitcher Hasidism, to spiritually inspire audiences, and to connect to God through alternative rock. As such, the group represents the epitome of a new Hasidic music within which women have an ever stronger voice. The band is to modern (Jewish) female audiences what a Hasidic rebbe is to a tish: spiritual leaders who have the power to impart universal notions through music.

The entry of Hasidic spirituality into America's club scene constitutes a peak in a long phase of renewal that began in the 1950s, when segments of Orthodoxy went mainstream through recordings of noncantorial music. In the 1970s, Yossi Piamenta (1951–2015), a rock guitarist born in Israel whom *Time* magazine called the Sephardic Santana and the *New York Times* compared to Jimi Hendrix, began to bring his blend of rock and Middle Eastern music to a variety of New York clubs and also went on tour. A noteworthy recent formation is the hipster band Zusha. Founded in 2014 in the East Village by "three neo-Hasidic dudes with less passion for college and more passion for music," the band imbues the Hasidic nigun with styles of folk, indie, reggae, and world soul. In October of that year, they made their debut at New York's Mercury Lounge, where indie headliners and up-and-comers have launched their careers since the 1990s. Since then, they have traversed the club circuit with appearances at the Highline Ballroom and the Bowery Ballroom and shared the concert stage with Lipa and others, most notably at the Kulturfest Yiddish Soul concert at Central Park's Rumsey Playfield. In January 2016, the band released its first full-length album, *Kavana*, which reached number 2 on Billboard's World Albums chart. The Hasidic contributions are perhaps the most unexpected of the Jewish influences on America's club scene.

Looking back, it was in the 1980s that progressive forms of Jewish music that traversed denominations and genres began to appear among a secular Jewish crowd in pubs and clubs. A district where Jewish immigrants left their mark since the end of the nineteenth century, the grungy Lower East Side became again a site of cultural innovation but of a different kind. In 1987, Michael Dorf and Bob Appel opened the Knitting Factory in an old, dilapidated Avon Products office on Houston Street between the Bowery and Broadway in New York. Initially, the venue was meant to be an art gallery with a performance space and café. The club quickly emerged as a home for the sounds that did not neatly fit any established categories. Within this environment, such musicians as John Zorn, David Krakauer, Marc Ribot, Anthony Coleman, and Frank London passionately explored the possibilities for new forms of Jewish music, emancipating themselves from conformity and inconspicuousness. Bands that performed there—Hasidic New Wave,

Paradox Trio, Zohar, and many others whose eclectic styles encompassed hard-core and acid rock, neo-Yiddish cabaret, free verse, free jazz, and electronica—began to frequent the club scene in other parts of America. As the home to the so-called downtown music scene, the Knit, however, remained the veritable temple of New York's avant-garde (in 1994, Dorf would move the club to Tribeca and in 2008 to Brooklyn; a satellite location existed in Los Angeles from 2000 to 2009). It became one of the epicenters of the klezmer revival and of J.A.M. (short for Jewish Avant-Garde Music and more often used for the record label Jewish Alternative Movement).

In this venue, Jewish music and the American club scene met through what composer John Zorn termed Radical Jewish Culture (RJC), an avant-garde Jewish music moment that developed within the downtown scene in the early 1990s. It became the banner under which many artists in Zorn's circle performed, produced, and circulated their music. A native New Yorker born in 1953, Zorn is known as a saxophonist, an arranger with a keen ear for instrumental color, a proficient organizer of new and innovative music groups, and an avid collector of recordings. His early works as a composer are eclectic and experimental; many contain sudden shifts of mood. RJC was born out of Zorn's *Kristallnacht*, which he wrote for the Festival for Radical New Jewish Culture at the 1992 Munich Art Project and recorded the same year. The cycle of seven compositions for chamber octet consisting of violin, clarinet, trumpet, electric guitar, sampling keyboard, contrabass, percussion, and waveform oscillator reflects on the infamous Night of Broken Glass in November 1938, when Jews were targets of violence and destruction in Germany and Austria. As such, it is a very personal reading of the Jewish experience before, during, and after the Holocaust. It begins in the eastern European shtetl, continues with the Holocaust and its aftermath, and moves to notions of healing and hope. With a shift to militancy and subsequent redemption, it ends with survival and the building of a Jewish state.

Kristallnacht was Zorn's first unified piece to employ more than one compositional method. A true musical ritual, the work is one of the most kaleidoscopic pieces Zorn ever created. It combines prerecorded sounds and abstract music. Noises such as burning paper, footsteps, and trash metal (played on an electric guitar) meet free jazz and rock. It contains references to Jewish numerology (its seven parts represent wholeness and completion), employs Arnold Schoenberg's twelve-tone technique in the third movement, and inserts evocations of oompah rhythm and waltz fragments in the first, fifth, and sixth movements. It relies on sonic maximization in that Zorn inserted extreme and sudden shifts of volume within and especially between tracks of a scale that requires electronic amplification. Through these shifts, Zorn wanted the listener to experience a small part of the pain the European Jews endured, not merely emotionally but physically. During the premiere, while the audience perceived the performance as disturbing, they were asked not to leave the room.

The second movement, "Never Again," is the longest and also the most extreme. It is also the only one with a bilingual title in Hebrew *and* English, permitting a broader reach. It consists of three parts, the bookends of which closely resemble each other, projecting a long, almost three-minute blast of glass breakage interspersed at an excruciatingly loud level with piercing sine tones. White noise with synthesized bamboo wind chimes and glockenspiel plates creates this continuous sound of broken glass. When this painful and violent section comes to a sudden halt, several sets of running footsteps open the middle section, evoking the presence of Jews hunted by Nazis. Different, often ominous sounds are layered. Intermittently soft cymbals come in, the sounds of hand drums, and quite prominently a high repeated chime on a glockenspiel or triangle that stands out from the other sounds. This sound will continue to resurface. There are chorused and electronically manipulated samples, accompanied by a light, rapid guitar tremolo. There is also a low bass solo that at times produces threatening sounds when rumbling underneath the other layers. There are excerpts of Nazi propaganda speeches and police shouts that have been already heard in the first movement, "Shtetl," and samples of chanting crowds, screams, and dogs barking in the background. Their ugliness and aggression is heightened by looping them to different lengths, layering them, and repeating them. In strong juxtaposition, we hear cantorial singing, which is also looped and layered over a sustained bass. The prayer song is answered by the only other lyrical sound in the movement, produced by a klezmer-invoking violin that emerges in the midst of this chaos (it otherwise produces rather unconventional plucked sounds).

The underlying sonic continuity is produced by a waveform oscillator that generates high sine tones that disrupt any sense of chronology or order. While it resurfaces intermittently, it is loudest in the beginning and at the end—a physical assault on the ear and a continuous one given its unpredictable recurrences. It is important to note that the piece also contains inaudible high-spectrum frequencies, some of which are of greater amplitude than the audible ones and beyond the limits of human hearing. These can induce nausea, headache, and other ill feelings. The history of the persecution of Jews in Germany is not merely remembered but also physically felt. In the moment of listening, it becomes reality. But also, these sine tones make it impossible to listen to the movement in detail—it can never be fully heard. "Never Again" exemplifies how Zorn pushes the boundaries of sound through maximizing sonic elements and through juxtapositions. Clearly, the extremes of timbre and amplitude create disturbing effects and an extreme psychological intensity.

Kristallnacht represents an informed engagement with Jewish history using a new sonic language. Creating it prompted Zorn to explore his heritage more deeply and examine compositional methods using Jewish modes like the freygish. He shares, "After [*Kristallnacht*] I wanted to do something that was not about the history of pain and suffering, but about the future and how bright and beautiful it can be." He set himself the task of writing 100 pieces within a year that would advance the form of Jewish music into the twenty-first century. Within several years, the number of compositions had grown to more than 200 and became known as *Masada Book I* (1993–1997). In 2004, *Book II: Book of Angels* followed, and *Book III: The Book of Beriah* (2009–2014) completed the project, at least for now.

Zorn named his mammoth project after the ancient fortification in the Judean desert, where Jewish rebels committed suicide rather than surrender to the attacking Roman army. Masada became a controversial symbol of Jewish national resistance against the enemy. For Zorn, it is a symbol of Jewish cultural identity. *Masada* is the result of his search for a grammar of new Jewish music and the attempt to give a "tune-book" to the Jewish people, writing melodies that take up no more than five staves on manuscript paper, can be played on any instrument, and inspire the creativity of musicians who want to use them. Informed by group improvisation, they operate like jazz charts, supplying a melody and some chords, often a bass line, and directives for tempo and mood.

Some of these sketches Zorn conceived at the rate of five compositions per hour.

Just as the number of commandments in the Torah, *Masada* consists of 613 tunes with Hebrew titles referring to Jewish artifacts, events, mythology, and true names, plus one long song to go with the "don't give Hitler a posthumous victory" commandment. (Zorn references here Rabbi Emil Fackenheim's 614th "commandment," a moral imperative that Jews not use the Holocaust to give up on God, Judaism, or the continuing survival of the Jewish people.) "Numbers mean a lot, especially if you're Jewish," said Zorn.

So how do *Masada*'s tunes work in performance? Let's look at "Ner Tamid," a reference to the eternal light that hangs above the ark in every synagogue and that symbolizes God's everlasting presence. It is a lyrical melody accompanied by straightforward simple harmonies. "Ner Tamid" features a distinct pattern of two quick notes followed by a longer held-out jazzy note. This pattern is frequently broken up through a series of quick notes that have a downward motion. Imagine it like an ornate eternal light whose hanging quality is being translated into melody and rhythm. In *Masada*, Zorn clearly recognizes the historical importance of melody as an expression of the Jewish soul. In his arrangements, he maintains it and makes it clearly recognizable. But nothing overshadows the melody.

The earliest recorded rendition of "Ner Tamid" can be found on the album *Tet* (the ninth *Masada* CD) also released in 1998 by DIW Records and recorded by the Acoustic Masada in April 1997. In 1993, Zorn had formed that quartet in order to record and perform *Masada*. It had the same instrumental makeup as the pioneering free-jazz group led by saxophonist Ornette Coleman in the late 1950s and early 1960s. The quartet rehearsed every Wednesday night at Café Mogodor on St. Marks Place and also at the Knit, where in 1993 Zorn had curated the Radical New Jewish Culture Festival. The four-minute rendition of *Tet* begins with Zorn on the alto saxophone clearly stating the melody, quickly joined by Dave Douglas, who with his muted trumpet sounds elegantly and unobtrusively renders melodic variations. They improvise on the "Ner Tamid" sketch in solos, while bassist Greg Cohen and drummer Joey Baron provide the rhythm section supporting the elegance of the melody with brush sounds and soft accents. The arrangement clearly intermixes free improvisation with the Jewish material that

"Ner Tamid" provides: it offers a melody with a Middle Eastern touch played over short repeating passages while bringing to mind the music of Ornette Coleman, though in contrast to Coleman, the improvisations of trumpet and saxophone often occur simultaneously—indeed, they are a prominent feature of *Tet*.

A shorter rendition of the tune can be heard on *The Circle Maker*, a double album recorded in December 1997 and released in 1998 on Zorn's Tzadik label. This arrangement was also made by Zorn. (Only with *Book II* did he begin to invite other artists to write, perform, and record their own interpretations of his tune sketches.) On this early recording, "Ner Tamid" is performed by the Bar Kokhba Sextet, which brings together six core members of the Masada family, which over time has featured different makeups and also included an Electric Masada. Expanding on tone color, "Ner Tamid" is first stated on the guitar (Marc Ribot) and countered by the violin (Mark Feldman) and violoncello (Erik Friedlander), accompanied by the rhythm section consisting of bass (Greg Cohen), drums (Joey Baron), and percussion (Cyro Baptista). There is also a live-at-Tonic version of the Masada quartet from June 2001, eternalized on a double album. In early 2007, the Masada quartet officially parted ways but performed once more with a different expanded bill in 2008. In the following years, Zorn staged several Masada marathons—hour-long concerts that draw from his songbook—in San Francisco and New York.

Through RJC, Zorn and other musicians turned their attention to writing and performing unconventional music that drew on Jewish music and heritage in idiosyncratic ways. The roots of this radicalism as a form of social and cultural critique lie in avant-garde aesthetics and Jewish political activism more than in religious Orthodoxy or folkloric heritage. The music blends experimental music with blues and jazz and with rock and punk in an effort to combine the unconventional, uncategorizable nature of downtown music with sounds that were recognizably Jewish. Although relatively fleeting in music history, RJC produced a burst of conversations, writing, and music—including festivals, international concerts, and nearly 200 new recordings of experimental music as well as funk, jazz, and klezmer fusions on Zorn's record label, Tzadik.

For Zorn, "All music is on equal grounds and there's no high art and low art." With RJC, he forged a new vision of Jewish identity in the contemporary world, one that sought to restore the bond between past and present, to interrogate the limits of racial and gender categories, and to display the tensions between secularism and observance and between traditional values and contemporary concerns. John Zorn saw RJC as a challenge posed to adventurous musical thinkers. He asked, "What is Jewish music? What is its future? If asked to make a contribution to Jewish culture, what would you do? Can Jewish music exist without a connection to klezmer, cantorial or Yiddish theatre?" The musicians' involvement in RJC sought to address these issues through the vision and imagination of individual musical minds.

Shifting coasts. It is 1992 in Los Angeles. The rap icon Eric "Eazy-E" Wright hosts a gang-truce event at Gazzarri's (now the Key Club), the infamous nightclub on Sunset Strip in West Hollywood, California. He invites a new rap duo, MCs Benyad and Mazik, underground hip-hop–styled, politically minded Jews from the Valley. After they win over a skeptical audience, Eazy-E persuades them to sign with his Ruthless Records—an odd fit for the rap mogul. Still, the duo, whose songs openly confronted the Middle East situation and the role of religion in war, presented the cutting-edge side of rap Eazy-E favored.

Blood of Abraham, as the duo came to be known, was one of many Jewish rap groups that gained public recognition in the United States from the mid-1980s on. But while groups such as the Beastie Boys and Michael Berrin (known as MC Serch) are white hip-hoppers who helped introduce rap to a broader white audience, Benyad and Mazik remained Afrocentric, catering to a black audience. When Blood of Abraham emerged in the early 1990s, the group stood as a testament to hip-hop's ever-burgeoning ability to defy cultural boundaries. One reason for this may lie in their heritage.

Benyad was born Benjamin Mor in Israel to Moroccan Jewish parents and raised in Nigeria until the age of ten, when his family moved to Los Angeles. Mazik was born David Saevitz in Santa Monica to a part-Irish father and a Jewish mother and raised in Las Vegas. As musicians, Benyad and Mazik were self-taught, drawing their inspiration from deejays and the cinema. They cite as extramusical influences the occult documentarian Manly P. Hall, psychologist C. G. Jung, pre-Christian world history, Egyptology, Gnosticism, the Masonic symbolist fine-art graffiti of Doze Greene, surreal art, and architecture. But the key characteristic of the group was an unapologetic Jewish identity. Blood of Abraham chose its name to relay its Jewish heritage while projecting an aggressive agenda, just as many rappers had done with their African-Americanisms. But they explored Jewish identity with a less self-conscious subversion of racial or ethnic stereotypes.

Under Eazy-E's mentorship, the group recorded its first CD in 1993 at the height of the strained black–Jewish relations in America. Released a year later, *Future Profits* is different from other rap in its provocative lyrics that draw on the politics of race and religion from a universal perspective. Instead of glorifying street stories, it promotes equality for all cultures, people, and religions. Although Jews have made prominent contributions to hip-hop, it is rare to actually hear Jewish religious beliefs in rap. Blood of Abraham created fourteen songs that all include references to Judaism, instilling a deep sense of Jewish identity into a genre associated with African American youth. Beginning with the bouncy, reggae-flavored "This Great Land Devours," the duo address rednecks in "Southern Comfort," asserting that "The God you pray to is a black Jew." Other tracks dealing with overtly Jewish themes are "Father of Many Nations" (a tribute to the biblical patriarch Abraham) and "Stick to Your Own Kind" (a line taken from Leonard Bernstein's *West Side Story*), which preaches solidarity between Jews and blacks. For "Stabbed by the Steeple," the duo shot a video at the Western Wall in Jerusalem; the track attacks the history of Western imperialism in Africa—particularly Christian missionaries' suppression of Ethiopian Jewry. The group's best-known track is "Niggaz and Jewz (Some Say Kikes)," an irreverent call for black–Jewish unity in the face of the shared struggle against bigotry. Provocative and epithet heavy, it is a comically potent statement on persecution, castigating anti-Semitism. It effectively addressed larger issues of racism and bigotry that occupied the Los Angeles rap scene yet offered a different perspective respected by the scene as an honest airing of personal epistemology. Its chorus samples an actual recording of the ravings of a Ku Klux Klansman. All tracks rely heavily on jazz samples, but hard-rock and spoken-word snippets are also utilized. *Future Profits* also features a spirited verse from Eazy-E as well as the first recorded appearance by will.i.am of the Black Eyed Peas, known then as Will 1X (the group was then known as A.T.B.A.N. Klann).

The album received a generally positive response among rap and hip-hop fans and artists, but when Eazy-E became terminally ill, its promotion stopped, and *Future Profits* disappeared from sight. Eazy-

E's death in 1995 and the end of the Ruthless label left the duo without support. Blood of Abraham fell into anonymity. Mazik and Benyad went on hiatus until 2000, which saw the unofficial release of the LP *Eyedol-lartree* on Mastergrip Records. With a pun on "idolatry" in its title, the album condemns greedy consumerism. Universal themes succeeded Jewish rap. But hints of Jewish themes remain present, such as in the opening of "I Know the Half":

> I believe in the philosophy of Abraham
> It's not just a philosophy, It's a movement
> It's a movement that will become, the international legacy of the world

The accompanying bonus DVD contains a ten-minute experimental film, codirected by Benyad and Mazik with filmmaker Brian Beletic. Featuring noir-ish black-and-white photography combined with stock and new footage, the film is an impressive display of the duo's multifaceted talents. Most recently, Benjamin Mor has resurfaced as an in-demand music video director, with clips for Katy Perry and Matisyahu.

Although short lived, Blood of Abraham offered a self-consciously Jewish alternative in rap that emerged from and addressed the greater hip-hop scene. Benyad and Mazik operated and performed entirely outside the Jewish communal realm, incorporating their own diverse Jewish experiences and backgrounds into tracks exploring more expansive rap discourses. They blazed the trail for other hip-hop artists, such as Yitzchak Jordan, known as Y-Love, who since 2001 rhymes in extensive freestyling with a mixture of English, Hebrew, Yiddish, Arabic, Latin, and Aramaic, often covering social, political, and religious themes. Rappers such as Ross Filler, known as Remedy, and Eden Daniel Pearlstein, known as Eprhyme, continue the legacy of the Beastie Boys but with a more overt Jewish message. All represent the multivalent relationship of Jews with hip-hop performance and as such contribute another facet to a people's attempt at musical change in order to ensure preservation and survival of Jewish heritage in the modern world.

9

BEYOND A SINGLE VENUE
Klezmer Everywhere

Klezmer has been everywhere. Name a venue and a time period you like, and I will tell you what style of klezmer music to find there. By the same token, klezmer resists precise specification. While klezmer music, klezmer musicians or klezmorim, and klezmer revitalization are commonly heard terms, clarinetist Andy Statman asserts that the music he plays is not klezmer but Hasidic music, and Giora Feidman has declared that all music is klezmer as long as one feels it. Many agree with trumpeter Frank London that klezmer "has gone from an underused term to being overgeneralized." Indeed, klezmer music transcends any one cultural affinity, style, or venue. What then is it? And in what guises can we find it in America?

Contracting two Hebrew words, *klei-zemer* means literally "vessel of song" and has originally designated the musical instrument. Taken literally, it is a fitting metaphor for the idea that a musician should make his instrument sing. The term has existed for ages but over time was filled with different content. In central and eastern Europe, it was used from the late sixteenth century on for Jewish guild musicians, who primarily played at weddings and other festivities outside the synagogue when music for ritual or for processions was needed. The exact sounds of their repertoire are unknown, though from the naming of some pieces we can discern that the musicians adapted dance music they learned from their non-Jewish neighbors and infused it with the sounds they heard in the synagogue. Nigun, Yiddish folk song, and Gypsy music were further significant influences. The birthplace of this unique musical repertoire can be traced to the southern areas of the Pale of Settlement, and it also evolved in the Austro-Hungarian Empire, thereby making its way westward.

The musicians initially did not accompany any vocal music. However, at weddings and festivities, they sometimes provided instrumentation to the rhymes of the badkhn (wedding jester). In the early seventeenth century, ensembles consisted of one or two fiddles, a bass, a tsimbl, and sometimes a flute. The violin or fiddle, classically the leader in ensemble settings in all kinds of musics, not only led the rest of the instruments but also assumed a solo role. With its high-pitched sound, it reigned over the other instruments and lent itself to all kinds of embellishments and expressive variations. In the musician's mind, touching the fiddle freed the sounds of crying from the instrument—a clear analogy to the human voice and the cry of the cantor. Over time, ensembles evolved, but until the later nineteenth century and even beyond, the fiddle continued to embody the essence of the music and led the ensemble. The musicians were exclusively male and learned their craft from family members. They often supplemented their income with hat making or barbering, with the exception of the leader, who was usually a full-time musician.

It was not until the late twentieth century that klezmer music came to firmly refer to repertoires that had absorbed and transformed a variety of musical traditions, including eastern European, Turkish, and Greek. The American Yiddish press had first used the term in the 1920s but without giving it any specific definition. The immigrants themselves largely avoided it, as it had become synonymous with a generation of musicians of low status, musically and otherwise. Clarinetist Dave Tarras (1897–1989), with Naftule Brandwein (1884–1963) among the greatest proponents of klezmer music of the first generation in America, recalled that "a klezmer was a guy that couldn't play," that is, someone who had a very limited skill set. Such association also led to recordings made between 1913 and 1942 avoiding the term but today would be clearly identified as klezmer music. Early twentieth-century recordings and writings most often refer to the repertoire as Yiddish or sometimes *freylekh* (happy) music. Groups chose names according to their leader's name, such as Kandel's Jewish Orchestra or Art Shreyer's Yiddish Orchestra. Some circumvented Jewish association altogether, such as the Oriental Orchestra. Only in the 1970s did klezmer music begin to designate a broad variety of styles with a common soundscape that is associated with the heritage of the Yiddish-speaking people of eastern Europe. The first recordings using klezmer to refer to repertoire were the Klezmorim's *East Side Wedding* and *Streets of Gold* in 1977 and 1978, followed by Andy Statman and Zev Feldman's *Jewish Klezmer Music* in 1979. From the 1980s on, klezmer music has evolved as a worldwide phenomenon just like jazz or tango, and its practitioners proudly refer to themselves as klezmer musicians and klezmorim.

But there is still little consensus as to what klezmer music is precisely. Does it refer to a purely instrumental repertoire, or can it include vocals? And what instruments are involved? Is it a genre or a style of performance? Is it composed or improvised? The extremely rich content and the wide spectrum of this repertoire with diverse origins and a long history from the Middle Ages to the present can hardly be captured with one musical concept. Klezmer captures attitude and lifestyle and repertoire and performance style, and, depending where and by whom it is performed, it can sound very different. As with other types of music (one might think here of jazz), the uniqueness of klezmer as music lies between the musicians and their repertoires. And as generations and tastes change, you can imagine that the sounds of klezmer music are changing as well. To explore klezmer music's evolution in and for America, let us travel back in time to the early twentieth century on the East Coast when the first generation of eastern European immigrants put their unique stamp on it.

Imagine we crashed a wedding in early twentieth-century Philadelphia, a celebration that has originally defined the klezmer's role. The ballroom of the Ambassador Hotel in North Philadelphia's Strawberry Mansion was one of the many halls used for life cycle celebrations, including bar mitzvahs and circumcisions. Being a wedding crasher would not have posed a problem, as the event was a public affair. The venue indicates a stark change of customs from the Old World, reflecting the (newly) acquired status of being Jewish in America. But this should not imply an abandonment of Jewish practices. There would be a chuppah, a canopy under which the Jewish couple stand during the ceremony. A rabbi would be present to preside over the ceremony and make a blessing, and a fiddler would provide background music. At the end of the ceremony, the groom would break the glass wrapped in a cloth napkin with his right foot, an act that remembers the destruction of the Temple in Jerusalem in the first century and also symbolizes the absolute finality of marriage. Just as the broken pieces of glass can never be put back together and returned to their original state, so the covenant of marriage irrevocably binds husband and wife in their new status. It is at that very moment that the guests shout "mazel tov" and the band would begin to play "Khosn, kale, mazel tov" (Congratulations to Groom and Bride), a well-known festive melody native to the wedding ceremony that has been around for ages. This posits the beginning of a night of music making.

After the well-wishes, the band would accompany the so-called grand march, where the family leads other guests around the room, while the bride and groom would disappear for a short period. The guests would proceed into the dining room, where the band would now play quietly. On the return of the bride and groom, it is time for dancing, with the first freylekhs reserved for the immediate family of the bride. Dancing would get serious after dinner. The band would play a bulgar, which had its roots in the march-like Romanian bulgaresca, with couples performing square dance-like figures and other steps in circles; it also allowed for individuals showing off his or her special steps. But one of the most essential wedding dances unique to the Philadelphia klezmer repertoire was the sher medley. It rose to prominence in the nineteenth century and remained an integral part of Philadelphia's weddings through the 1960s. It was not a standard part of the repertoire but a request number, and the person who asked for it had to pay the musicians a substantial tip. In turn, the bandleader would dedicate the number to the patron, who would invite others to join him in dance.

Originally, the sher is a western European contra dance that entered Jewish folklore in the eighteenth century and became a common social dance. Its literal meaning, "scissor," might derive from the figure that imitates the cutting action of scissors: the quick movements of straight legs, reminiscent of the shears of tailors. It involves four couples in a square formation who dance figures through which they advance (promenade), retire (lead out), change places (cross), and circle. After all the steps are completed, the entire dance would be repeated three more times.

Music for the sher was sequenced in long medleys, with musical material deeply anchored in Jewish tradition (unlike the borrowed bulgar), consisting mostly of oompah-rhythm freylekhs with a lively tempo. What is interesting about the Philadelphia sher medley is that its features are distinct from those heard in New York or Milwaukee. For one, the Philadelphia sher medley is exceptionally long, about twenty minutes or sometimes more. It is highly structured with distinct sections. This provides a feeling of consistency and stability. As such, it is profoundly different from the loosely improvised sher medleys performed elsewhere in the United States.

Indeed, just by traveling ninety miles northeast, we find a different klezmer scene, one with considerably more diversity but also defined by discontinuities. In 1908, clarinetist Naftule Brandwein arrived on Ellis Island. Like many others in those days, he hoped for a better life and an assured future. He belonged to the first wave of klezmorim who came from the Old World with a solid musical background. As many other musicians at the time, he was from what is now Ukraine, born into a family of klezmorim who lived in a small town in Galicia. Like others, he was unable to read music, which made his engagement by established bandleaders and composers like Alexander Olshanetsky, Joseph Rumshinsky, and Sholom Secunda quite impossible. Brandwein earned a living by dominating the wedding circuit. He also played for the Jewish underworld. A womanizer, gambler, and drinker with an eccentric personality (he liked to wear outrageous outfits or play with his pants down with his back facing the audience to conceal his fingering), Brandwein fit the stereotypical description of a klezmer. Given his eccentricities, it is no surprise that he played only and recorded briefly with established bands, such as the Abe Schwartz Orchestra, Joseph Cherniavsky's Yiddish American Jazz Band, and the Leo Reisman Orchestra. In the 1920s, he began recording under his own name and for a short while became a star of the 78-rpm-record era and the self-proclaimed "King of Jewish Music."

In February 1926, Naftule Brandwein recorded "Von tashlach / New Year's Prayer at the River," accompanied by the Naftule Brandwein Orchestra, which at the time consisted of a violin, trombone, piano, and cymbal. The orchestration alone shows a shift from earlier klezmer ensembles. The clarinet had been incorporated into klezmer music in the second half of the nineteenth century, introduced by Jewish musicians who played in military bands. It soon became an integral part of the ensemble and, with the advent of recording, the definitive solo instrument of klezmer music in the early days, as it was difficult to record string instruments for their high-frequency and low-intensity sound. (If many melodic instruments were present in the band, the fiddle or clarinet played the lead voice, and other instruments took over for only short moments for contrast.) The piano had been seldom used by European musicians. As an instrument of the middle class, it was not easily affordable and, due to its size, not easy to include in street music or at weddings. However, it became popular among the immigrants at the end of the nineteenth century as part of their socialization into American life. The trombone as a replacement of the string bass created balance in timbre, provided rhythmic accents, and added to harmony. Through its instrumentation, "Von tashlach" exemplifies the onset of Americanization of Old World klezmer music.

Since its inception, Brandwein's piece has become a klezmer standard. It references the symbolic rite celebrated on the afternoon of Rosh Hashanah, the Jewish New Year, when observant Jews assemble along the banks of a running stream, reciting penitential prayers and shaking their garments as if casting away sins into the water to be washed away. As such, it reminds us of klezmer music's religious influence. Assigned titles such as "Von tashlach" had not been the norm. As common in an oral tradition, tunes were originally played without any composer's credit and without names. The musicians often called their tunes only by the dance form—freylekhs and khosidl, along with borrowed forms such as the bulgar and the hora—or the rite they accompanied or by the musician who taught them. Titles became necessary with the advent of recordings in the first decades of the twentieth century. Most of the early titles relate to life cycle or refer to the state of mind of the musician. Brandwein's "Fufzehn yahr fon der heim awek" (Fifteen Years Away from Home, 1924) and Dave Tarras's "Mayn tayere Odessa" (My Dear Odessa, 1926), evoke the nostalgia of the immigrant experience and a longing for the lost home. Why Brandwein titled his piece "Returning from Tashlikh" is not known; however, the melody has a wavy quality to it. It flows like a river, and its overall joyful expression might refer to the light and happy feeling that sets in after having cast away sins.

Technically, "Von tashlach" is a freylekhs. It is something of a catch-all term with equivalent names such as hopke (hop), dreidl (spinning top), and rikudl (dance) and interchangeably used with skotshne, sher, and khosidl to designate an upbeat dance tune. The variant names imply different dance steps, but there is little difference in the actual music. They may even refer to a single musical entity. Freylekhs can be considered the default Ashkenazic celebratory tune, commonly played in procession to and from the wedding canopy. Their function during weddings eventually disappeared, but the pieces themselves remained in the repertoire. They usually consist of two or three sections, with distinct changes in mood, held together by an underlying oompah rhythm. Although freylekh means "cheerful" or "happy," this denotes mood, not necessarily speed. Older tunes are slower, but most are in a moderate walking tempo.

Brandwein's extremely fast-pace piece consists of three contrasting sections. The first opens with the piano and trombone, which set the oompah rhythm and introduce a repetitive pattern that changes harmonies only infrequently. The clarinet quickly comes into the foreground with a light tripping melody that contains many fast passages. The cymbal occasionally accentuates the beat. Indeed, the accompaniment provides more rhythmic than harmonic support. Think of it as a timekeeping bottom and an improvisational top. This represents klezmer music's tension between rhythm and melody. What is most characteristic of the clarinet tune is its very first step (a diminished fifth interval), which is commonly found in prayer chant. This incipit recurs and gives the tune a distinctive and unusual musical signature not often found in other tunes. What is common, however, is the repetition of each section, followed by a repeat of the whole tune three times. But each repetition happens in true klezmer fashion: never play the same tune twice. Liberties in tempo and the addition and omission of notes are joined by improvisational gestures that include specific technical uses of instruments unique to klezmer music that support the rhythm. We hear cries or sobs that emote a weeping sound, yearning slides, inflexions (using microtones) that create a crying quiver in the instrument, and different types of trills—these are all reminiscent of the human voice with its unique range of expression. Indeed, klezmer music is easily identifiable by such characteristic expressive melodies, complete with laughing and weeping. This is not a coincidence. These gestures bring out the heart of the melody and move it closer to vocal music, alluding to synagogue chant as a major influence of klezmer music. "Von tashlach" ends, like many other klezmer tunes, with a long, ascending, continuous glide and three descending chords that are rendered slower. Originally, such a formula might have been practical to finish quickly a tune when it was needed in a ceremony (i.e., at the entry of the bride, when a gift was announced, etc.) or at the end of an old recording roll, such as the one Brandwein used in 1926. This arch-form ending quickly became a standard.

Brandwein's recording displays his personal style as a musician. In general terms, his art is fluent and inventive with much emotional depth; there is an overall raw and gutsy expression to his sound. His playing is effortless, and he easily changes registers. The liveliness of his playing is evident in that he constantly jumps up and down the scale, covering an impressive range, all the while expressing himself in slides and trills. While some players tend to overembellish and thus overshadow the melody, Brandwein reveals himself as a relatively restrained master. His gestures support the rhythm and help the melody to flow freely, like a river, sometimes tumultuous and frantic and sometimes quiet and lamenting. During all of this, he gives the impression of spontaneity and ease, an unadulterated expression of joy and creativity. Even if the tune is well known and has been played a thousand times, it seems as if Brandwein just invented it.

Brandwein stands in stark contrast to the other legendary clarinetist, Dave Tarras, whose musical literacy, cultured playing technique, and professionalism led him to take over the space Brandwein had carved out. In comparison, his style is much more polished and conservative and varies from tune to tune. He clearly had a different way to apprehend the repertoire and the profession. A sober, dignified, and hardworking musician, he was born Dovid Tarrashuk in a shtetl farther east in Podolia. He learned from his father and by the age of nine had mastered the guitar, balalaika, flute, and mandolin, finally taking up clarinet in his early teens. At the age of eighteen, he was drafted into the army of Czar Nicholas II and served in a military band until the army's collapse amid political chaos and revolution in 1918. In 1921, he joined the flood of emigrants heading for New York. He is credited with being the chief proponent of the bulgar, which by the mid-twentieth century had become the principal repertoire among musicians.

While Tarras's career took off, Brandwein's soured from the mid-1920s on in spite of his unique talent. He made his last recording in 1941 and lived his final years in relative obscurity, playing occasionally in the Borscht Belt, a popular vacation spot in the Catskill Mountains for New York City Jews from the 1920s to the 1970s. By the late 1940s, klezmer music's popularity and commercial viability began to ebb. After World War II, it began to fade out, with the exception of Philadelphia, where musicians held on to their Old World repertoires and which continued to boast an enduring klezmer scene.

Brandwein did not live to witness the resurgence of interest in klezmer music that began in the late 1970s. But his influence was vast. A new generation of musicians saw him as a source of inspiration and continued his legacy. As the intricate details of klezmer music are not well preserved in sheet music, his and others' recordings were important sources for recovering the early twentieth-century style of playing. Brandwein is regarded as an important pillar of klezmer history and a vivid inspiration to young players all over the world. His influence is evident in the numerous arrangements of "Von tashlach" from the 1980s until today. Albums that feature the tune in unique new arrangements range from *Bessarabian Symphony* (1994) by Joel Rubin and Joshua Horowitz and *KlezSqueeze* (1996) by the Sy Kushner Jewish Music Ensemble to *Klez Klez Goy Mit Fez* (2000) by Yid Vicious, *Kleztory and I Musici De Montreal* by Kleztory, and *First Klez* (2008) by Salomon Klezmorim. As evident from these album titles, the so-called revivalists maintain a playful relationship to klezmer music's past. They identify with its history, but most of all they proudly identify themselves and their music as klezmer, a designation that an earlier generation of musicians had considered an insult.

Klezmer music's revitalization began when flutist Lev Liberman discovered old 78 rpms of the repertoire and subsequently founded the California-based group the Klezmorim in 1975. It became one of four bands that regenerated klezmer music in different parts of the United States. In New York, Andy Statman and Zev Feldman headed the movement, Hankus Netsky followed in Boston, and Henry Sapoznik founded Kapelye in New York in 1979. A new generation of klezmorim was born. The musicians involved had diverse backgrounds, from folk to classical music, but they did not imbue klezmer music with it. Instead, they aimed at re-creating the sound of the late Naftule Brandwein and of Dave Tarras, who was still alive and could provide guidance firsthand.

In the subsequent decade, however, bands emerged that took a different approach. One of them is the Klezmatics. After making their debut in April 1986 at the now defunct Café Daro on St. Marks Place in Manhattan's East Village, the band paved the way for klezmer music's presence in hip rock and jazz clubs, literally moving klezmer sounds from the synagogue social hall to the American club scene. With this move to new venues, the band also revamped the "classic" repertoire. Like other bands of its generation and beyond, the Klezmatics approached klezmer music in two ways: by arranging preexisting standard tunes and by writing new compositions. In both ways, they expanded on earlier styles, going beyond historicization. Indeed, the Klezmatics discovered the rich improvisational potential of klezmer melodies and combined them with the agility and finesse of a jazz ensemble, with pop and rock, or with a punk attitude. They fused popular and world-music styles. For example, they would underlay an original melody with a funk undercurrent or a reggae pulse or transform freylekhs or bulgars to resemble Jamaican ska and include a solo reminiscent of Frank Zappa. This eclectic style could emerge only because of the band members' different backgrounds in rock and jazz.

While the Klezmatics' approach brought the instrumental music of the golden age into a new era, they preserved the essentials of the older repertoire—the tunes, the ornamental gestures, and even parts of the arrangements. They just imbued them with a contemporary sensibility. Connecting the old with the new undoubtedly fueled the Klezmatics and has accounted for their popularity among a broad audience. "We gave ourselves a job years ago, and it is to always walk the line of never getting too far away from the Jewish klezmer tradition, but never just slavishly copying and reproducing either," confirmed trumpeter-composer Frank London in a 1997 interview. Or as the group's former violinist Alicia Svigals put it, "We're not about 'authenticity.' We're about folk fetishes and fetishizing what's supposed to be a Jewish band." The Klezmatics have also described themselves as "the planet's radical Jewish roots band." But klezmer music has always remained at their core.

Although the band's style has been evolving, their balancing of old and new remains constant and is recognizable from the 1989 debut recording *Shvaygn=Toyt* to the 2006 Grammy-winning album *Wonder Wheel* (in the category of Best Contemporary World Music Album). Fans consider *rhythm + jews* of 1990 their most "traditional" album. It is the first revivalist recording to feature the word "Jew" on the cover. The rousing opening track, "Fun Tashlikh," is a signature piece and reveals the Klezmatics' approach on many levels. It employs new studio techniques, layers drums and percussion, and takes the use of vocals and instruments to an extreme: Lorin Sklamberg's ghostly moaning and nigun-like vocalizations are put through a guitar effects pedal, while David Krakauer on the growling bass clarinet goes from one extreme to another. This is not your grandfather's klezmer. Yet Naftule Brandwein's 1926 tune is one that your great-grandfather might have known.

"Fun Tashlikh" begins with a free-styled introduction that features Middle Eastern drumming, provided by guest artist Mahmoud Fadl, set against David Krakauer's wailing bass clarinet solo. This was Krakauer's first recording with the Klezmatics (the group has performed with different bills). His instrument is at times barely recognizable. He plays with timbral contrast evoking the sound of the Arabic double-reed instrument known as mizmār when he moves to the lower registers and imitates a woman's vocal ululations in the higher registers. He incorporates klezmer music's unique embellishing gestures. In his solo, Krakauer also includes a few short repeated phrases reminiscent of jazz before giving the listener a taste of Brandwein's tune, whose first section he plays twice in a lower register.

After this idiosyncratic opening with a hint of Brandwein, the tune then appears in its three-part repeating structure. But there are twists. The rhythm of the bass line following this opening is evocative of Middle Eastern music. So are ululating vocals, which are evocative of zagareet, a sound of encouragement, an expression of joy and excitement in Arabic culture produced by alternating rapidly between two high pitches. Violin and bass clarinet play the first section of the tune in call-and-response. Frank London's blues-inspired "wa-wa" trumpet in the background of the second section foreshadows the interplay between him and Sklamberg in the short passage following the tune. The second section almost has a Celtic sound, similar to what one would hear in *Riverdance*. Only in the third section do we hear the tune straightforward, played in unison by all the instruments. In the ensuing repeat, the bass clarinet solos over the melody. A lengthy interlude follows that preserves the Middle Eastern rhythm in the bass and percussion, while the bluesy trumpet draws out long notes for a solo that joins the nigun-like vocals (the bass clarinet is harmonizing in rhythmic unison) in call-and-response fashion. This seamlessly merges into the third repetition of the tune, which is similar to the beginning with a bluesy trumpet in the interlude. "Fun Tashlikh" ends with a percussion solo that brings back the Middle Eastern rhythm, while the other instruments play in unison the opening motive of the tune with its unique interval. All accelerate and close with the motive that also closes Brandwein's third section. But the overall result is a sound almost closer to Middle Eastern music than klezmer music.

With "Fun Tashlikh," the Klezmatics blend a tune from the standard klezmer repertoire with Arabic and Middle Eastern sounds, free jazz, and Celtic music—elements not found in Brandwein. But the ululating melodies of the violin and clarinet recognizably evoke klezmer music. As the first track on *rhythm + jews,* this arrangement is very important in conveying to the listener that, while the Klezmatics act from a deep appreciation and understanding of historical styles and pay homage to Brandwein, they embody an eclecticism in keeping with their time. Not only is this track a powerful opening for the whole album, but it is also a political statement given the involvement of the Egyptian drummer and the Arabic zagareet.

"Fun Tashlikh" sets the tone for the rest of the album, which brings out Middle Eastern characteristics in klezmer tunes by way of free jazz. The solo parts on each track reflect the implicit connections between the two genres—listen to Matt Darriau's occasional excursion into free-jazz improvisation on the saxophone and Frank London's use of mutes to trigger sounds reminiscent of Bubber Miley and Miles Davis. While the Klezmatics' style might seem expansive, it is part of a resurgence with crossovers between seemingly adverse styles and genres and new musical ideas. David Krakauer, who played with the Klezmatics for six years, puts this into context: "We were doing a highly amplified, irreverent, improvisation infused, anti-nostalgic/almost punk style of klezmer music. At the same time Don Byron was also putting forward a very urban/modern view of Jewish music with his take on Mickey Katz's music and Ben Goldberg, who was doing his thing on the west coast with the New Klezmer Trio. Plus there were other related projects at the time like Anthony Coleman's *By Night* that looked at eastern European culture through an avant-garde lens." But this is not where klez-mer music's journey ends.

Fast-forward to 2015 and 2016, when the reigning violin virtuoso, Itzhak Perlman, gave a number of concerts around the country, cele-brating the twentieth anniversary of *In the Fiddler's House*. I was lucky to get a ticket for the Carnegie Hall show on March 31, 2015, which doubled as a gala concert of the National Yiddish Theatre Folksbiene's centennial. Many key players of the klezmer scene shared the stage with the Israeli American violinist. Aside from London, Sklamberg, and Statman, there were Michael Alpert, Alan Bern, Kurt Bjorling, Judy Bressler, and Hankus Netzky with his Klezmer Conservatory Band. Clearly, klezmer music was not crossing over into the classical world—it was the other way around. Klezmer music moved maestro Perlman from Beethoven to bulgars.

Seating close to 3,000 people, Carnegie Hall in midtown Manhattan is the ideal venue when large crowds are expected. And, indeed, the klezmer all-stars and the classical violinist faced a sold-out hall. The venue had klezmer history. On February 20, 1983, Carnegie Hall first opened its doors for two triumphant sellout shows by the Klezmorim. But the collaboration with Perlman was different both in nature and in its effect. It marked a new stage of klezmer music's evolution. It began in 1995, when Perlman embarked on a widely publicized tour, jamming with several musicians in New York City and Krakow. The tour focused on both: Perlman's exploration of his heritage and of klezmer music in its different phases and stylistic evolution. PBS chronicled it in a docu-mentary that in its title, *In the Fiddler's House*, put a spin on the ac-claimed musical *Fiddler on the Roof*, equating the iconic shtetl musi-cian with klezmer. Simultaneously with the broadcast, EMI Classics/ Angel Records released a recording with the same name—certainly an intriguing move for a major label and a superstar artist such as Perlman.

In his introductory notes to the CD, Perlman stressed that he em-braced klezmer as his own music and asserted that it is "what you might hear if you came to my house and I decided to jam with some friends." And jamming he does—with some very talented bands: the Andy Stat-man Orchestra, the Klezmer Conservatory Band, Brave Old World, and the Klezmatics. These four bands represented the status quo of the klezmer scene at the time with the first two generally performing a more historical or conservative repertoire, the latter having a more progressive and hybrid approach to klezmer music. But in their collaboration with Perlman, the dichotomy does not quite hold. Indeed, there is more complexity in each group's balancing of tradition and innovation. To be sure, Perlman was deeply involved in choosing the material and worked together with the bands to achieve a perfect blend (he shares writing credits for two tracks). This was a showcase for neither the bands nor Perlman. It was a unique opportunity for all musicians to display their skills and abilities by way of klezmer music. For example, the first track, "Reb Itzik's Nign," bridged the gap between Perlman's background and the klezmer world by starting off as a duet between the violinist and Alan Bern from Brave Old World on piano. Bern composed it in a style that is reminiscent of Joseph Achron and Ernest Bloch. For the last third of this song, the entire band joins in at an increased tempo, playing the main tune as a freylekhs, thus creating a crossover between classical and klezmer music.

With the incorporation of other musical styles, *In the Fiddler's House* offers a great variety of sounds. Another number that must be mentioned here is "Ale Brider" (We're All Brothers) in an arrangement by the Klezmer Conservatory Band. The piece has been revolutionary in several ways. For one, it is not instrumental music but rather relies on lyrics—these are rooted in Morris Winchevsky's "Akhdes" (Unity), which was published in August 1890 in a monthly journal of Yiddish culture. The poem promulgates peoplehood and equality, which were central themes for turn-of-the-century Jewish socialists and those active in the labor movement. About thirty years later, the journalist and folklorist Shmuel Hurwitz, known by his pseudonym A. Litvin, added a melody to the adapted text and claimed it to be a highly popular folk song from the Old Country. In 1988, the Klezmatics arranged text and music. In line with their activist stance, they added a queer verse in which the word "freylekh" serves as double entendre ("Un mir zaynen ale freylekh, oy, oy, ale freylekh / Vi Yoynoson un Dovid HaMelekh, oy, oy, oy"). Not only did they bridge gender divides, bringing the themes of inclusivity and unity into the realities of a new era, but they also introduced song into a genre that had been almost exclusively deemed instrumental music. Indeed, klezmer music in the late twentieth century enabled new paradigms for the performance and arrangement of Yiddish song—and vice versa. Since its klezmer incarnation, "Ale Brider" has become the Klezmatics' signature number and often serves as an encore at their concerts. It has been arranged and recorded by countless klezmer ensembles.

To be sure, the 1995 rendition by the Klezmer Conservatory Band and Perlman omits the couplet with the daring reference to Jonathan and King David (not so the 2008 version, a twelve-minute track in which "Ale Brider" is integrated into a *Klezmer Suite*). Characteristic of klezmer music, the melody is repetitious with added variation as the piece continues. It includes a section toward the end where different instruments infectiously render the tune, at times in virtuosic fashion, beginning with the violin, followed by mandolin, clarinet, and flute (all in duet with Perlman). This inclusion of improvisations over a short repeating passage, also noticeable on other tracks, was a significant innovation among klezmer groups of that time. Perlman shows his absorption of the klezmer style with gestures such as bends and slides that sound like laughing.

In the Fiddler's House topped world and classical-crossover music charts internationally, becoming one of the top-selling klezmer CDs of the late twentieth century. Together with the film, which won an Emmy Award, it played an important role in substantially increasing the visibility of klezmer music. The successful releases were followed by an abundance of activities the following year. Together with the klezmer bands, Perlman did a summer festivals tour, drawing sold-out houses and collecting material for the CD sequel, *Live in the Fiddler's House*, which was released the same year. Given Perlman's superstar status as a classical musician, klezmer music became known to a very broad audience. He greatly helped in widely popularizing it. Indeed, the scene never again became as prominent as it had been during its association with Perlman. There was a flourishing of awareness among the general public, and klezmer music became a sphere where non-Jews and Jews from across the spectrum met.

While the scope of klezmer music began expanding, few groups continued in the vein of *Fiddler's House* classical crossover; an exception was Boston's Shirim with a program of restyled classical pieces on *Klezmer Nutcracker*. Likewise, a few composers of classical music have incorporated klezmer sounds into their concert hall compositions, such as David Schiff in the *Divertimento from Gimpel the Fool* (1982) for clarinet, violin, violoncello, and piano and Simon Sargon in *KlezMuzik* (1995) for solo clarinet and piano.

To be sure, klezmer music's rising success triggered a plethora of new bands and recordings for a growing market, culminating in the peak year of recordings in 1998. Crossover developments broadened further as musicians sought to depart from the mainstream. Many klezmer musicians aligned themselves with world music, with bands like Klezmos identifying their repertoire as "world Klez music" and Rubinchik's Orkestyr performing "old-world beat" (contracting Old World and world beat). Ben Brussell defined the style of his band Klezmania! as "definitive world music." Some fusions of klezmer music created a new eclecticism. Take, for example, the Freilachmakers Klezmer String Band from Sacramento, California; on *The Flower of Berezin*, the band replaces the iconic clarinet with the clawhammer banjo to play klezmer tunes mixed with Irish and country sounds.

Popular music has found itself in klezmer, too. Shloinke, a garage klezmer band from Chicago, imbued traditional sets of klezmer music with an irreverent rock-and-roll attitude. And Yid Vicious, a band from Madison, Wisconsin, has offered high-energy klezmer dance tunes with a hint of rock (viz. the band's name, a pun on punk rocker Sid Vicious). HaLaila calls its music "tribal Jewish funk, or depending on our mood, 'acid klez.'"

Some bands took fusion to farther extremes. Charming Hostess, a band that grew out of the avant-rock scene of Oakland, California, mixed Yiddish, Sephardic, and other folk songs with driving art-rock instrumentals, such as on the album *Eat*. Rabbi Bob Gluck's *Stories Heard and Retold* experiments with ambient collages of Jewish folk and ritual sounds. And King Django put forward a klezmer–ska hybrid with Yiddish translations of the British ska band Madness as well as a Jamaican-styled rendition of "Hevenu Shalom Aleichem."

In order to set themselves apart, klezmer bands identified ever more eclectic and specific musical alignments and orientations. The Cayuga Klezmer Revival band has characterized its style variously as "folk, roots, electric, acoustic" and "jazz, rock, swing, folk, ska, and reggae" and defined its repertoire as "a mixture of traditional Eastern-European tunes, Ladino, Israeli, and original tunes."

America has had its influence, too. On the album *The Hidden Light*, clarinet and mandolin master Andy Statman and his quartet offer jazz-infused klezmer improvisations on Hasidic tunes and original meditations on spiritual themes. Bruce Kaminsky's *And the Angels Swing* alludes to the classic Benny Goodman song "And the Angels Sing"; with its powerful trumpet solo from Ziggy Elman, the album features strong klezmer renditions of jazz classics like Dizzy Gillespie's "A Night in Tunisia" and jazz stylings of standards such as "Hava Nagila." Americana can be also found in *Back in the Shtetl Again* by western Massachusetts–based Klezamir; they include songs with a swing feel and instrumental tracks that occasionally borrow from country music.

Women have carved out a space as well, both as musicians and as leaders of ensembles (previously women had played a marginal role as klezmorim). Noteworthy are the groups Isle of Klezbos and Mikveh, an all-women's sextet and quintet, respectively, both formed in 1998.

As we have reached the twenty-first century, anything goes klezmer. There are musicians and bands who attend to historical conceptions and pay tribute to early recording-era musicians (think of the Tarras Band, which preserves the style of the acclaimed clarinetist after whom it is named), and in parallel there is ever more diversification and eclecticism with musicians incorporating various styles of music. There are musicians of the "next generation" who bridge both if not all worlds, such as the Brooklyn-based clarinetist and composer Michael Winograd (b. 1982). Since 2007, he has been the clarinetist of the Tarras Band, which he formed together with trumpeter Ben Holmes and pianist Pete Sokolow. He is a member of the Yiddish Art Trio (YAT), which has existed since early 2009 and aims at redefining the scope of contemporary Yiddish music. Deeply rooted in klezmer and Yiddish music, YAT uses historical idioms to explore new kinds of sounds, thereby vastly expanding klezmer music's vocabulary. Winograd is also the cofounder and director of the groundbreaking "borderless world fusion band" Sandaraa. Founded in the fall of 2013, it includes accordionist Patrick Farrell and percussionist Richie Barshay, both also rooted in klezmer music. Winograd has collaborated with musicians involved in other genres as well. He occasionally joins Ahava Raba, a duo of Cantor Yaakov "Yanky" Lemmer and trumpeter Frank London that explores the spiritual sides of Jewish music; he has played alongside Itzhak Perlman and Socalled. If you want to get a taste of his versatility, listen to the album *Storm Game* of 2013.

The ever more divergent scenes represent the truly diverse nature of klezmer music in the twenty-first century. Aside from fusing a multitude of musics (from Arabic and Balkan to Hungarian, from classical to jazz and pop) in a variety of ways, klezmer music is also informed by new immigrants, such as Roberto Juan Rodriguez, who blends the Afro-Cuban melodies of his homeland with classic klezmer tunes. Klezmer music has proven to be flexible enough to mix with whatever it meets. It provides musicians with a frame in which they can freely develop new sound worlds—a creative foil of some sort. If it used to be the duty of klezmorim to bow to the audience's wishes, in the twenty-first century musicians cater to their audiences with individuality and unique inter-pretations. They continuously challenge prior perceptions and encour-age you to think of klezmer music not simply as Jewish music but beyond. Klezmer music has begun to take a stance in relation to minor-ities and crises, such as AIDS. Social and political activism has ex-pressed itself in all-women bands, titles of albums, and lyrics. By ad-dressing wider issues, klezmer reflects the ever-changing social fabric of Jewish music.

With new productions of sound and meaning, klezmer music has also expanded its performance contexts. Indeed, its venues changed and diversified. In its early days, it was heard during weddings, in the Yid-dish theater and vaudeville, and in music halls and wine cellars. Today, klezmer music can be heard in a wide range of venues, from smoky dives to the synagogue social hall, on street corners, on radio and in film, and, not the least, on the concert stage and during music festivals. There are festivals devoted to klezmer music, such as the long-running but now discontinued KlezKamp in the Catskills, KlezCalifornia, Yid-stock, and the recently founded KulturfestNYC and Yiddish New York. Aside from performances, they offer lectures, master classes, and work-shops.

Indeed, the transmission of the art of klezmer changed as well, from oral methods to the revivalists' reliance on scores and recordings to more formalized musical training that requires the ability to compose and arrange in the vein of conservatory education. There are klezmer ensembles at universities, and there are conservatories that offer spe-cialized training. No doubt, each new way to learn music implies a change for klezmer music's interpretation.

For the musicians, there are many incentives to play. Of course, there are always those for whom a new niche presents an opportunity, economic and otherwise. Many are truly drawn to the music; some want to rediscover the European roots of their families and reconnect with the Yiddish culture of their ancestors. For others, klezmer music serves spiritual, even religious purposes. The scene counts a substantial number of non-Jews and secular Jews who comfortably express themselves through Yiddish culture. Klezmer music thus constitutes an alternative form of and space for cultural expression, serving as a relatively neutral option in relating (to) the Jewish experience. Similarly, many different audiences of all backgrounds—and regardless of age or gender or heritage—embrace klezmer. Klezmer music has become part of American culture across the fifty states (and beyond), transcending ethnicities and communities and other possible boundaries. Indeed, America is klezmerized.

Klezmer music is paradigmatic for most musics discussed in this book and for Jewish music in America at large. Notwithstanding the impossibility of exact definition, it is clearly an amalgamation of the cultures that surround it. It is a conscious musical construction that is constantly defining and redefining itself. From the eighteenth century to the twenty-first, Jewish music has adapted but never assimilated completely. It is reflexive of external challenge and internal contradictions. It consciously and subconsciously borrows liberally but never sacrifices its inherent Jewish sensibility. The internal rhythms of Jewish languages and the sounds of the synagogue and of folklore have all enabled the music to retain a unique imprint that separates it from that of the surrounding community, sometimes more, sometimes less.

Jewish music in America has assumed different meanings in historical and cultural contexts. It has continuously evolved and transformed. Like all music, it is a product of its time and creators. Secularization and technology have opened up new possibilities and with it opportunities but also challenges. Its role as a conduit for the enactment and negotiation of Jewishness continues to offer experiences of embodied belonging that are shaped, in each instance, by sets of associational values. Therefore, and given its fluidity and even ambiguity, it will continue to evolvel, continuing the Jewish experience in sound in all its meaning and diversity. With ever-new generations of Jews in America to emerge, it will grow out of its legacy or preserve it and will continue to flourish.

SELECTED READING

Barzel, Tamar. *New York Noise: Radical Jewish Music and the Downtown Scene*. Blooming-ton: Indiana University Press, 2014. A pioneering study of the Radical Jewish Culture movement, a banner under which many artists in the circle of John Zorn performed and produced an experimental music shaped by jazz, rock, free improvisation, and avant-garde concert music with the aim to forge a new vision of Jewish identity.

Beeber, Steven L. *The Heebie-Jeebies at CBGB's: A Secret History of Jewish Punk*. Chicago: Chicago Review Press, 2006. This volume looks at punk's beginnings in Manhattan's Lower East Side in the early 1970s, asserting that it was the most Jewish of rock move-ments. It is offers biographies of Jewish punks, alongside a historical overview and some musical analysis.

Benarde, Scott R. *Stars of David: Rock 'n' Roll's Jewish Stories*. Hanover, NH: Brandeis University Press, 2003. A collection of short vignettes of Jewish musicians, singers, and songwriters who frequented the rock scene from 1953 on, revealing the sheer variety of the Jewish experience in rock and roll in surprising and provocative new ways.

Brinkmann, Reinhold, and Christoph Wolff, eds. *Driven into Paradise: The Musical Migra-tion from Nazi Germany to the United States*. Berkeley: University of California Press, 1999. A collection of essays focused on émigré conductors, professors, and composers and their contributions to American cultural history. Among those discussed are Erich Korn-gold, Ernst Krenek, Arnold Schoenberg, and Kurt Weill.

Cohen, Judah M. "Hip-Hop Judaica: The Politics of Representin' Heebster Heritage." *Popu-lar Music* 28, no. 1 (2009): 1–18. Explores the use of rap and hip-hop conventions as they have developed within the self-consciously contemporary American Jewish hipster scene between circa 1986 and 2006.

———. *The Making of a Reform Jewish Cantor: Musical Authority, Cultural Investment*. Bloomington: Indiana University Press, 2009. An insightful study of the training and transformation of cantorial students into invested cantors, focusing on American Reform at the turn of the twenty-first century.

Croland, Michael. *Oy Oy Oy Gevalt! Jews and Punk*. Santa Barbara, CA: Praeger, 2016. This book explores the cultural connections between Jews and punk in music, documentaries, young adult novels, zines, and so on. Jews played a prominent role in the history of punk, including such major bands as the Ramones, the Dictators, the Clash, Bad Religion, and NOFX.

Feldman, Walter. *Klezmer: Music, History, Memory*. New York: Oxford University Press, 2016. The first comprehensive study of the musical structure and social history of klezmer from the sixteenth to the twentieth century, written by an accomplished musician and leading authority in Eastern European Jewish dance.

Gottlieb, Jack. *Funny, It Doesn't Sound Jewish: How Yiddish Songs and Synagogue Melodies Influenced Tin Pan Alley, Broadway, and Hollywood.* Albany: State University of New York in association with the Library of Congress, 2004. A slightly controversial but entertainingly written volume that draws parallels between melodies written for synagogues and the Yiddish theater and popular music written in the years 1914–1964 that do not necessarily sound Jewish.

Hecht, Stuart J. *Transposing Broadway: Jews, Assimilation, and the American Musical.* New York: Palgrave Macmillan, 2011. This comprehensive study of the Broadway musical eschews a chronological approach to demonstrate how the (Jewish) American experience has manifested itself in popular music over the course of the twentieth century and into the first years of the twenty-first.

Hersch, Charles. *Jews and Jazz: Improvising Ethnicity.* New York: Routledge, 2017. The first in-depth study of the Jewish involvement in the world of American jazz, with focus on such prominent musicians as Michael Brecker, Stan Getz, Benny Goodman, Dave Liebman, Lee Konitz, Red Rodney, and Artie Shaw.

Hillman, Jessica. *Echoes of the Holocaust on the American Musical Stage.* Jefferson, NC: McFarland, 2012. A pioneering study on the traces the Holocaust left directly or indirectly in eight musicals: *Milk and Honey, The Sound of Music, Fiddler on the Roof, Cabaret, The Rothschilds, Rags, Ragtime,* and *The Producers.*

Katz, Israel J. "The Sacred and Secular Musical Traditions of the Sephardic Jews in the United States." *American Jewish Archives* 44, no. 1 (1992): 331–56. A historical overview of Sephardic music, commencing with the arrival of the first Jewish settlers from Recife, Brazil, in Nieuw Amsterdam (New York) in 1654 and the subsequent arrival of Sephardim from the eastern Mediterranean region at the turn of the twentieth century.

Kligman, Mark. *Maqām and Liturgy: Ritual, Music, and Aesthetics of Syrian Jews in Brooklyn.* Detroit: Wayne State University Press, 2009. A thorough study on the interaction of music and text in Sabbath prayers of the Syrian Jews, in which Arab and Jewish practices have merged. A twenty-three-track audio supplement of liturgical chants can be downloaded at http://www.wsupress.wayne.edu/maqamandliturgy.

Koskoff, Ellen. *Music in Lubavitcher Life.* Urbana: University of Illinois Press, 2000. An illuminating study of the musical world of the Lubavitcher Hasidim in the Crown Heights neighborhood of Brooklyn, New York.

Kun, Josh. "The Yiddish Are Coming: Mickey Katz, Anti-Semitism, and the Sound of Jewish Difference." *American Jewish History* 87, no. 4 (1999): 343–74. Explores the reception and race politics of the bandleader, clarinetist, and Yiddish-English parodist Mickey Katz in post–World War II America.

Lehman, David. *A Fine Romance: Jewish Songwriters, American Songs.* New York: Nextbook, 2009. A poetically written book on the formation of the American songbook, which was written almost exclusively by Jews.

Levine, Joseph A. *Synagogue Song in America.* Crown Point, IN: White Cliffs Media Company, 1989. Written from a practitioner's perspective, this historical examination of cantorial music focuses on its four basic components: reciting prayer texts, cantillation, *nusaḥ,* and performance technique, as well as their various alterations and combinations.

Melnick, Jeffrey P. *A Right to Sing the Blues: African Americans, Jews, and American Popular Song.* Cambridge, MA: Harvard University Press, 1999. A fascinating study of Jewish songwriters, composers, and performers—among them Irving Berlin, George Gershwin, and Al Jolson—who made "black" music in the first few decades of this century.

Most, Andrea. *Making Americans: Jews and the Broadway Musical.* Cambridge, MA: Harvard University Press, 2004. An analysis of Broadway songs from classics such as *Oklahoma!, Annie Get Your Gun, Babes in Arms,* and *South Pacific,* aimed to show how Jewish composers formed their vision of America on the musical stage.

Nahshon, Edna, ed. *From the Bowery to Broadway: New York's Yiddish Theater.* New York: Columbia University Press, 2016. A collection of essays from leading historians and critics with vivid illustrations that recount the heyday of the "Yiddish Broadway." A fantastic introduction to important figures in Yiddish theater history who in many cases are not well known.

Netsky, Hankus. *Klezmer: Music and Community in Twentieth-Century Jewish Philadelphia.* Philadelphia: Temple University Press, 2015. A comprehensive portrait of Philadelphia's Jewish musicians, the environment they worked in, and the repertoire they performed at local Jewish lifestyle and communal celebrations.

Ophir, Natan. *Rabbi Shlomo Carlebach: Life, Mission, and Legacy.* New York: Urim Publications, 2014. The first extensive biography of Shlomo Carlebach, considered one of the influential composers of Jewish religious music of the twentieth century and a progenitor of the modern neo-Hasidic renaissance.

Rapport, Evan. *Greeted with Smiles: Bukharian Jewish Music and Musicians in New York.* New York: Oxford University Press, 2014. This is the only monograph in English on Bukharian Jewish music and musicians and thus an important contribution to the small body of writings about the rich musical tradition of the Jewish communities of the former Soviet Union.

Rogovoy, Seth. *The Essential Klezmer: A Music Lover's Guide to Jewish Roots and Soul Music, from the Old World to the Jazz Age to the Downtown Avant-Garde.* Chapel Hill, NC: Algonquin Books of Chapel Hill, 2000. A lightly written overview of klezmer, accompanied by a comprehensive discography, a thoughtful guide to building your own klezmer library, and a tour of klezmer on the Internet.

Ross, Sarah. *A Season of Singing: Creating Feminist Jewish Music in the United States.* Waltham, MA: Brandeis University Press, 2016. This lively study describes the multiple roots and development of feminist Jewish music in the last quarter of the twentieth century, focusing on the work of prolific songwriters such as Debbie Friedman, Rabbi Geela Rayzel Raphael, Rabbi Hanna Tiferet Siegel, and Linda Hirschhorn.

Schiller, David M. *Bloch, Schoenberg, and Bernstein: Assimilating Jewish Music.* Oxford: Oxford University Press, 2003. This incisive study sheds new light on an important aspect of the cultural and aesthetic achievements of three seminal Jewish composers.

Shansky, Carol L. *The Hebrew Orphan Asylum Band of New York City, 1874–1941: Community, Culture and Opportunity.* Cambridge: Cambridge Scholars Publishing, 2016. Tells the story of a boys' band that was not only an important educational component of one of the largest Jewish charitable organizations of its time but also a significant source of music making and performance in New York.

Shelemay, Kay Kaufman. *Let Jasmine Rain Down: Song and Remembrance among Syrian Jews.* Chicago: University of Chicago Press, 1998. Tells the story of songs with sacred Hebrew texts and melodies from Arabic and other sources, as they have continued to be composed, performed, and transformed through the present day in the large Syrian Jewish community in Brooklyn, New York, as well as Mexico and Israel.

Slobin, Mark, ed. *American Klezmer: Its Roots and Offshoots.* Berkeley: University of California Press, 2002. This outstanding collection of essays, written by academics of all stripes and practitioners, covers the many angles of klezmer in America.

———. *Chosen Voices: The Story of the American Cantorate.* Urbana: University of Illinois Press, 1989. This fascinating volume traces the nebulous beginnings of the cantor as a recognizable figure to the heyday of the superstar sacred singer in the early twentieth century, providing a diverse portrait of the cantorate. A later added website, http://canto rate.wesleyan.edu, provides audio examples, images and videos, and many other materials.

———. *Fiddler on the Move: Exploring the Klezmer World.* Oxford: Oxford University Press, 2000. Focuses on klezmer as heritage music, community, style, and statement through systematic musicological analyses and anecdotes.

———. *Tenement Songs: The Popular Music of the Jewish Immigrants.* Urbana: University of Illinois Press, 1996. A look into the rich musical world of immigrant Jews: the rise of Yiddish popular music in vaudeville dives and Yiddish theater and on parlor pianos in tenement homes during the era of mass migration to the United States.

Solomon, Alisa. *Wonder of Wonders: A Cultural History of* Fiddler on the Roof. New York: Picador, 2013. An engagingly written history of the beloved Broadway musical that puts

Fiddler in the context of twentieth-century Jewishness, American theater history, Broadway musicals, and theater productions overseas.

Strom, Yale. *The Book of Klezmer: The History, the Music, the Folklore.* Chicago: A Cappella, 2002. An entertaining and carefully documented study of klezmer from its origins in Renaissance Europe through its reemergence as a popular art form in the late twentieth century in the United States. The interviews with forgotten klezmorim, as well as luminaries such as Theodore Bikel, Joel Grey, Leonard Nimoy, Andy Statman, and John Zorn, are invaluable.

Summit, Jeffrey A. *The Lord's Song in a Strange Land: Music and Identity in Contemporary Jewish Worship.* New York: Oxford University Press, 2000. Relying on oral history and analysis of recordings, the full range of contemporary Jewish practices in the Boston metropolitan area is examined.

———. *Singing God's Words: The Performance of Biblical Chant in Contemporary Judaism.* New York: Oxford University Press, 2016. The first in-depth study of the experience and meaning of chanting or reading Torah among contemporary American Jews.

Walden, Joshua S., ed. *The Cambridge Companion of Jewish Music.* Cambridge: Cambridge University Press, 2015. A kaleidoscope of introductory essays on Jewish liturgy, klezmer music, music in Israel, the music of Yiddish theater and cinema, and classical music from the Jewish Enlightenment through the twentieth century.

———. "The 'Yidishe Paganini': Sholem Aleichem's *Stempenyu*, the Music of Yiddish Theatre and the Character of the Shtetl Fiddler." *Journal of the Royal Musical Association* 139, no. 1 (2014): 89–136. Explores the music of Yiddish theater in early twentieth-century New York by considering multiple adaptations of the Russian Jewish author Sholem Aleichem's 1888 novel *Stempenyu*, which was adapted into two theatrical productions and finally inspired a three-movement recital work for accompanied violin by Joseph Achron.

Wood, Abigail. *And We're All Brothers: Singing in Yiddish in Contemporary North America.* New York: Routledge, 2014. Discusses Yiddish song as a potent medium for musical and ideological creativity at the twilight of the twentieth century.

Zuckerman, Bruce, Josh Kun, and Lisa Ansell, eds. *The Song Is Not the Same: Jews and American Popular Music.* West Lafayette, IN: Purdue University Press for the USC Casden Institute for the Study of the Jewish Role in American Life, 2011. This collection of essays covers a large range of topics and musicians, including the Jewish sheet music trade, musical comedy, the role of music in shaping Henry Ford's anti-Semitism, and Bob Dylan's Jewishness.

SELECTED LISTENING

Almost all the pieces discussed in this *Listener's Companion* can be found on YouTube. Additionally, there are several repositories with Web-based access that offer a diverse array of streamed recordings related to the content of this book.

Dartmouth Jewish Sound Archive
http://djsa.dartmouth.edu
The Dartmouth Jewish Sound Archive hosts more than 75,000 tracks of Jewish music, with
    many thousands being still in the queue and many not commercially available. Its content
    spans folksongs, synagogue music, Jewish radio programs, humor, children's stories, and
    anything that reflects the Jewish experience—in English, Hebrew, Yiddish, Ladino, Rus-
    sian, Arabic, French, and other languages. You can browse by album, genre, theme,
    language, and occasion. Publicly accessible, image and audio content is available to Dart-
    mouth users who have an active NetID or guests via a social media account.

KlezmerShack
http://www.klezmershack.com
Everything you always wanted to know about klezmer.

Milken Archive of Jewish Music
http://www.milkenarchive.org
With roughly 600 recorded works, this is one of the largest collections of American Jewish
    music ever assembled. It also contains more than 800 hours of oral histories; nearly 50,000
    photographs and historical documents; thousands of hours of video footage from record-
    ing sessions, interviews, and live performances; and an extensive set of program notes and
    essays that illuminate the music's historical and cultural context.

Recorded Sound Archives—The Judaic Collection
https://rsa.fau.edu/judaic
The Recorded Sound Archives (RSA) is part of Florida Atlantic University Libraries Special
    Collections and Digital Library. Its Judaic Collection is dedicated to the preservation of
    recorded Jewish music and currently boasts nearly 6,000 recordings from cantorial to

Yiddish, from the early twentieth century to the present, many of which can be heard at full length. You can browse by performer or album.

Robert and Molly Freedman Jewish Sound Archive
http://sceti.library.upenn.edu/freedman
One of the most complete listing and indexing of Yiddish music in the world, with more than 4,000 Yiddish and Hebrew recordings, searchable by author, title, key word, or the first line of the song.

Central Asia in Forest Hills, N.Y., Music of the Bukharan Jewish Ensemble Shashmaqam. Smithsonian Folkways, 1991. Ceremonial music and ritual song former Soviet Central Asia performed principally in Tajik.

From Avenue A to the Great White Way: Yiddish & American Popular Songs from 1914–1950. Sony, 2002. This two-CD set contains 50 songs that trace the early recorded history of Jewish music in New York and the subsequent influence that music had on American popular song. It includes rare recordings from early stars of the Yiddish theater, such as Molly Picon, a klezmer piece by Abe Schwartz, and a beautifully operatic performance by Yossele Rosenblatt.

The Golden Age of Cantors: Musical Masterpieces of the Synagogue. Tara Music, 2006. A double-length recording featuring many of the great cantors that served in America's synagogues during the 1920s and 1930s.

Golden Chants in America: Commemorating 350 Years of Jewish Music, 1654–2004. Bari Productions, 2005. Cantor Rebecca Garfein performs a wide variety of songs—from Ashkenazic and Sephardic and popular to sacred—that reflect the diversity of the American Jewish experience.

Historic Music of the Spanish and Portuguese Synagogue in the City of New York. Shearith Israel League, 2003. This three-CD set features remastered recordings of the Sabbath and holiday services as well as miscellaneous selections from decades ago. It features the voices of Dr. David de Sola Pool (rabbi from 1907 to 1956), Dr. Louis C. Gerstein (rabbi from 1956 to 1988), Rev. Abraham Lopes Cardozo (hazan from 1946 to 1990), and the Shearith Israel Choir under Leon Hyman.

Yiddish, Hebrew & Jewish Music: An Anthology of Klezmer, 1905–1952. Retro, 2006. In the ever-expanding jungle of klezmer recordings, this two-CD collection offers a solid compilation of performers and styles prevalent in the early twentieth century.

DVDS

Broadway Musicals: A Jewish Legacy. Athena, 2013. Jewish composers and lyricists played a unique role in the creation of the modern American musical. The film showcases the work of legends such as Irving Berlin, Jerome Kern, George and Ira Gershwin, Lorenz Hart, Richard Rodgers, Oscar Hammerstein II, Leonard Bernstein, and Stephen Sondheim.

A Cantor's Tale. Ergo Media, 2007. Follows the Brooklyn-born Cantor Jacob Mendelson in exploring the roots of Jewish liturgical music. Appearances by renowned cantors and aficionados are included; among them are Erik Anjoy, Alan Dershowitz, Frank London, Matthew Lazar, Joseph Malovany, Jackie Mason, Ben-Zion Miller, Alberto Mizrahi, and Neil Shicoff.

The Golden Age of Second Avenue. Arthur Cantor Films, 1968/1987. This documentary chronicles the early twentieth-century halcyon days of Yiddish theater in New York City, featuring photos, music and archival clips from historic Yiddish films, and candid interviews with luminaries such as Isaac Bashevis Singer. Narrated by noted Broadway and Hollywood actor Herschel Bernardi, the program also includes performances by Paul Muni, Molly Picon, Maurice Schwartz, and other Yiddish theater icons.

Great Cantors of the Golden Age: Great Cantors in Cinema. National Center for Jewish Film, 2006. A compilation of famous cantors in the cinema: Mordechai Hershman in *The*

Voice of Israel (1931), Leibele Waldman in the cantor–search committee comedy *A Cantor on Trial* (1931), Yossele Rosenblatt in *Dream of My People* (1933), Moishe Oysher in *Overture to Glory* (1940), and Moshe Koussevitsky in *We Who Remain* (1946).

The Klezmatics: On Holy Ground. 7th Art Releasing, 2010.

Jewish Soul, American Beat: The Return. 1999. An exploration of American Jewish identity and its future, explored through interviews of artists, composers, and musicians, such as Ephraim Buchwald, Arthur Hertzberg, Annette Insdorf, Tony Kushner, Egon Mayer, Cynthia Ozick, Ann Roiphe, Steve Reich, Elizabeth Swados, Moshe Waldoks, and John Zorn.

A Jumpin' Night in the Garden of Eden. Filmmakers Collaborative, 2000. A portrait of the late twentieth-century resurgence of klezmer, with focus on the careers of two bandleaders: Henry Spoznik from New York and Hankus Netsky from Boston.

Sabbath in Paradise. Tzadik, 2007. This documentary examines contemporary Jewish musical culture in the context of New York's avant-garde jazz scene in the 1990s with a focus on Andy Stateman and John Zorn as well as Anthony Coleman, David Krakauer, Frank London, and Marc Ribot.

A Sacred Noise: The New Jewish Music. Jewish Theological Seminary of America, 2000. Featuring artists Debbie Friedman, Seth Glass, and Craig Taubman as well as the groups The Klezmatics, Pharaoh's Daughter, and Vocolot, to show a generation of musicians who have broken new ground in order to transmit the Jewish experience. The sound track is interlaced with commentary by the artists as they describe their connections to Judaism and its musical heritage.

A Tickle in the Heart. First Run Features, 2004. Follows the New York–born Epstein brothers, who are klezmer musicians and at the time were living in retirement communities in Florida as they toured the United States and Europe.

Yiddish Theater a Love Story. New Love Films, 2007. A portrait of Zypora Spaisman, founder and grand dame of the Folksbiene Yiddish Theatre.

The Thomashefskys: Music and Memories of a Life in the Yiddish Theater. Docurama Films, 2012. A celebration of Yiddish theater pioneers Boris and Bessie Thomashefsky.

INDEX

ABOUT THE AUTHOR

Tina Frühauf serves on the faculty at Columbia University and is associate executive editor at Répertoire International de Littérature Musicale in New York. She serves also on the doctoral faculty of The Graduate Center, The City University of New York. An active scholar and writer, her research is centered on music and Jewish studies, especially in religious contexts but also art music, historiography, and Jewish community (through participatory action research), often crossing the methodological boundaries between ethnomusicology and historical musicology. She has received most recently fellowships and grants from the American Musicological Society, the Leo Baeck Institute, and the Memorial Foundation for Jewish Culture. She has written widely about the German Jewish music culture; aside from book chapters and encyclopedia articles, her work appeared in *The Musical Quarterly*, *Musica Judaica*, and *TDR: The Drama Review*. She is the author of *The Organ and Its Music in German-Jewish Culture* (Oxford University Press, 2009/2012; also available in German through G. Olms), editor of *An Anthology of German-Jewish Organ Music* (A-R Editions, 2013) and *Hans Samuel: Selected Piano Works* (A-R Editions, 2013), and coeditor of *Dislocated Memories: Jews, Music, and Postwar German Culture* (Oxford University Press, 2014), which won the Ruth A. Solie Award and the Jewish Studies and Music Award of the American Musicological Society. She has written several books for a general readership. She is currently completing a comprehensive monograph on music in the Jewish communities of Germany after 1945. She has organized the 2015 conference Postmodernity's Musical Pasts: Rediscoveries and Revivals after 1945, hosted by the Barry S. Brook Center for Music Research and Documentation, to venture into new areas of musicological inquiry. An edited volume is in preparation.